The Hulton Getty Picture Collection

The British
Millennium

**1,000 Remarkable Years
of Incident and Achievement**

D1400687

The Hulton Getty Picture Collection

The British Millennium

1,000 Remarkable Years
of Incident and Achievement

Nick Yapp

KÖNEMANN

Frontispiece: St Paul's Cathedral, Sir Christopher Wren's, and London's, Baroque masterpiece. Completed in 1710, the original medieval cathedral had been destroyed during the Great Fire of London in 1666.

First published in 2000 by Könemann Verlagsgesellschaft mbH,
Bonner Strasse 126, D-50968 Köln

© 2000 Könemann Verlagsgesellschaft mbH
Photographs © 2000 The Hulton Getty Picture Collection

This book was produced by The Hulton Getty Picture Collection,
Unique House, 21–31 Woodfield Road, London W9 2BA

Design: Mick Hodson and Alan Price
Project manager and editor: Richard Collins
Picture editors: Jack Connelly, Tom Worsley
Proof reader and indexer: Liz Ihre
Editorial assistance: Tom Worsley, Gill Hodson
Scanning: Antonia Hille, Dave Roling, Mark Thompson

Publishing director: Peter Feierabend

Typesetting by Mick Hodson Associates
Colour separation by Omniascanners srl
Printed and bound by Star Standard Industries Ltd
Printed in Singapore
ISBN 3-8290-6011-4
10 9 8 7 6 5 4 3 2 1

Based on an original idea and concept by Ludwig Könemann

CONTENTS

General Introduction

For almost nine hundred years, from 1066 to the mid-20th century, Britain enjoyed the good fortune of being physically separated from the rest of Europe. The Channel was narrow enough to allow early trade with near neighbours, but wide enough to make it impossible for any army, no matter how strong, successfully to invade. While hostile hordes scorched mainland Europe from end to end, the British Isles remained inviolate and unplundered.

The British fought on the seas, their invincible navy protecting and policing the trade routes of the world and playing a major part in the establishment of the greatest Empire the world has ever known. Behind these 'wooden walls', as the old sailing ships were called, the British were able to steal a march on their closest rivals in political, industrial and agrarian development.

Linguistically, Latin was abandoned early by all but the Church, and, apart from an uncomfortable flirtation with Norman French, nothing stood in the way of the English language. In the beginning there was Langland and Chaucer, then Shakespeare, and an unending stream of great writers – Milton, Pope, Swift, Keats and Wordsworth, Austen, the Brontës, Eliot, Dickens and a hundred of others. Then the Empire was blown away by the winds of change, industry fell into decline and recession, farming became a mad scramble of scandals and subsidies, but the glories of British art and architecture, fashion and theatre, and the language itself somehow survived.

The British developed a talent for travel, for poking their noses into other people's business. They were to be found all over the world – climbing mountains, seeking the sources of great rivers, staggering across deserts, sailing vast oceans single-handed. Wherever they went, they took their culture and their sport: football, cricket, golf - even 'ping-pong', as they loved to call table-tennis. In the age of the amateur, the British were the finest amateurs, and, when the world turned professional, they accepted strings of defeats with as good a grace as any.

In May 1712, the English essayist Joseph Addison reflected on the greatness of the 'British Nation'. He listed what he regarded as the 'honest prejudices' of the British: 'that one Englishman could beat three French-men, that we could never be in danger of Popery so long as we took care of our fleet; that the Thames was the noblest river in Europe; that (old) London Bridge was a greater piece of work than any of the Seven Wonders of the World'. All nonsense, of course, but the proud belief of a nation that has spent almost all the last thousand years being at ease with itself.

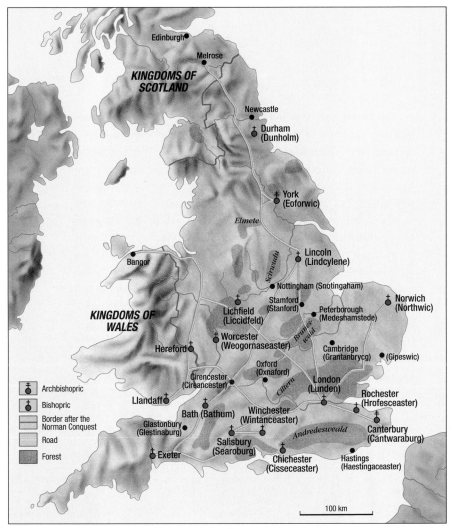

Map 1 The British Isles in the 11th Century

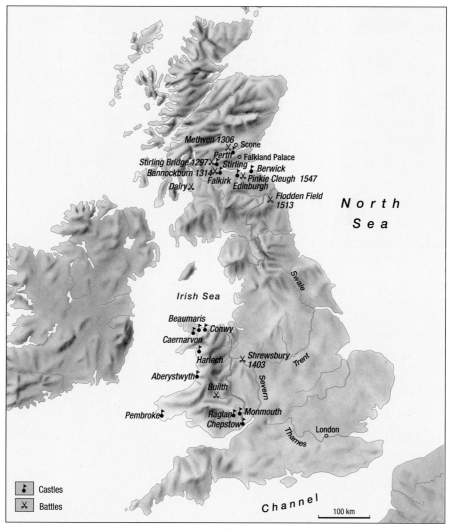

Map 2 The Conquest of Wales and Scotland, 1200–1550

Thames London

Deal
Walmer

Dover Rye
Winchelsea

Southampton Portsmouth

Calais

Etaples **Artois** **Burgundian**
Netherlands

Crécy-
en-Ponthieu Agincourt

Sluis

Luxem-
burg

Amiens

Harfleur Rouen

Normandy Seine

Falaise Verneuil Paris

C h a m p a g n e

Brest

Rennes

B r i t t a n y

M a i n e

Troyes

A n j o u Loire

T o u r a i n e

Orléans

B u r g u n d y

B e r r y

Poitiers

P o i t o u

B o u r b o n

F R A N C E

Bay of

Biscay

L i m o u s i n

D a u p h i n é

Bordeaux Castillon

G u i e n n e

Rhône

English possessions in France
at the outbreak of war

First campaign of Henry V

Battle or siege

A r m a g n a c

100 km

Map 3 The Hundred Years' War, 1337–1453

Map 4 Wool Production and Trade in 1500

Map 5 The Civil War, 1642–1660

Map 6 The Industrial and Agricultural Revolutions, 1760–1820

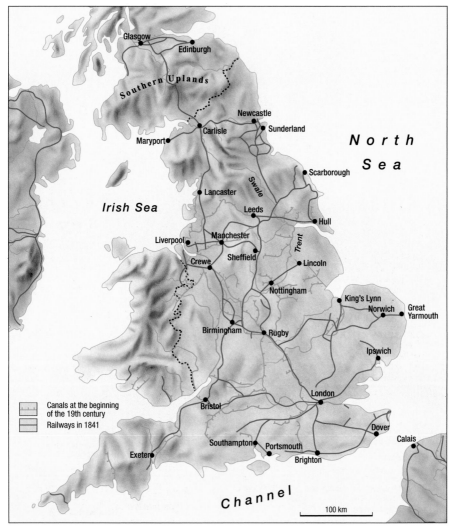

Map 7 Railways and Canals in 1850

Glasgow
Edinburgh
Southern Uplands
Newcastle
Carlisle
Sunderland
Maryport
North
Sea
Scarborough
Lancaster
Swale
Irish Sea
Leeds
Hull
Liverpool
Manchester
Trent
Crewe
Sheffield
Lincoln
Nottingham
King's Lynn
Norwich
Great Yarmouth
Birmingham
Rugby
Ipswich
London
Bristol
Dover
Calais
Southampton
Portsmouth
Exeter
Brighton
Channel

Canals at the beginning
of the 19th century
Railways in 1841

100 km

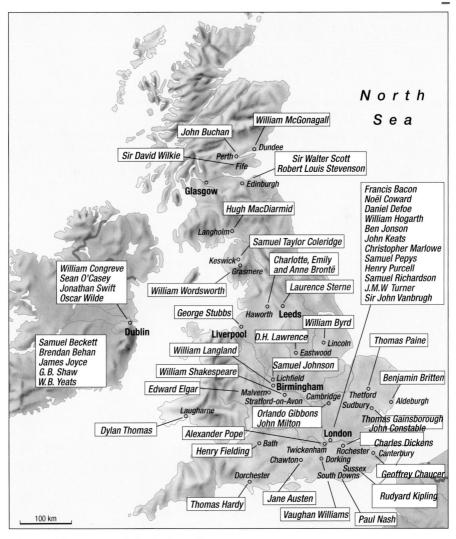

Map 8 Literary and Artistic Britain

North Sea

William McGonagall

John Buchan

Sir David Wilkie

Perth
Dundee
Fife

Sir Walter Scott
Robert Louis Stevenson

Glasgow
Edinburgh

Hugh MacDiarmid

Langholm

Francis Bacon
Noël Coward
Daniel Defoe
William Hogarth
Ben Jonson
John Keats
Christopher Marlowe
Samuel Pepys
Henry Purcell
Samuel Richardson
J.M.W Turner
Sir John Vanbrugh

Samuel Taylor Coleridge

Keswick
Grasmere

Charlotte, Emily
and Anne Brontë

William Congreve
Sean O'Casey
Jonathan Swift
Oscar Wilde

William Wordsworth

Laurence Sterne

George Stubbs

Haworth
Leeds

William Byrd

Dublin

Liverpool

D.H. Lawrence

Samuel Beckett
Brendan Behan
James Joyce
G. B. Shaw
W.B. Yeats

William Langland

Eastwood
Lincoln

Thomas Paine

Samuel Johnson

Benjamin Britten

William Shakespeare

Lichfield
Birmingham

Thetford
Sudbury
Aldeburgh

Edward Elgar

Malvern
Stratford-on-Avon
Cambridge

Thomas Gainsborough
John Constable

Laugharne

Orlando Gibbons
John Milton

London

Dylan Thomas

Alexander Pope

Charles Dickens

Bath
Twickenham
Rochester
Canterbury

Henry Fielding

Chawton
Dorking
Sussex
South Downs

Geoffrey Chaucer

Dorchester

Rudyard Kipling

Thomas Hardy

Jane Austen

Vaughan Williams

Paul Nash

100 km

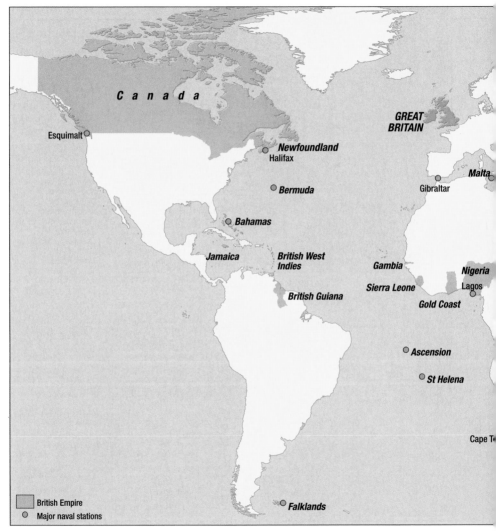

Map 9 The British Empire in 1914

Introduction to
Period 1 – 1000–1500

In 1012, the King of Anglo-Saxon England paid £48,000 in Danegeld. This was just one instalment in a sum regularly paid to buy off attacks by the Danes. It was an enormous amount, an expensive revelation of the relative weakness of a kingdom that had been united for little more than a hundred years. Alfred the Great had done his best to protect Wessex, his part of England, in the late 9th century, but the navy he had built no longer existed. The 2,000-mile coastline of Britain was again unprotected, as its last Saxon king was fatally to discover fifty-four years later.

But, for Scots, Welsh and English alike, life was hard at the beginning of the 11th century. The scattered population lived in isolated settlements, scratching a living from the land, the sea or the forest. Central control, such as existed, lay in the hands of Ethelred in England, Malcolm II in Scotland, and a group of warring princes in Wales. But king and court lay far distant from most villages.

Of more immediate importance to the peasant was the local lord. Rural society was divided into those who owned the land and those who worked it. There were several independent specialists – blacksmiths, carpenters, fishermen, tailors, salters, millers and bakers – but most people laboured in the fields. Families worked together, women and children alongside men. How they lived depended very much on where they lived, and on the vagaries of the weather. A generous lord, a good harvest, the absence of plague and pestilence meant better times for everyone. A series of damp summers could bring death and would certainly mean destitution, for few had reserves of food or money on which to draw. Survival was a gamble each winter, a time when the land yielded no crops, neither grain nor vegetables. The store of salted meat, so carefully laid down in the late autumn, when most animals had been slaughtered, was almost exhausted. It was not difficult for most Catholics to give up eating meat during Lent. None was available.

Death was a preoccupation in medieval life. Poets – save Chaucer – wrote of little else. But with the coming of spring, and April's sweet showers, came new hope. On big estates there was work for all, and some estates were very big indeed. Wulfric Spott, founder of the monastery at Burton-on-Trent in 1004, owned land in more than a dozen English counties. As forests were cleared, land owners needed labourers to work the land made available. So, a bargain was struck. The peasant promised two days' work on the lord's land in spring and summer, three days at harvest time, and the payment of rent. In return, his lord gave him seven acres of land, two oxen, a cow and six sheep, tools for work and utensils for his house.

Most houses were simple wooden frames, packed with wattle and roofed with thatch. Humans shared the one large room with poultry and animals. Food was cooked over an open fire on the earth floor, the smoke going out through a hole in the roof, after (it was to be hoped) choking at least some of the parasites that lived on humans and animals alike. The lord's house was not much grander. It centred round a great hall, where everyone ate, business was conducted, justice dispensed and where visitors and retainers slept. The lord and his family occupied separate rooms. Nearby were 'bowers', barns and outhouses, surrounded by wooden stockades. Furniture consisted of trestle tables, benches, mattresses, pillows, wall-hangings and chests. The poor had palliasses; the rich had good bed linen. The peasant ate with their fingers off a wooden platter or from the common pot; the rich with spoons or knives (but not forks) from imported tableware.

At the bottom of the social order were slaves, mere chattels, whose owners could kill them with impunity – though ecclesiastical law frowned upon such wickedness. Slaves had no belongings, no property, no money and no rights. Anyone who killed a slave simply paid the price of the value of the slave to the owner. This was reckoned at one pound, or eight oxen.

Change was slow, but relentless in the way it altered people's lives. The ingenuity of engineers and early scientists could not be denied. Better ploughs were invented; mills were powered by wind as well as water; time was measured by mechanical clocks instead of hourglasses. Houses were built of stone. Glass windows were installed, though for a long time they were not permanent fixtures, but were simply inserted in the wall at night or during bad weather. Clothing improved in comfort and style, though the basic costume remained much the same – a mantle over knee-length tunic and trousers for men, a kirtle reaching to the ground with tunic and mantle for women. Jewellery became more elaborate, more finely decorated. More people learnt to read. Superstition gave way to science – and the pace of change accelerated.

By 1500, the Crusading spirit had died in Britain. The code of chivalry, that had once been the rulebook of the 'parfit gentil knyght', had degenerated into mere pomp and ceremonial. Tournaments, banquets and heraldry were all that remained, though in the 14th century Edward III attempted to revive King Arthur's Court of the Round Table. The Church, which had once established a vice-like grip over the hearts and minds and souls of the faithful, was losing influence. New voices were raised in protest. The old order, almost as soon as it was established, was challenged by writers, philosophers, by Roger Bacon and other scientists, and by John Wycliffe and other preachers.

Though the vast majority stayed on the land, almost imperceptibly people drifted to towns. In 1066, the population of York (the second largest city in Britain) was reckoned to be 10,000, that of Norwich 6,600. Five hundred years later, York had grown to 25,000, and Norwich to 15,000. Even London, the proud capital of a united England in 1500, had only 75,000 inhabitants – bigger than any German city, but only one third of the size of Paris. Towns were ill-paved, smelly and unhealthy – but they did offer work and the chance to make a fortune.

During these five hundred years there was much jockeying for power – between kings and barons, Church and State, and – near the end of the period in England – between the Houses of York and Lancaster. The prize for which all these parties competed was power. England was increasingly a country worth ruling – rich, independent and well-protected. Scotland, too, was proudly independent. For centuries the Scots had fought the English, but in September 1497, James IV signed the treaty of 'perpetual peace' with Henry VII of England, and six years later married Henry's daughter. The Welsh had not been so fortunate. Edward I had invaded Wales and sealed his conquest by building a series of noble and forbidding castles from Conway to Caernarvon.

There was to be no repeat of the conquest with which the period had begun.

1
THE NORMAN CONQUEST
1000–1100

Castrum Royale Londin

The Tower of London – fortress, palace, prison and symbol of Norman power over the Saxons. In the centre is the White Tower, the innermost part of the Tower during Norman times. It was designed by William the Conqueror's architect, an emotional monk named Gundulf, a great designer of castles and fortresses who later became Bishop of Rochester. Work began almost immediately after William's entry into London, for the Conqueror was anxious to awe the people of London into submission. The Tower was built of Caen limestone and Kentish ragstone, thus combining and symbolising William's two territories. The walls are 5 metres thick at the bottom, and 4 metres thick at the top.

Introduction

The greatest invention of the age was the mouldboard plough. This not only cut a furrow through the soil, but also turned the earth, bringing the richer bottom soil to the top of the furrow. 'Thus,' Walter of Henley proudly proclaimed, 'it be cleansed and rid of the water the which maketh the tillage good.' For the masses, it simply meant life-saving bigger harvests.

The villain of the age was the miller, suspected in every village of stealing grain from his customers and overcharging them for grinding their corn. An 11th-century riddle asked: 'What is the boldest thing in the village?' The answer was: 'A miller's shirt, for it grips a thief by the throat every day.'

It was an age when might was right. Kings could be elected by men or appointed by God, but their ability to stay on their thrones depended on strength alone. In Scotland Macbeth killed his cousin Duncan I in battle in 1040, but was himself killed at Lumphanan near Aberdeen in 1057. In 1039 Llywelyn ap Gruffydd, king of Gwynedd and Powys, began his campaign to become king of all Wales. It took him sixteen years. England had four kings in seven years following the death of Canute, the last of them being Edward the Confessor.

And it was Edward who unconsciously paved the way for the Norman invasion in 1066. Edward spent twenty-five years exile in Normandy and acknowledged his cousin William, Duke of Normandy, as his rightful successor. When Edward returned to England in 1042 he spent most of his time in pious works – the building of Westminster Abbey began in 1050. Edward was not well enough to attend the consecration of the Abbey at Christmas 1065, and died eight days later. Harold Godwinson was immediately appointed King by the Council of England.

In Harold's nine-month reign, he successfully beat off a Danish invasion in the north, at Stamford Bridge, but was killed by a Norman arrow at Senlac near Hastings (otherwise known as the Battle of Hastings) three weeks later. The Norman conquest was swift and efficient. On 26 December 1066, William crowned himself King in Westminster Abbey.

The greatest achievement of the age was Domesday Book, an investigation into the taxable value of William's new realm. William wished to know exactly what lands his barons owned, how many feudal knights were bound in homage to support him, 'how England was peopled, and with what sorts of men'. Local juries of eight men had to list the number of ploughs, freemen, serfs, animals, mills and fisheries, cottages and barns, beehives and doves that existed in each village. 'There was,' complained a Saxon chronicler, 'no single hide nor yard of land...left out.'

In a scene from the Bayeux Tapestry, Harold of England takes leave of his King, Edward the Confessor, probably some time in 1064. Harold was on his way to Normandy, to swear allegiance to Duke William.

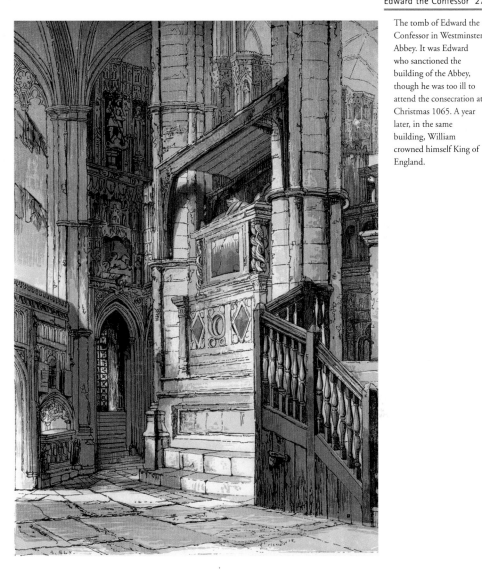

The tomb of Edward the Confessor in Westminster Abbey. It was Edward who sanctioned the building of the Abbey, though he was too ill to attend the consecration at Christmas 1065. A year later, in the same building, William crowned himself King of England.

Ego Wullms cognoie Baftard° Rex Anglie do t
t ocedo tibi Depoti neo Alano Britannie Conuti
t heredib; nuf mypfim om̃ Villaſ t ñaſ que
nup fuerut Conutiſ Ed̃Wyni in Eboracſhi
ñ cũ feodiſ Militut eccliſ t aliſ libtat
pſuetudib; ita libe t honopfice ſicut iſe
Ed̃Win ea tenunt. Dat m obſidione coram
Cuntate Eboz.

(*Left*) William the Conqueror sits on a well-cushioned English throne. His Coronation was a rushed affair. During the ceremony, shouts could be heard coming from outside Westminster Abbey. Fearing an uprising against him, William grabbed the crown and placed it on his own head. (*Opposite, below*) The Battle of Hastings, 14 October 1066. After almost a day of fighting, the contest was evenly balanced, but a feigned retreat by the Normans lured the Saxons from their position at the top of a hill. Harold and his two brothers were killed, and the Saxons were left without a leader.

(*Left*) William the Conqueror grants the honour of Richmond to his ally Alan Rufus, Earl of Brittany. The Bretons had played a large part in the defeat of the Saxons at Hastings.

The Bayeux Tapestry was made in England some time after 1070 and was probably commissioned by Odo, Bishop of Bayeux and half brother of William the Conqueror. It is 70 metres long and portrays events leading up to the Norman Conquest. (*Top*) Harold visits William in Normandy and pledges support for William's claim to the English throne.

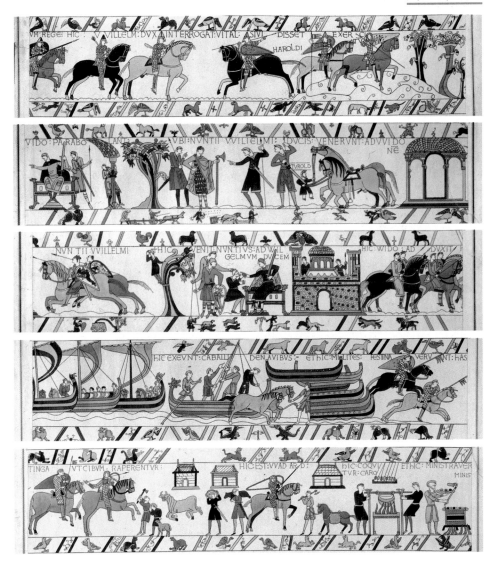

In the summer of 1086, William 'held very deep speech with his council about this land [England] – how [it] was peopled, and with what sorts of men'. So in 1086 he commissioned the Domesday (literally 'the Day of Judgement') survey, a detailed account of land ownership and taxable value throughout the country. William was eager to gain this information, but his people were not so eager to supply it. (*Left*) The ancient chest in which Domesday Book was preserved for hundreds of years.

As well as recording details of land ownership, the Domesday commissioners were instructed by William to discover the strengths of the barons, and how many knights they were bound by feudal duty to supply. At the time, William needed war funds to combat a threatened Scandinavian invasion, hence the speed with which the survey was compiled. (*Left*) The old cover of Domesday Book. Although the metal corners are of later date, the covers are certainly extremely old.

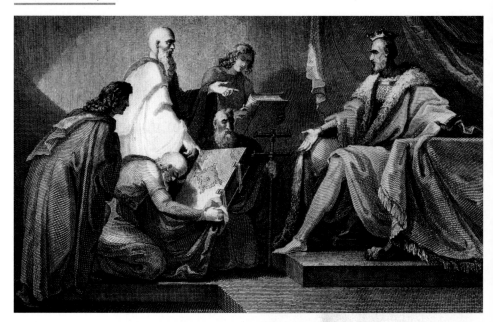

(*Above*) Domesday Book is presented to William the Conqueror by members of his council in 1087. It is doubtful that he ever had time to read it, for he died a few weeks later, on 9 September 1087. (*Right*) A page from Domesday Book. It is part of the description of Westminster. The details are almost certainly accurate, for William ordered a second set of chroniclers to tour England, checking the findings of the first.(*Opposite*) A portrait of William the Conqueror. He was the bastard son of Robert I of Normandy, and his mother was a tanner's daughter from Falaise. Although an able ruler, William was primarily a soldier, a harsh and brutal man.

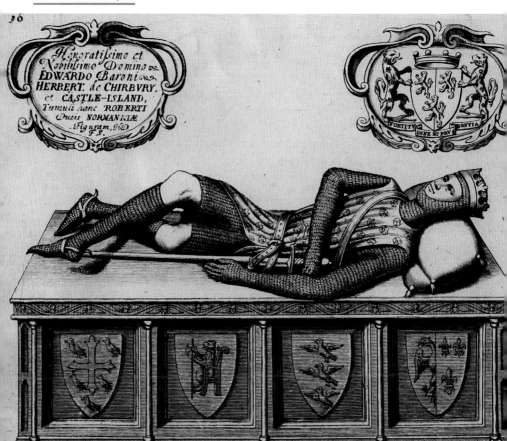

The tomb of Robert of Curthose, Duke of Normandy. Robert was the eldest son of William the Conqueror and Matilda of Flanders. Robert rebelled against his father and was exiled to France. He disputed the succession of both William Rufus and Henry I to the throne of England, but was captured and imprisoned at Devizes, Bristol and Cardiff. He died in 1134 at the age of eighty.

In general, Norman soldiers were far better armed and protected than their Saxon opponents, though the Saxon two-edged axe could slice through chain mail. The mounted knight, however, was one of the most powerful and terrifying warriors on the battlefield. The bow had yet to have the range or accuracy of the later English longbow.

The vast majority of people lived and worked on the land, with a task for each season and hopes for each harvest. (*Left*) A group of labourers. The tools they carry are simple – a dibber, a shepherd's crook or possibly a simple hook to reach nuts or berries on high branches, and a hoe. (*Below*) A farmer sows seed by the broadcast method. The dog is there to scare birds, though two are happily eating from the sack of seed.

An early ploughing scene from the beginning of the 11th century. The draught animals are probably small oxen, and the plough is almost certainly made of wood.

God spede ye plouz: & sende us korne Inolk

A Saxon ploughman. Wooden ploughs were not very efficient at breaking up the earth, especially where the soil was wet or heavy. The ploughman carries an axe to break up clods of earth left by the plough.

Cliffords Tower, York. The first English castles were built by the Normans, and were all built to the same pattern. They were known as 'motte and bailey' castles. The bailey was the palisade or fortified fence that ran round the perimeter of the castle. The motte was the steep-sided mound of earth with a flat top. Later, as in this picture of the medieval castle at York, fortified towers or 'keeps' were erected on the motte. Castles were both the instruments and symbols of Norman domination.

(*Opposite*) William Rufus, or William the Red, King of England from 1087 to 1100. He was the second son of William the Conqueror, but succeeded to the throne after his older brother was exiled. He promised the people good government, a relaxation of the harsh forest laws that denied them rights to hunt and collect fuel, and a reform of the tax system. He failed to keep these promises. (*Above*) The death of William Rufus. He was killed while hunting in the New Forest by an arrow fired by a knight named Walter Tyrell. No one knows whether this was an accident or murder. (*Right*) The Rufus Stone, marking the place where William Rufus died.

(*Above*) St George slays the dragon. It was not until Norman times that he became the patron saint of England. (*Opposite*) Lady Godiva, wife of Leofric, Earl of Chester. In protest at the taxes raised by her husband, Godiva rode naked through the streets of Coventry. Legend has it that she asked all the citizens to stay indoors, and that all obeyed save 'Peeping Tom', who was immediately struck blind.

An 'Ancient View of St James's Westminster Abbey and Hall from the village of Charing'. The numbered buildings are: 1. St James's Palace. 2. A public house at the village of Charing. 3. Westminster Abbey. 4. Westminster Hall. 5. A wall belonging to the Palace (now Pall Mall). 6. Fields near St James's Park. 7. A conduit (on the site of the present Palace of St James's). The village of Charing is now the area around Charing Cross and Trafalgar Square, and the hill in the distance may well represent that leading up to Clapham Common. In Norman times, Westminster was almost entirely separate from London, with Charing and other villages in between.

2
MAGNA CARTA
1100–1215

To Western contemporaries, the clash between Crusaders and
Saracens was personified in the meeting between Richard I and
Saladin, by the battle between axe and lance, might and right
pitted against dark arts and cunning. The Arabs regarded the
Crusaders as among the most mysterious of the Creator's works:
'animals possessing the virtues of courage and fighting, but
nothing else; just as animals have only the virtues of strength and
carrying loads...'

Introduction

and and sea yielded more and more. Annual rents along the coast were reckoned in fish – 38,500 herrings for Southease in Sussex; 60,000 herrings for Dunwich in Suffolk. New tin mines were opened in Cornwall, new lead mines in Derbyshire. Iron-working increased in Yorkshire and Lincolnshire, Sussex and Kent, and the Forest of Dean in Gloucestershire. Tidal mills were established on the Deben estuary in Suffolk, supplying greater power to more and more machines.

Great castles descended upon Dover and Pembroke, Colchester and Chepstow as the Normans strengthened their hold on England and Wales. Strongbow began the process of colonising Ireland that was to haunt Britain for the next eight hundred years. The great cathedral rising in glory at Ely looked out across the Fens where Hereward the Wake maintained the last Saxon resistance to Norman rule. Ranulf Flambard, bishop of the wonderful new cathedral at Durham, became the first prisoner to escape from the Tower of London. Thomas à Becket died at the altar of his cathedral in Canterbury. He was murdered by four knights of Henry II, who managed to break almost every rule laid down by John of Salisbury for chivalrous behaviour: 'to defend the Church, to assail infidelity, to venerate the priesthood, to protect the poor from injuries...to pour out their blood for their brothers.'

Despite frequent wars, trade and communication with mainland Europe greatly increased. With imported goods came imported ideas, covering everything from how to make soap in hard cakes to how to make 60 per cent proof alcohol. There were revolutionary new techniques in architecture (the flying buttress and ribbed vaulting), in farming (harnessing draught animals in sequence and the cross-breeding of sheep), in industry (the loom with two treadle-operated leashes), and in art (woodcuts for ornamental letters in manuscripts).

The Scots, under David I, Malcolm IV and William the Lion, maintained their raids on the northern counties of England with varying success, though they had still to deal with separatist risings in their own country. The Welsh, under Owain Gwynedd, rallied and drove the English out of Wales.

And, on 15 June 1215, at Runnymede, near Windsor, John of England put his signature to one of the greatest documents in British history – the great charter of liberties, known as Magna Carta. It was an attempt to assert the rule of law over arbitrary rule, and its words still have force and relevance. 'No freeman shall be arrested or imprisoned or disseised or outlawed or exiled...except by the lawful judgement of his peers and by the law of the land...To none will we sell, to none will we refuse or delay right or justice.'

KING IOHN.

(*Left*) John Lackland, king of England from 1199 to 1216. Few monarchs have been subject to such appalling publicity as John. Although by no means loveable, he was an able administrator and spent more time in England than his predecessor and elder brother, Richard I. (*Opposite*) Arthur of Brittany with his gaoler. Arthur was born in 1186, the posthumous son of another of John's brothers, Geoffrey. He was hailed as Richard's successor by the barons of Anjou and Philip II of France, but was captured by John and imprisoned in Calais. It was, and sometimes is, popularly believed that John was responsible for Arthur's murder.

(*Left*) Durham Cathedral, one of the most impressive of all Romanesque ecclesiastical buildings. William of St Carileph, Bishop of Durham, began work on it at the end of the 11th century and the bulk of the building was finished in 1133. William was succeeded by Ranulf Flambard, whose main claim to fame is that he became the first prisoner to escape from the Tower of London. (*Opposite*) The nave of Durham Cathedral, with its massive rib-vaulting, was completed in the 12th century. The pillars are over 2 metres in diameter.

An early view of Durham Cathedral, standing like a fortress 22 metres above the River Wear. It was built partly as a place of worship and partly as a fortress for defence against raids by the marauding Scots. It was a place of sanctuary for hunted men and women, and a place of pilgrimage, for it contained the bones of St Cuthbert. It was also the burial place of the Venerable Bede, author of the 8th-century *Historia Ecclesiastica Gentis Anglorum* (*Ecclesiastical History of the English People*).

Hereward the Wake (literally 'the Watchful') was the last of the great Saxon folk heroes. In reality he was a Lincolnshire squire who led a raid on Peterborough Abbey in protest against the appointment of a Norman abbot. In legend, Hereward became the leader of a band of freedom fighters, cheating and cheeking the Normans before disappearing into the Fens. The images of Hereward rescuing a young girl from the Normans (*above*) and of his heroic death (*right*) spring from legend.

Mort de Hereward.

Robin Hood

C. Wilhelm 1904

Robin Hood – also known as Robin o' Locksley and the Earl of Huntingdon (*left*) – is, probably and sadly, a creation of romantic imaginations. For seven hundred years or more he has been the hero of books, poems, plays and films, all of which depict him as a brave, handsome, generous-hearted fellow. Legend has it that in the late 12th century he lived in Sherwood Forest, with a band of jolly outlaws who included Little John (*opposite*, with sword – an ironic depiction), Will Scarlet, Friar Tuck and Alan a' Dale. If Robin really did exist, it is almost certain that he was not a Saxon, though his enemies may well have been the Norman Sheriff of Nottingham and Prince (later King) John.

Richard I, also known as Richard the Lion Heart (*opposite*), was King of England from 1189 to 1199, although he spent only six months of his life in England (August–December 1189 and March–May 1194), and probably could not speak English. He was a soldier king and a crusader. Contemporary opinion varied about him. To some he was hot-tempered and irresponsible, 'bad to all, worse to his friends, and worst of all to himself'. To others he was generous and accomplished, a lover of music, and, of course, a man with the heart of a lion. He was the second Angevin king of England, and his arms (*right*) subsequently became those of England.

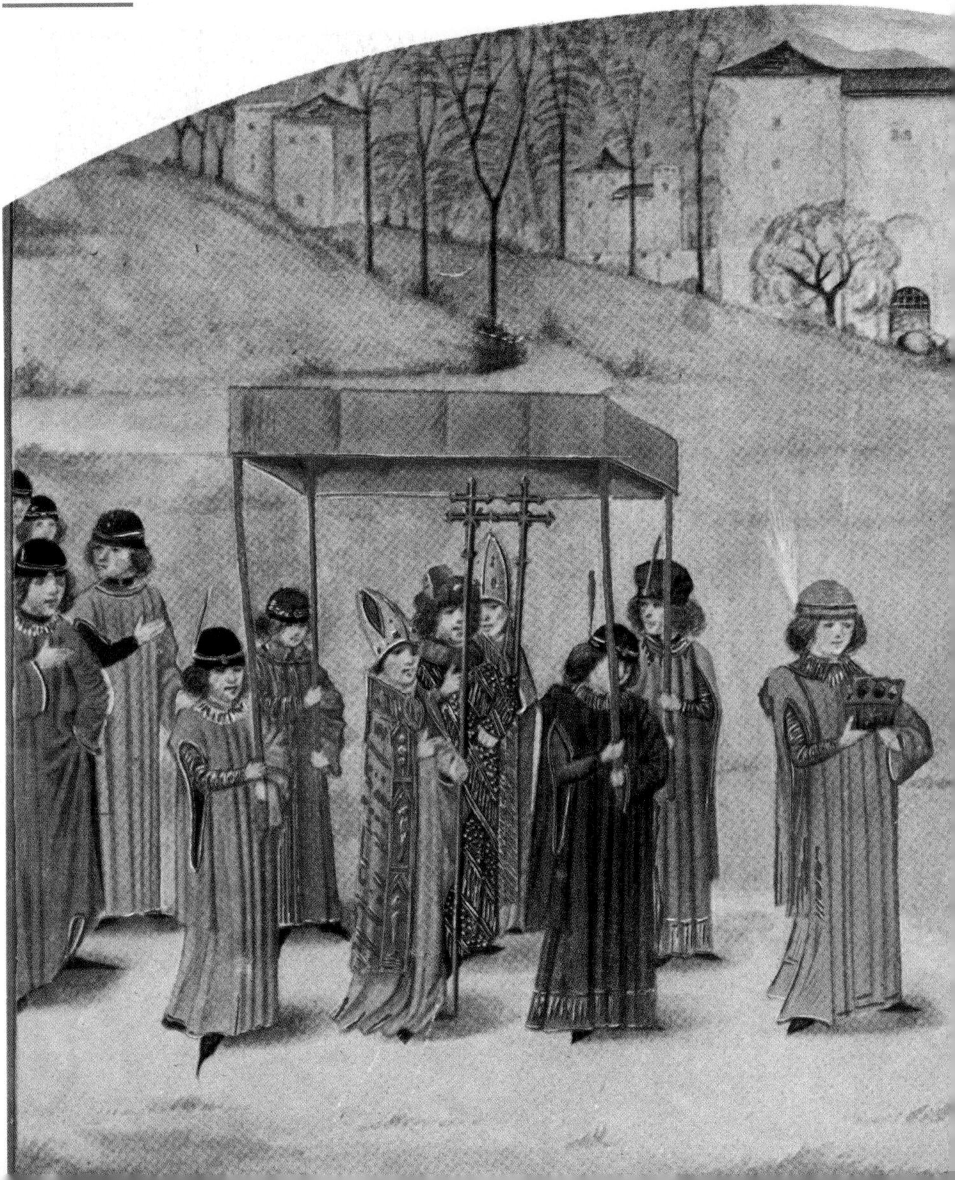

(*Left*) The Coronation Procession of Richard I, 3 September 1189. Roger of Wendover wrote an eye-witness description: 'Duke Richard, when all the preparations for his coronation were complete, came to London, where were assembled the archbishops of Canterbury, Rouen and Treves…the archbishop of Dublin, with all the bishops, earls, barons and nobles of the kingdom…Proceeding to the altar, Duke Richard swore, in presence of the clergy and people, that he would observe peace, honour, and reverence all his life, towards God, the holy Church and its ordinances: he swore also that he would exercise true justice towards the people committed to his charge.' Some were extremely happy to see Richard crowned (*below*), for that day he released all those unjustly or arbitrarily imprisoned. For Richard, the day ended in feasting with 'wine flowing along the pavement and walls of the palace'.

Seljuk Turks captured Jerusalem in 1075. The Holy City was in infidel hands. Twenty years later, at the Council of Clermont, Pope Urban II urged 'men of all ranks, knights and foot soldiers, rich and poor, to hurry to wipe out this evil race'. Thus were the Crusades born. A contemporary described the departure of Crusaders for the Holy Land (*left*): 'And so, when they had embarked there were, between galleys and lenys and ships and terides, thirty six sails; and there were one thousand five hundred horsemen…and there were fully 5000 men afoot…' All Crusades started with glorious expectations of victory, but all ultimately failed.

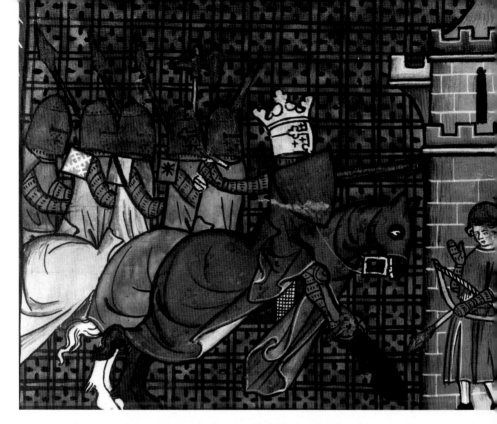

French and English knights fighting at Gisors, Normandy, *c.*1190 (*above*). The Crusaders were well practised in the art of fighting. When not holding tournaments, knights frequently met on the field of battle, as their kings contested the right to disputed territory. Soldiers who did their duty were regarded as little lower than the saints, and the Crusades gave thousands the opportunity to prove their courage in the noblest of Christian causes. They also offered the wayward and the profligate remission from sins and a moratorium on any debts.

(*Below*) A Saracen attack on Crusaders, *c.* 1200. An anonymous Crusader left a vivid account of the first contact between Crusaders and Turks: 'The Turks surrounded us on all sides, fighting, throwing javelins and shooting arrows marvellously far and wide…We nevertheless met that encounter with united spirit. And our women on that day were a great help to us, in bearing drinking water to our fighters… and always comforting those fighting and defending.'

Thomas à Becket was the son of a wealthy Norman merchant who entered the Church and became Archbishop of Canterbury in 1162, at the age of forty-four. He was a champion of the Church against the nobles, many of whom he excommunicated (*opposite, top left*) for their theft of Church property. He was also prepared to argue with kings, including Louis of France and his own King Henry II (*opposite, top right, and below*). In 1170, four knights, who had heard Henry utter the fateful words 'who will rid me of this turbulent priest?', burst into Canterbury Cathedral and murdered Becket at the altar (*left*).

Cantuariensis ecclesiæ cath:
ab occidente prospectus.

Tho: Johnson delin:
Daniel King sculp:

Becket was canonised in 1173 and Henry did public penance at his tomb a year later. Canterbury Cathedral (*left*) became a shrine, the destination for thousands of pilgrims from all over England and Europe, including the pilgrims described by Chaucer in his greatest work. It also became one of the most beautiful buildings in England (*above*), for, after the martyrdom of its popular Archbishop, the Cathedral was greatly enlarged. This work was begun by William of Sens, one of the finest builders of the age, but an accident left him disabled when he fell from scaffolding. His place was taken by William the Englishman, and the main body of the cathedral was completed at the beginning of the 13th century.

(*Left*) The south doorway of Kilpeck parish church in Herefordshire. The 12th century witnessed a great surge in English church building, with a flowering of decorative stone carving, often centred around the south door. At Kilpeck the entire arch is covered in Norman grotesques – dragons, monsters, birds and humans. (*Right*) The church of St Mary at Iffley, Oxfordshire, built *c.* 1170-80, is one of the best preserved 12th-century village churches in England.

Henry I (*right*) was the only English-born son of William the Conqueror. He was posthumously styled 'Beauclerc' ('The Scholar'), though he was not particularly learned. He was cold-blooded and crafty, and could be very cruel. But he was an able administrator who master-minded popular reforms of the system of justice. He strengthened his position by marrying Matilda (sometimes known as Edith) of Scotland (*above*).On 25 November 1120, their eldest son William was drowned with three hundred other young noblemen in the wreck of the *White Ship* (*opposite*). Henry was said never to have smiled again.

Henry, 1st King of England &c

By the 12th century wool was one of the chief products and exports of England. It was a cottage industry; women often took spindles into the fields with them to spin wool while they minded the pigs or fed the cattle. Even weaving was done in the open air on simple hand-looms (*above*). Land owners took to raising sheep, a far less labour intensive occupation than growing crops. One shepherd could look after a great many sheep (*opposite, below*). Many labourers lost both job and home as land was converted to pasture. Life was far more secure for the craftsman, and there was always work for the village blacksmith (*opposite, above*).

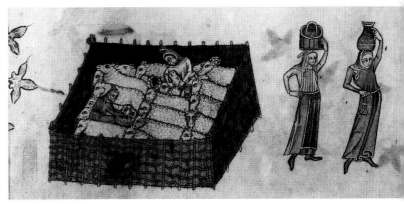

3
FORGING THE NATION
1215–1300

An English port in the mid-13th century. English and Scottish merchants and traders were quick to take advantage of the Italian revolution in banking in the 13th century. No longer did goods have to be paid for in coin. A simple entry in a ledger marked how much money a man had made. This led to a rapid growth in trade all over Europe. Wool was England's chief export, but there was a staggering variety of imports: lead and alum from Romania, cloves from the Black Sea, silk and glass from Venice, leather and oranges from Spain, wine from France. The English Channel was as busy seven hundred and fifty years ago as it is today.

Introduction

The pace of change quickened. Walter of Henley and other agriculturists praised the development of the broad-wheeled plough, which enabled the earth to be turned even when wet. The downland and hills of England, Wales and Scotland were increasingly dotted with sheep – 32,000 sacks of wool were exported to mainland Europe in 1273 alone.

More and more forest fell to axe and saw. Timber was needed in building (though the new Chapter House of Westminster Abbey had an iron frame), in machinery, for vats and casks, in ship-building, tanning and rope-making. This led to shortages and to the first imports of timber from Norway to Grimsby in 1230. It also led to environmental concern, and tree-felling was restricted in the Forest of Dean in 1282.

Timber was also needed as fuel, though sea-coal was gathered on the beaches of Northumberland, and there were already many 'bell' coal mines in Britain. In 1257 Queen Eleanor was driven from Nottingham Castle by the smoke from coal fires throughout the town. London became the first city officially to suffer from air pollution. In 1285 the citizens of Wapping, Southwark and East Smithfield complained about the coal fumes from the kilns that produced lime for building and farming. A royal proclamation forbade the burning of coal.

The age produced extraordinary men. Robert Grossetete (1175–1253) was born of humble parents in Stratbrook, Suffolk. He studied at Oxford and Paris, and became Bishop of Lincoln and the first Chancellor of Oxford University. As well as being the author of many books and commentaries, he was a learned mathematician and wrote the first treatise on lenses and optics. In his wake came Roger Bacon, known to his contemporaries as Doctor Mirabilis. Bacon's ideas played a leading part in the invention of the magnifying glass, gunpowder, lighter-than-air flying machines, the microscope and the telescope. He may be credited with the invention of spectacles, but his far-sighted imagination got him into trouble, and he was imprisoned for heresy.

In 1271 Robert the Englishman reported that 'clockmakers are trying to make a wheel which will make one complete revolution for every one of the equinoctal circle...', in other words, a mechanical clock. Fifteen years later, Bartholemew the Orologist of St Paul's Cathedral succeeded.

It was an age when St George's Day became a public holiday and when marrying for love was a luxury known only to the poor. For others it was a purely business arrangement. In 1274 the Abbot of Hales in Lancashire ruled that: 'John of Romsley and Nicholas Sewal are given to next court to decide as to the widows offered them.'

Edward I (*opposite*) was King of England from 1272 to 1307. At the age of fifteen he married Eleanor of Castile (*above*), a loving union that lasted almost forty years. Edward was raised as a soldier by his father, Henry III, and spent much of his reign fighting the Welsh and the Scots. In 1284, in an attempt to capture the loyalty of the Welsh, Edward presented his infant first son to them as the first Prince of Wales (*left*). By then, Edward and Eleanor had already been married for thirty years.

Edward spent much of his life fighting the Scots. Though he had his victories and captured the Coronation Stone of Scotland at Scone, total success eluded him. In the summer of 1307, though old and infirm, he marched north one last time, but died at Carlisle. He had charged his son to carry his bones with the army until the Scots were completely subdued, but the Prince buried his father in Westminster Abbey, inscribing *Scotorum Malleus* (Hammer of the Scots) on his tomb.

Eleanor of Castile was nine years old when she married Edward and only fifty-four when she died. From 1270 to 1273 she accompanied Edward on a Crusade to the Holy Land, where she is said to have saved his life by sucking poison from a wound. She died at Hadby in Nottinghamshire, and her grief-stricken husband commanded that 'Eleanor Crosses' should be erected at each of the nine places where her cortège halted on its journey to London. The Cross at Waltham, Hertford-shire (*opposite*), is one of three that survive. Eleanor's tomb (*above*) is in Westminster Abbey.

XIII

(*Opposite*) A portrait of Edward I's Parliament, *c.* 1270. Edward is seated on the throne (top, centre), with his brother-in-law, Alexander III of Scotland, to his right, and Llywelyn ap Gruffydd, Prince of Wales, to his left. Edward was known as the English Justinian, for he spent much of his reign refining and reforming the law of England. He was also the first English king to accept the notion that the law could only be changed with the consent of Parliament. His relations with the Church were less cordial, and he had in Archbishop Pecham (*left*, centre) a man who was prepared to follow in the footsteps of the martyred Becket.

(*Left*) Crowds in Cheapside attend the parade that carries the head of Llywelyn ap Gruffydd through the streets of London. Gruffydd was killed in battle near Builth, stubbornly resisting English domination to the last, and with his death Wales lost her political independence.

(*Right*) Sir William Wallace, champion of Scottish independence. He was a doughty warrior, a good tactician and a cunning guerrilla fighter. In 1297 his army routed the English at Stirling Bridge, but the following year suffered a defeat at Falkirk. Wallace was betrayed and captured by the English in Glasgow in 1305. He was tried in London, condemned, and immediately dragged by a horse from Westminster Hall to the Tower, where he was hanged and quartered.

SIR WILLIAM WALLACE, FROM AN ANCIENT PAINTING IN THE POSSESSION OF SIR JOHN MAXWELL OF POLLOK

ROC:BACH.

(*Above*) A medieval astronomer studies the heavens. In his hand is an astrolabe, with which he is calculating distances. (*Opposite*) Roger Bacon, English philosopher and scientist. Bacon studied at Oxford and Paris, and became a Franciscan monk, though he was later expelled from the order and imprisoned for his 'suspected novelties'. He was a brilliant and original thinker, whose works on mathematics, philosophy and logic were way ahead of his contemporaries.

It is easy to dismiss medieval physicians as at best bungling, at worst greedy. John of Salisbury claimed that their attitude was 'never mind the poor; never refuse money from the rich'. But medicine was becoming a science. Doctors worked in their laboratories (*right*), made house calls to the sick (*above*), struggled and studied to improve their knowledge. Identifying those parts of the body where the Actual Cautery (a hot iron) should be applied (*opposite*) may have been a hit or miss affair, but knowledge was increasing all the time.

The wealth of England, Wales and Scotland was increasingly to be found on the backs of sheep. From the west of Wales to East Anglia, from the Cheviots to the South Downs, the hills and plains of all three countries were covered with fleeces that could be turned into gold. Tending sheep was a job for man or woman; shearing and carding (*opposite*) were mainly man's work. Spinning was primarily done by women, either on a distaff (*left*) or the faster and more efficient spinning wheel (*below*). The finest wool was said to come from Tintern, and fetched twenty-eight marks a sack. Most English wool was exported to Flanders, France or Brabant to be made into cloth, in which form it was then sent all over Europe. The wool trade was attractive enough for Edward I to plan to make it a royal monopoly late in his reign.

In many parts of England entire towns and communities were devoted to the production of wool. One of the richest areas was Suffolk, where Eye, Coddenham, Kersey, Lindsey and Sudbury all became known as 'wool towns'. The richest and perhaps finest of them all was Lavenham, where merchants, among them generations of the local Spring family, met to discuss trade, wages, prices and prospects in the half-timbered Wool Hall (*right*).

Piety and pride went hand in hand in the 13th century. Those who made their fortune were prepared to display their wealth, and to spend part of that wealth in giving thanks to God for the gifts He had bestowed upon them. A favoured way of doing this was church-building. The richer you were, the more elaborate the church. At Lavenham, the Sprying family built a church (*opposite*) that was both beautiful and ostentatious, for its nave and the walls of its aisles were largely made up of massive stained-glass windows, and the entrance to the porch (*right*) was decorated with rich carvings.

Willemin del. et Sculp.

Giraldus Cambrensis, a Norman-Welsh chronicler and ecclesiastic who died in 1223, delighted in the art and practice of music. 'The sweet harmony of music,' he wrote, 'not only affords us pleasures, but renders us important services. It greatly cheers the drooping spirit, clears the face from clouds, smoothes the wrinkled brow, checks moroseness and promotes hilarity.' Many of his contemporaries would have agreed with him, for the 13th century witnessed a flowering of music throughout the British Isles. The first known English round song *Sumer is icumen in* ('Summer is a-coming in') was written at this time by an anonymous writer. Kings and princes played the harp (*opposite*), the lyre, the bagpipes, the viol and the tabor.

The wind organ (*opposite, below*) began to appear in churches and cathedrals. A carving of the mid-13th century on the Minstrels' Pillar in Beverley Minster, Yorkshire (*above*), shows a large band of musicians playing a variety of instruments. The sound they made would have much enlivened church services. 'In labour of various kinds,' continued Giraldus, 'the fatigue is cheered by sounds uttered in measured time. Hence artificers of all sorts relieve the weariness of their tasks by songs.'

4
MEDIEVAL MATURITY
1300–1450

In 1328 Edward III claimed a better right to the throne of France than the incumbent Philip VI. In retaliation, Philip threatened to help David II of Scotland in his war against Edward, and invaded the rich duchy of Aquitaine, then still an English possession. And so began the Hundred Years' War. The French raided Portsmouth and Southampton, and French ships were seen in the mouth of the Thames. On Midsummer Day 1340, the French fleet was sighted in the Channel near Sluys (*left*) – 'so great a number of ships that their masts seemed to be a great wood'. The English attacked and won a 'wild and horrible' victory.

Introduction

For much of the 14th and 15th centuries, England was at war – with the Welsh, with Scotland, with France, with itself. There were three famous victories against France (Crécy, Poitiers and Agincourt), and a dreadful defeat by the Scots at Bannockburn in June 1314 where the schiltrons of Robert Bruce routed Edward II's army of 20,000 men and guaranteed Scottish independence.

The war with France was a thing of fits and starts that lasted a hundred years, and, like all wars, hastened the development of technology. The invention of cast iron ushered in a new iron age which produced portable cannons, iron cannon balls and the first armoured carts. The other great weapon of the age was the English longbow, first used at the Battle of Falkirk in 1298. It had a range of over half a mile (850 metres) and was powerful enough to penetrate armour.

But such wars involved few English men or women. Far more destructive were the virulent outbreaks of plague in the 1340s. The Black Death first hit Britain in 1346 and reached its destructive peak three years later. No one knows how many died, but in some regions 50 per cent of the population was wiped out, and many villages disappeared for ever. The loss of life had two immediate effects – food became scarce and labour became expensive. Wages rose alarmingly and led to an early example of state intervention in the economy. The Statute of Labourers (1351) established a maximum wage, with penalties for those employers or landlords who exceeded it.

Many landlords responded by cutting back on the number of peasants they employed and switching from arable to cattle and sheep farming. Peasants, faced with the choice between being underpaid and overworked or homeless and without work, rose in protest. The Peasants' Revolt of 1381 was led by Wat Tyler, Jak Strawe and the egalitarian preacher John Ball. It greatly frightened the rich and the clergy, but achieved little in the end.

In a flowering of literature, William Langland and Geoffrey Chaucer respectively captured the miserable months and happy hours in a peasant's life. Langland's *The Vision of William Concerning Piers the Ploughman* graphically described the misery of 'a poor man hanging on to the plough'. Chaucer took a brighter view, declaring 'For I have seen, of a full misty morn, following full often a merry summer's day...'

Other innovations included iron needles, the fork, the slide trumpet and trombone, and Thomas Brightfield's water closet. This last was invented in 1449, and was flushed with water piped from a cistern. But the idea did not catch on, and four hundred years passed before it was reinvented.

WARD the third's eldest sonn;
id faigne ; he that wonn ,
the feild ; and did aduaunce ,
h the trembling hart of Fraunce.
ind , at Poitters I gaue fight ,
nd , slew and put to flight ,
t took prisoner their King ,
w-men with y̆ gray goose winge
es , weare euer tri'd ;
draw conquest to theire side ;
rran a part of Spaine :
ard , call'd King Pedros raigne:
heire come wee yet perceaue;
sh arrow: a full sheaf
torious battaile shew
e out of the trustly bow .
ers of arrows that day spent .
till vic̃torie as they went .
hts . the black Prince wonn .
nat his complec̃tion
es̆ memory hee erec̃ted:
chery, toe much neglec̆ted .

to all the worthy
ew louers of
Archery ⋆
Thos: Cecill
sculp:

Hee died
the 49 of his
age ano 1376
brunced at
Canterb:

POITIERS

Daniel at y̆ Angel in Lombar.

Edward III's first four years as King were difficult ones, for the country was virtually ruled by his mother and her lover, Roger Mortimer. In 1327, at the age of eighteen, Edward took control. He had Mortimer executed and sent his mother into exile. From then on, much of Edward's reign was taken up by war. In 1346 Edward invaded France, taking with him his eldest son Edward, dubbed 'The Black Prince' from the colour of his armour (*left*). At the Battle of Crécy, the Prince 'won his spurs', leading the right wing of the English army in a memorable victory. Edward then granted him the conquered provinces of France (*opposite*). Ten years later, the Black Prince was back in France, commanding the entire army at Poitiers. In 1361 he married Joan, 'the Fair Maid of Kent', who bore him two sons. The elder died in 1370; the younger became Richard II.

The Battle of Crécy, 26 August 1346. 'Then there began a terrible encounter between the armed men, with lances, spears, and battle-axes. Nor did our archers neglect their duties, but rising from their places of safety shot their arrows over the tops of ditches and hedges, to prevail over the armed soldiers, and their arrows flew more swiftly and more profusely than the weapons of those who fought in arms.' It was a famous victory.

The death of Sir William Wallace (*right*) did little to lessen Scottish resolve to resist English attack. The new hero of the Scottish Wars of Independence was Robert Bruce (*opposite, far left*). Bruce was a formidable man who murdered his way to the throne of Scotland in 1306. Within three months he had been driven into exile, while the rest of his family were killed or imprisoned. His sister was suspended in a cage from the walls of Roxburgh Castle (*opposite, left*). Bruce returned, waged a successful guerrilla war and built up enough strength to drive the English from Scotland. By the spring of 1314 England's last outposts were Berwick and Stirling. Edward II's attempt to relieve Stirling resulted in the Battle of Bannockburn, a humiliating defeat for the English. In 1327 Bruce was recognised by Edward as king of an independent Scotland. He died in 1329 and was buried at Melrose Abbey (*above*).

In 1284 the Statute of Rhuddlan divided Wales into the borderlands, ruled by the Marchers on behalf of the English crown, and the rest of Wales, directly ruled by England. To hold the population in check, Edward II and Edward III established a chain of massive fortresses, at Conwy (*right*), Builth, Aberystwyth, Flint, Rhuddlan, Caernarvon, Harlech and Beaumaris.

The outer walls of Conwy Castle are 5 metres thick, half a mile in length, and built in the shape of a Welsh harp. There are eight great drum towers, and twenty-one semi-circular towers at intervals along the walls. When it was built, it seemed virtually impregnable. In 1399 Richard II, abandoned by his allies in his struggle for power with Henry Bolingbroke, withdrew to Conwy Castle with just one hundred men. He accepted terms from the Earl of Northumberland and left the castle, only to fall into an ambush. He was taken as a prisoner to Flint, Chester and then Pontefract, where he was murdered the following year.

In 1381 a poll tax of four pence for all lay people was introduced to pay for the wars against France. In late May, entire villages in south-east England refused to pay. People armed themselves with axes and sickles, and elected Wat Tyler and Jak Strawe as their leaders. They marched on London where they released a radical priest named John Ball (*opposite, below*, on horseback). The ragged army reached Smithfield and Richard II rode out to them. Accounts differ as to what happened next, but it seems that William Walworth, Mayor of London, mortally wounded Tyler (*opposite, above*). In the Victorian engraving of the event (*above*), an incredibly young Richard is threatened by armed peasants. The King rode bravely forward and placed himself at the head of the rebels. Subsequently, Ball was executed and all promises made to the peasants were broken.

John Wycliffe (*opposite*) was a scholar and cleric who became increasingly disenchanted with the Church of Rome. He questioned its doctrines and practices, as well as the authority of kings, popes and bishops. He paved the way for the translation of the Bible into English, and was an uncompromising preacher (*left*). His followers were derisively called 'Lollards', from the Dutch for 'mumblers'. Among them was Sir John Oldcastle, who suffered martyrdom by being burned alive (*below*).

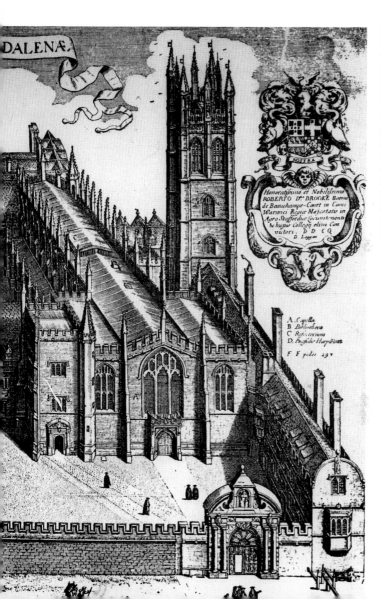

(*Left*) The College of the Blessed Mary Magdalen, Oxford University, soon after completion in the mid-15th century. It was founded by William de Waynflete to accommodate forty fellows, thirty scholars, four chaplains, eight clerks and sixteen choristers. It was only one of many centres of learning founded at this time – nine of the Oxford and Cambridge colleges were established between 1438 and 1496.

(*Left*) The twin towers, spires and rooftops of All Souls College, Oxford University. It was founded in 1438 as a memorial to the soldiers of Henry V killed at the Battle of Agincourt, twenty-three years earlier. Forty fellows were to spend their time there praying for the souls of Henry, the Duke of Clarence and the English captains who had died. The windows in the library were executed by John Prudde, the King's glazier, who charged eight pence a foot for glass 'powdered' (ornamented) with figures of the prophets, and ten pence a foot for glass 'flourished with roses and lilies and certain arms'. Stained glass was much admired in the 15th century, but such beauty was not cheap.

Few people avoided violence in the 15th century. It was an almost everyday feature of life. Animals were hunted for sport, for meat, for their skins, for their transgressions – every creature from rats to deer (*left*). Crowds gathered to watch cock-fights, badger-baiting and bear-baiting (*below*), but animals were not alone in their suffering. The most spectacular sport was jousting (*opposite*), where bold, brave knights risked injury and death, and all for a lady's favour.

Fact and legend are inextricably linked in accounts of the life of Richard 'Dick' Whittington (*opposite, below right*). Legend suggests he was a poor youth, whose life in the kitchen of a London merchant was so miserable that he ran away. But on Highgate Hill (*right*) he heard the sound of the bells of Bow Church saying: 'Turn again, Whittington, thrice Mayor of London.' In fact, he was the son of a rich merchant and worked his way up through the Mercers' Company to become Mayor of London four times. He was a philanthropist, who gave money to build almshouses, a college, a library at Greyfriars (*above, left*), and London's first public lavatory. The legend that his sole childhood friend was a cat (*opposite, below left*) dates from some two hundred years after his death.

It took well over a hundred years to build Salisbury Cathedral (*left*), whose 125 metre high spire is the tallest in England. The interior, with its columns of grey Chilmark and varnished Purbeck stone, is one of the greatest glories of mid-14th century architecture.

1402

GEOFFREY CHAUCER.

Geoffrey Chaucer (*opposite*) was in turn page boy; soldier; 'yeoman of the king's chamber'; Comptroller of the Customs and Subsidy of Wools, Skins and Tanned Hides in the Port of London; and knight of the shire of Kent. But he is remembered for his spare time occupation – that of poet. Between 1369 and his death in 1400, Chaucer was the voice of English poetry. His most famous work is *The Canterbury Tales*, a witty and colourful account of the lives and fortunes of a group of pilgrims – such as The Cook (*above, right*), The Pardoner (*above, left*) and The Merchant (*right*) – on their way from the Tabard Inn, Southwark, to the shrine of Thomas à Becket.

The Coronation of Henry V (*right*) took place in April 1413. Henry was twenty-six and had been, by all accounts, a wild youth. He spent most of his nine-year reign in a vain attempt to conquer France. His army consisted principally of two units: the men-at-arms (*below, far right*), 'armed and arrayed as belonging to their estate'; and archers (*below, left*). Both were contracted to serve the King for a limited period: there was no standing army. Men-at-arms often wore surcoats over their armour (*opposite*), decorated with the device or emblem of the captain they served.

The expedition of 1415 landed near the Seine estuary on 14 August. Five days later, Henry's army surrounded the port of Harfleur. Henry (*above*) expected Harfleur to surrender within the month, though the wait cost him 2,000 of his troops, victims of dysentry. Harfleur capitulated on 18 September 1415; Shakespeare's portrayal of Henry storming the 'breach' is totally inaccurate. Late in October, the French and English armies met at Agincourt. The English were cold, tired, hungry, and outnumbered by the French. Again, historically, there is no record of Henry inspiring his men with a great speech on the morning of the battle (*opposite*), but the English archers poured their arrows into the massed ranks of the French and the day was won. French losses were appalling. Fewer than three hundred Englishmen were killed.

The Hundred Years' War spluttered like a firecracker. Periods of peace and calm were noisily punctuated by campaigns and expeditions as a succession of English kings, from Edward III (*opposite, below*) to Henry VI, sought to recapture lost possessions in France. When there was no fighting, kings of France and England were personally on good terms. One of Edward's first acts as King was to do homage to Philip VI of France (*opposite, above*), but it did not take much for English resolve to harden, and for diplomatic relations to break down. (*Above*) Edward III sends his challenge to Philip. The Bishop of Lincoln and others have vowed to wear a patch over one eye until they have performed some gallant deed on the field of battle.

The Church's virtual monopoly on literacy was coming to an end. The finest calligraphy and the most beautiful illuminated manuscripts were still produced in monasteries by monks like Edwin (*opposite*), seen here writing with both hands at once, but more and more ordinary folk could read and write. Written reports were compiled (*above*) of government transactions, of judgements in law suits, of the deliberations of Parliament. And the vast increase in trade meant that merchants had to employ clerks and accountants to keep records of stock and write the all-important invoices.

Wives obeyed their husbands; children obeyed their parents. The medieval family was a unit of strict control at all levels of society. Generations lived together, from tiny babies to the old and infirm (*left*). Birth and death were no strangers to any home in the 14th and 15th centuries. Young children were indulged with toys and games (*opposite, below*), from rag dolls and spinning tops to hobby horses and skipping ropes. With so many children dying in infancy, those that survived were all the more valued.

The rejoicing that accompanied the birth of a baby was sadly often a prelude to a period of mourning for mother, child or both. A woman might live through many pregnancies, but half her children were likely to die in infancy. To speed the birth process, bunches of herb agrimony or semi-precious stones were attached to the mother's thigh. To hasten healing after childbirth, midwives rubbed the end of the umbilical cord with saliva, the ash of a snail, cumin or cicely. Immediately after birth (*above*), midwives bathed the baby in warm water, swaddled it in a warm cloth, and placed it in the mother's arms.

5
THE COMING OF THE TUDORS
1450–1500

For the poor, the staple diet was dark bread, curds, weak ale and boiled beans, prepared in the corner of a room that served as bedroom, living room, kitchen and animal shelter. For the rich, not only was the kitchen (*right*) a far grander and more hygienic place, the diet was also more varied and far tastier. Meat was displayed as a sign of wealth. The typical rich man's table might include a handsome array of beef, mutton, pork, poultry, venison, pigeon, goat, lamb, wild boar, rabbit and several freshwater fish. He ate few vegetables and little fruit, much of which was regarded as unwholesome: 'Beware of salads, green foods and raw fruit.' Apples, cherries, pears and plums were either preserved in honey or cooked in pies and pastries. Not surprisingly, constipation was a major problem, and, since the diet lacked vitamin C, rickets and scurvy were widespread.

Introduction

Life in this period offered more comfort and beauty and greater luxury. A visitor to Sir John Fastolf's castle at Caister in Norfolk in the 1450s would have been dazzled by the gold ewers, silver platters and the gilt gallon-pots enamelled with Fastolf's arms. There was still comparatively little furniture, even in well-to-do households, but Fastolf's chamber was rich with bed-hangings round his feather bed and 'six white cushions'. A hundred miles away there were all the glories of John of Utyman's stained glass in the windows of Eton College. John had been granted the earliest known English patent for this work.

In the 1460s, Margaret Paston of Norwich bequeathed to her daughter curtains, brass pots and 'two pairs of my finest sheets'. Elizabeth Poynings gave her daughter a generous wedding present that included plate, jewels, clothes, napery, seven great coffers, six chests, two cabinets, eleven joined stools, a 'little' table that was

2 metres long, and a round table – almost all she had save for 'such stuff as cannot be kept from the moths'.

Food was better and tastier. For hundreds of years stews and casseroles had been flavoured with herbs or with flowers such as violets, lilies, roses and primroses; the palates of the rich could now be tempted with regular supplies of spices from the east.

Trade was increasing rapidly. The world was shrinking slowly. In the wake of the voyages of Vasco da Gama and Christopher Columbus, British explorers set sail across vast oceans that were still said to contain sea monsters and mermaids. In 1497 John Cabot (born in Genoa but adopted by England) sailed west from Bristol with his three sons, in search of a sea route to Asia. Fifty-four days later he sighted Cape Breton Island, Nova Scotia, and claimed North America for England.

But the change that was to have the greatest effect on the entire world was the invention of printing by Johannes Gutenberg in the 1440s. England's first printer was William Caxton, who learned the art during a visit to Cologne in 1471–2. Four years later, he set up his wooden press in Westminster. In all, Caxton printed over a hundred books, including Chaucer's *Canterbury Tales* and Malory's *Morte d'Arthur*.

In 1485 at Bosworth Field, Richard II, last of the Plantagenet kings, was defeated and killed by the followers of Henry Tudor. The Wars of the Roses, which had seen the deaths of four kings of England and the murder of two royal princes in the Tower of London, were at last over. A battle in which barely 10,000 men took part had decided the fate of a nation. The Tudor Age began.

(*Right*) John Cabot kneels before Henry VII. Cabot was a Genoese navigator and explorer who settled in England. In 1497 he sailed with his three sons from Bristol (*below*), seeking a route to Asia, but landed in Nova Scotia, and claimed North America for England. His son Sebastian (*opposite*) was later made inspector of the navy by Edward VI.

EFFIGIES SEBASTIANI CABOTI
ANGLI FILII IOHANIS CABOTI VENE
TI MILITIS AVRATI PRIMI INVEN
TORIS TERRÆ NOVÆ SVB HERICO VII ANGLI
Æ REGE

SPES·MEA·IN·DE

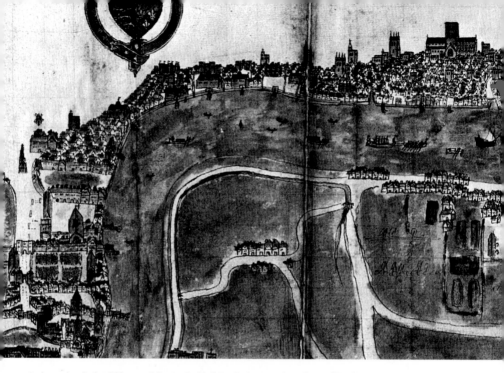

In the one hundred and fifty years following the Black Death, the size and population of London barely increased. There was still only one bridge across the Thames. Southwark, noted mainly for inns such as the Tabard, was the one settlement of any importance south of the river, and only a strip of houses joined Westminster and the City. The Tower of London (*above*, far right), Old St Paul's (centre, with square tower), the palace of Westminster (far left) and Southwark Cathedral (south of the river and next to London Bridge) were the only buildings of any great size. The contemporary German depiction (*right*) is more imaginative than accurate.

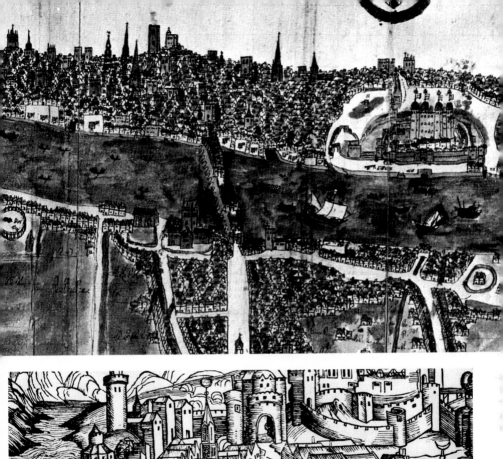

The scene is the Temple Garden. The time is 1455. This is the legendary beginning of the Wars of the Roses, as portrayed in Act 2, Scene 4 of Shakespeare's *Henry VI, Part 1*. Richard Plantagenet and the Earl of Warwick each pluck a white rose, the favour of the Yorkists. The earls of Somerset and Suffolk each pluck a red rose, the favour of the Lancastrians. The wars ended thirty years later.

Richard Neville, Earl of Warwick, was originally the wealthiest and most powerful supporter of the Yorkist cause. Offended by Edward IV's marriage to Elizabeth Woodville, and disappointed in his ambition to be appointed supreme commander, he defected to the Lancastrians. On 14 April 1471 Edward IV marched out of London with the trained bands to Barnet (*right*), where he attacked Neville's larger force at dawn on Easter Sunday. After three hours of fighting in thick mist, two separate divisions of Lancastrian troops mistakenly attacked each other, and Neville was killed in the struggle that followed (*opposite*).

The Wars of the Roses lasted intermittently from 1455 to 1485, though only thirteen weeks of that period were spent in actual fighting, and some battles lasted little more than half an hour. The decisive battle, and the largest battle ever fought in England, was at Towton on 29 March 1461, involving perhaps 50,000 combatants. Most battles were fought in open fields, and the picture (*left*) may well be of the Battle of Wakefield in 1460, when the Yorkists inadvisably left the safety of Sandal Castle and were defeated by the larger Lancastrian force.

In the confusion of the Wars of the Roses, it was not difficult for impostors to present themselves as rightful heirs to titles and even to the throne itself. Lambert Simnel was a baker's son who claimed to be the elder of the princes murdered in the Tower. His claim was backed by Margaret, Duchess of Burgundy (*opposite, top right*). With 2,000 German troops, Simnel invaded England in 1487. He was defeated, arrested and spent the rest of his life as a scullion (*right*). Perkin Warbeck (*opposite, top left*) was also a protégé of Margaret (*opposite, bottom right*), and claimed to be the younger of the two princes. He surrendered to Henry VII on the promise of pardon, but was executed in 1499 for attempting to escape. Jack Cade (*opposite, bottom left*) was a physician who was outraged by the misgovernment of Henry VI. With 40,000 followers he captured and held London for several days, but his troops dispersed. Cade fled, was captured and executed.

For much of the 15th century, Scottish kings battled to hold on to power. In 1437 James I was murdered in the Dominican friary at Perth, and the crown passed to his six-year-old son, James II, later known as 'James of the Fiery face' (*left*). The chief threat to James came from the Douglas family, of whom Archibald Douglas, known as Archibald the Grim (*opposite, left*), perhaps the most ambitious. In 1440 James II lured Douglas's son William into Edinburgh Castle where the poor man was beheaded. Fifteen years later the power of the Douglas family was finally broken. James III (*opposite, right*) was murdered by noble rebels in 1488, seemingly with the approval of his own son, who became James IV.

OFFER OF
THE KINGSHIP
TO RICHARD
DVKE OF GLOWCESTER
AT BAYNARD'S CASTLE
JVNE 26ᵗ
1483

Few kings of England have received such bad reviews as Richard of York, last of the Plantagenet line (*opposite, bottom right*). He was a capable man, but his brief reign was violent and vengeful. In 1472 he married Anne Neville (*opposite, bottom left*), younger daughter of the Earl of Warwick. Richard's brother, the Duke of Clarence, had already married Anne's older sister, and suspected that Richard was seeking to gain the Neville possessions. Six years later Clarence was impeached and executed, but there is scant evidence that Richard was involved.

In 1483, while at Bayward's Castle, Richard heard that Edward IV had died (*opposite*), and that he himself was to be the guardian of Edward's sons and heirs. Richard hurried back to London, where he accused Lord Hastings and other members of the Council of treason (*above*). Rivers, Grey and Hastings were all executed, Edward's sons were confined in the Tower of London, and Parliament offered Richard the crown. He reigned for just over two years.

Edward IV (*opposite, far left*) was handsome, popular and licentious. His ill-advised marriage to Elizabeth Woodville (*opposite, near left*) displeased many of the nobles and was followed by uprisings in the north of England. On Edward's death in 1483, the crown passed to his son who became Edward V. Two months later both he and his brother (*right*) fell into the hands of Richard of York (Richard III). They were imprisoned in the Tower of London and never seen again. They were certainly murdered, probably on Richard's orders.

Two months after the defeat and death of Richard III, Henry Tudor (*opposite, far right*) was crowned King of England. The Wars of the Roses had ended; the Lancastrians were victorious. England was, however, still a much divided country. Yorkist supporters regarded Henry as little more than a Welsh usurper, whose claim to the throne was weak – Henry was the grandson of Henry V's widow and Owen Tudor. Within three months of his Coronation, Henry did much to unite England and secure his tenure on the throne by marrying Elizabeth of York (*above*). The wedding (*centre*) took place on 16 January 1486.

The Wars of the Roses
came to an end with the
death of Richard of York
at the Battle of Bosworth
Field. Henry Tudor
became King of England.
His eldest son was Arthur,
Prince of Wales (*left*),
born in 1486. At the age
of two, Arthur was
betrothed to Catherine of
Aragon (*opposite, below*)
to facilitate an alliance
between England and
Spain. The wedding took
place in November 1501,
but Arthur died five
months later.

Although children of noble and wealthy families (*above*) often led pampered lives, both sons and daughters were seen as diplomatic and commercial pawns, with little say in when and whom they should marry. Thus it was not uncommon for boys to marry at the age of fourteen, girls at the age of twelve.

In 1476 William Caxton (*right*) set up his wooden printing press in Westminster (*below*). The stained-glass window at Stationers' Hall Court depicts Caxton presenting his first printed page to Edward IV and his Queen, Elizabeth Woodville (*opposite*).

Reverendo admodum viro
D: ZACHARIÆ CRADOCK
S.T.P. Præposito, omnibus
Socijs Collegij Etonensis,
hanc ejusdem Collegij Deli
neationem D.D.C.Q.
Dav. Loggan

COLLEGIUM REGALE de ETONA PROPE WIN

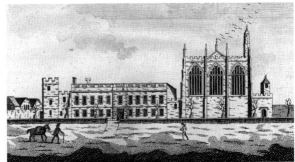

In 1440 Henry VI founded a college at Eton (*above*). Henry was a lover of learning, a 'royal saint' who might well have enjoyed being Master of Eton considerably more than King of England. The gatehouse leading to the quadrangle (*above, top*) bears similarities to those at Hampton Court. The College, with its magnificent chapel (*left*), was built on the water meadows just across the river from Windsor, giving Henry a fine view of his benevolence from the ramparts of the castle.

'The conditions required of a surgeon are four,' wrote a contemporary practitioner. 'The first is that he be educated; the second that he be skilled; the third that he be ingenious; the fourth that he be well behaved.' A surgeon's education was to include 'things natural, non-natural and unnatural'. So surgeons made use of animals, snakes and birds in their treatment of patients (*opposite, top left and bottom left*), as well as semi-precious stones (*opposite, bottom right*). A surgeon's ingenuity was to include the possession of 'slender fingers, hands steady and not trembling (*opposite, top right*), clear eyes, etc.' Allied to the skills of the surgeon was the wisdom of the pharmacist (*left*), who prepared pills, potions, powders, balms, salves and ointments for his fellow physicians.

Introduction to
Period 2 – 1500–1815

Henry VII worked hard to secure the hold on the throne of England that he had won on Bosworth Field in 1485. Above all, he wished to make the monarchy rich and its subjects obedient. His marriage to Elizabeth of York shrewdly united the Houses of York and Lancaster, but it was left to his second son to reap the rich harvest that the first Tudor king had sown. Henry VIII was a handsome, clever and combative young man, who promised much and delivered little. When he died in 1547, at the age of fifty-six, he left three children, religious friction throughout his kingdom and some pleasant pieces of music.

No matter – Britain's rise to the position of most influential nation in the world had little to do with kings or queens. Some monarchs (Elizabeth I and William III) helped the nation's drive to wealth and power; others (James II and most of the Hanoverians) merely got in the way. Charles I was the most obstructive, clumsy enough to jolt the newly united nations of England and Scotland into a civil war, which ended with his own execution and a brief and exciting period when Britain was a republic.

What really fuelled Britain's triumph was a mixture of luck, belligerence, imagination and hard work. Empires were won (and, in the case of the American colonies, lost) by the application of a very determined group of people. Spared the horrors and distractions of the wars that raged across mainland Europe throughout the 17th and 18th centuries, British minds could turn to more productive matters – in art, literature, architecture, philosophy, science and technology.

The age of printing ushered in a long and golden era for English literature. The age of Shakespeare included Francis Beaumont, John Fletcher and Ben Jonson, and Shakespeare himself (1564–1616) had hardly left the stage when a clutch of other playwrights entered – including John Dryden and Sir John Vanbrugh (dramatist and architect). The second half of the 17th century produced Jonathan Swift, Daniel Defoe, Alexander Pope, William Congreve and Samuel Richardson among others; the 18th century alone produced John Keats, Percy Bysshe Shelley, William Wordsworth, Henry Fielding, Sir Walter Scott, Tobias Smollett, Laurence Sterne, David Hume, Tom Paine and a dozen more great poets, philosophers and novelists. By 1770, English was spoken in every continent in the world.

Never before (and never since) had Britain been so rich in scientists and engineers. In 1628 William Harvey described the circulation of the blood. In 1662 Robert Boyle published his theories on the properties of the pressure and volume of gases. In the year that the Great Fire destroyed much of London and gave Sir Christopher Wren the sort of opportunity architects crave, Sir Isaac Newton watched an apple fall in his garden. It led to his formulation of the laws of gravity. Twenty years later, from the same brilliant mind, came the *Principia Mathematica*, later still his work on optics.

'Turnip' Townshend, Jethro Tull and Coke of Holkham revolutionised methods of farming. Arthur Young and William Cobbett toured Britain on horseback, spreading the word as to what to grow and how best to grow it. The Industrial Revolution, which had been simmering away since the invention of steam power by Newcomen early in the 18th century, boiled over with inventiveness. A single decade (1769–79) saw the arrival of the spinning jenny, the water frame, Matthew Boulton and James Watt's first steam engine, and Richard Arkwright's first spinning factory. Steam power and the machines it drove tripled Britain's industrial growth from

0.7 per cent per annum in the years 1710 to 1760, to 2.2 per cent per annum in the last twenty years of the 18th century.

The world was Britain's market. Elizabethan sea dogs (Sir Walter Raleigh, John Hawkins, Martin Frobisher, Sir Francis Drake and Sir Richard Grenville) had ensured English participation in the scramble for North America during the 16th century. Armies followed, pushing inland from the ports that had been captured or constructed. By the mid-18th century, Britain had taken possession of Canada, New England, India, Gibraltar and much of the West Indies. Australia, New Zealand and South Africa followed in the next fifty years. Only the American colonies escaped, to the consternation of the English and the strains of *The World Turned Upside Down*.

Accumulation on this scale required a certain ruthlessness and the British were not unduly sensitive people. The poor, the sick and the young were shown little sympathy in their times of need. The criminal was shown no forgiveness. Susannah Wesley, mother of the founders of the Methodist movement, declared that a child's spirit must be broken before it was seven years old, and there was a cruelly obvious way to break it. The law of

England held over two hundred crimes worthy of capital punishment in the late 18th century – including that of defacing London Bridge. Little progress had been made since laws passed against beggars in 1530 advised 'whipping and imprisonment for sturdy vagabonds. They are to be tied to cartwheels and whipped until the blood streams from their bodies, and then to swear an oath to go back to their birthplace or where they have lived for the last three years and to "put themselves to labour"…For the second offence the whipping is to be repeated and half the ear to be sliced off; but for the third offence the offender is to be executed as a hardened criminal.' Clearly, Tudor law-makers did not expect such severe punishments to deter the destitute from reoffending.

But the pace of change had quickened dramatically. The rich now lived in immeasurable comfort in grand houses (Vanbrugh, John Nash, Sir John Soane, James and Robert Adam), surrounded by beautiful paintings (Joshua Reynolds, John Constable, Thomas Gainsborough and J.M.W. Turner), exquisite furniture (Thomas Chippendale and Grinling Gibbons), and overlooking landscaped parkland (Lancelot 'Capability' Brown). Britain itself was no longer self-sufficient in food supplies, but most large estates produced their own meat, vegetables and fruit – including some exotic varieties, for the greenhouse was a British invention of the 17th century.

England had swallowed the parliaments of Scotland and Ireland – the first in 1603, the second in 1801. British prestige was at its height in 1825, for it was only ten years since Britain had formed the backbone of the alliance that had defeated Napoleon Bonaparte and restored peace and vestiges of the *Ancien Regime* to Europe. Ahead lay another ninety years of the *Pax Britannica*.

6
BLUFF KING HAL
1500–1550

Displays of wealth and power were much appreciated throughout medieval Europe. Patrons of the arts paid extra money for paintings that used luxurious colours. A palace was designed as much for ostentation as for comfort. The splendour of a servant's apparel reflected the splendour of the master. So it was with diplomacy. When Henry VIII embarked from Dover on 31 May 1520 (*left*) to meet Francis I at the Field of the Cloth of Gold, he took with him a retinue far larger than he could possibly have needed. The two kings met at a camp or 'tilting ground' in Picardy. For three weeks the two courts met in friendly rivalry – jousting and dancing, competing in sport and costume and courtesy.

Introduction

Descriptions of England were printed by Caxton in 1480 and Wynkyn de Worde in 1497, but both were little more than reworkings of the 14th-century *Polychronicon* of Ranulph Higden. Early in the 16th century, Erasmus wrote to a friend 'did you but know the blessings of Britain you would clap wings to your feet and run hither'. He was less happy on leaving Dover, where all his money was confiscated under a law of Henry VII forbidding the export of bullion.

A far lengthier account of early Tudor England came from Polydore Vergil di Urbino, who arrived in England in 1502, became an English citizen in 1510, and stayed until 1551. In 1534 Vergil published his *Anglica Historia*, to a mixed reception from English readers.

Vergil noted that southern England was far richer than the north, that much of the country was given over to cattle and excellent sheep, that enclosures were robbing the poor of their land to create deer and hunting parks for the rich. He admired London, particularly London Bridge, poised on arches 20 metres high and 10 metres broad. The shops and houses on it made it seem more like a street than a bridge. He regarded English men as tall, fair and 'good companions'. English women were of excellent beauty and 'in whiteness not much inferior to snow'.

Vergil described the English as great eaters: 'their beef is peerless, especially being a few days powdered with salt'. In the *Italian Relation*, a fellow-countryman of Vergil praised English beer and ale: '...nor are these liquors disliked by foreigners after they have drank them four or six times; they are most agreeable to the palate, when a person is by some chance rather heated'.

The great events of Henry VIII's reign escaped the attention of many foreign visitors. In 1513 an invading Scottish army under James IV was crushingly defeated by an English army commanded by the Earl of Surrey. Sometime in 1530, Henry (in his late thirties) first met Anne Boleyn (in her early twenties). He had already had brief affairs with her mother and her older sister, but Henry's lust for Anne was fanned by the pressing desire for a male heir. This yearning led, in rapid succession, to the break with Rome, the establishment of the Church of England, four further marriages, war with Spain, the imprisonment of his younger daughter by his older daughter, and the zealous persecution of Protestants by Catholics and Catholics by Protestants.

It was a busy, though not happy, reign.

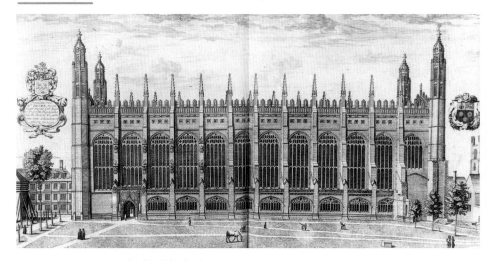

In England, the crowning glory of Gothic architecture was the Perpendicular style, and the finest example was the chapel of King's College, Cambridge (*above and opposite*). It was commissioned by Henry VI, but work was interrupted by the Wars of the Roses, and much of it was built during the reign of Henry VII (*left*). It was completed in 1515, and Flemish craftsmen spent the next twenty-six years inserting the stunning stained-glass windows.

As a young man, Henry was athletic, handsome and popular. He was a musician, dancer and skilled protagonist at the many tournaments he attended (*above*). He was not, however, a great negotiator. The splendour of the Field of the Cloth of Gold (*opposite*) was not matched by any great diplomatic coups. His concern to produce a male heir brought out the worst in him. Catherine of Aragon was discarded, Anne Boleyn executed. But even the birth of Edward (*top*, with Henry) was overshadowed by tragedy. Jane Seymour, Edward's mother, died twelve days later.

At the age of sixteen, Catherine of Aragon (*above, left*) was married to Arthur, Henry VIII's older brother. Arthur died six months later, and Catherine then married Henry. Twenty-four years later, Henry secretly married Anne Boleyn (*above, right*). Henry had already had an affair with Anne Boleyn's sister, and the marriage did not last long. Anne was accused of adultery with her brother and four commoners. She was beheaded in May 1536. Eleven days later, Henry married Jane Seymour (*left*), who died twelve days after giving birth to a son, later Edward VI.

For political reasons, Henry's next selection was Anne of Cleves (*above, left*), whom he married by proxy in 1540. She was not to Henry's taste, however, and the marriage was annulled by Parliament six months later. Catherine Howard (*above, right*) had the misfortune to be Henry's fifth wife. She was charged with having committed adultery before the marriage, and was executed in 1542. Catherine Parr (*right*) married and tended the ailing lecher in his last years. Soon after Henry's death in 1547, she married a former lover and died in childbirth.

In 1512 Henry made an alliance with the Pope and the King of Spain against Louis XII. He then set out to campaign in France, and James IV of Scotland (*opposite, left*) took the opportunity to make an unwise attack on England. Thomas Howard, Earl of Surrey (*opposite, far left*), marched north with an English army, and on 9 September 1513 inflicted a crushing defeat on the Scots at Flodden Field (*above*). James, his earls and archbishops and 10,000 of his men were killed. Howard had a mixed career. As a military leader he was highly successful. He raided the French coast, devastated the Scottish borders, and pacified those who protested at Henry's destruction of the monasteries. Politically, however, Howard was far less able or admirable. He acquiesced at the execution of his niece, Anne Boleyn, but subsequently lost Henry's favour and was condemned to death. Henry himself died just in time to save Howard from the executioner's axe. Howard is now best remembered for his poetry.

Sir Thomas More (*opposite, above*) was Henry VIII's most able chancellor. He was a man of the Renaissance – lawyer, philosopher, writer and statesman. He was also a devoted husband and father, and, above all, a pious Roman Catholic. His most famous work was *Utopia* (title page by Ambrosius Holbein, *left*), a search for the best possible form of government.

Henry was well aware of More's brilliance, and the strength of his chancellor's religious faith. When Henry proclaimed himself Head of the Church, it was inevitable that the two men would clash. Those who stood in Henry's way – even those he claimed to love – invariably ended up on the scaffold. More did not escape this fate. In 1535, he was led from his cell in the Tower of London and beheaded (*below*).

Thomas Wolsey (*opposite, bottom right*) was the brilliant son of an Ipswich butcher. He entered the Church and became Archbishop of York, cardinal, and the most influential member of Henry's Council. He lived and travelled in style (*right*) and was the King's favourite. (*Opposite, below left*) Henry even sent the royal physician, Dr Thomas Butts, to attend an ailing Wolsey. When he failed to obtain the Pope's permission for Henry's marriage to Anne Boleyn, Wolsey's fall was swift. He was summoned before Henry (*opposite, top*) and forced to surrender his seal of office (*top*).

Wolsey marked his rise to power by building the magnificent palace of Hampton Court (*opposite and above*) on the banks of the Thames a few miles upstream from London. The Palace was constructed round a series of courtyards and contained an impressive central hall, still known as Wolsey's Hall (*right*). When Wolsey fell from power, all his possessions, including Hampton Court, were forfeited to the Crown.

Henry annulled his marriage to Catherine of Aragon in 1533, on the basis that she had been previously married to his brother Arthur, and that the marriage was therefore invalid. Pope Clement VII refused to sanction Henry's marriage to Anne Boleyn and excommunicated the English king in 1534. The allegorical portrait (*left*) shows Henry with his feet on the Pope, receiving supplication from members of his Council – among them Chancellor Cromwell; Thomas Cranmer, the man who sanctioned Henry's marriage to Anne Boleyn; Bishop John Fisher, who was subsequently to be executed for refusing to recognise Henry as the Head of the Church of England. (*Above*) A representation of those Catholics who were suspected of plotting against Henry following his break with the Roman Catholic Church.

William Tyndale (*left*) was born in 1494. He was a bold religious reformer who shared Martin Luther's views of the Church. Tyndale went to Germany in 1525 and began printing his English version of the New Testament in Cologne (*below*, opening page of St Matthew's Gospel). Henry wanted Tyndale sent back to England to stand trial, but the poor man was arrested in Antwerp, tried by a court of Catholic zealots, and condemned to death. He was strangled and burnt at the stake in 1536 (*opposite*).

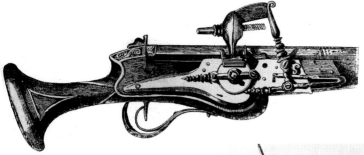

In the early 16th century, many English gentlemen of means and stature set aside one room in the house as an armoury (*opposite*). Here they kept an assortment of weapons (spears, swords, axes, mace and chain) – many of them well past their 'best before' date – and suits of armour. Although England was far more peaceful and law abiding than during the days of the Wars of the Roses, these weapons were not merely for display. If called upon by the King to raise a force for the defence of England or for service overseas, it was the duty of such men to equip and arm themselves and their followers for battle. It was also the time when plate armour became as effective as it could ever be, clothing both rider and horse (*right*) from head to toe. The greater number of joints in the armour allowed far more freedom of movement, but the weight proved exhausting. The invention of such weapons as the wheel-lock pistol (*above*) sounded the death knell for the knight in armour. Henceforth war was to be far more mobile.

The cheapest form of domestic lighting was the rush dip, a taper made from the stalks of rushes, peeled down one side, cut into lengths of about 30 centimetres and then dipped in hot melted fat, preferably lard. The rush was left to dry and then placed in a small receptacle called a 'nip'. It provided a weak light for about half an hour. Outside, and when travelling, cressets were used *(opposite and right)*. These were vessels of iron which held grease or oil, pitched rope, wood or coal. Sometimes they were suspended from the edges of roofs, but more usually they were carried on the ends of long poles.

7
SHAKESPEARE'S BRITAIN
1550–1600

The signature that could bring death or delight. Elizabeth
laboured long and hard over her duties as Queen of England, and
took considerable time and trouble over her signature. This was
not an age when documents were hurriedly approved by the
dozen. The flourishes reflect her pride in her role, and perhaps
something of her determination to yield to no one. 'I am your
anointed Queen,' she once observed in a speech. 'I will never be
by violence constrained to do anything.'

Introduction

The reign of Elizabeth I has traditionally been seen as marking the first fine flowering of English culture. This was the age when the most famous Englishman of all time wrote the most famous plays in history, and a fellow dramatist, Christopher Marlowe, added such masterpieces to the repertoire as *Tamburlaine*, *Doctor Faustus*, *The Jew of Malta* and *Edward II*.

In the great drawing rooms and galleries of such fine dwellings as Burghley House, Hatfield House and Hampton Court, the music of John Byrd and Thomas Tallis was played and sung. For John Day, having succeeded Caxton as England's leading printer, published music for choirs, stringed instruments and the virginals – as well as Foxe's *Book of Martyrs*, a warning to all good Protestants such as the Queen herself, and a later inspiration to John Bunyan.

English dancers and actors were popular at

home and abroad. English players of the viola da gamba were reckoned the finest, and many continental musicians came to England for instruction. The masques and dances held for the court at such venues as Richmond Palace, Nonesuch Palace and Middle Temple Hall in London outshone all previous entertainment.

But all this took place towards the end of Elizabeth's forty-five-year reign. When she ascended the throne in 1558, England was in a parlous state – crippled with a debt of over £266,000, 'ragged and torn with misgovernment', threatened by the close alliance between Mary, Queen of Scots, and Henry II of France, threatened even more by the sea power of Spain, and with the principal fortress defences of Berwick and Portsmouth falling into ruin.

The recovery was led by Elizabeth herself – a skilled diplomat, a forceful ruler, a true lover of her country and the discerning employer of bold adventurers. Her dealings with Drake, Raleigh, Hawkins and other buccaneers may have been secretive and illicit but they were certainly effective. The oceans and the ports of the world were plundered to bring Elizabeth the treasure she most desired – England's security. Drake was her greatest hero. It took him three years to complete the second circumnavigation of the globe in the *Golden Hind*, and three days to play his part in the destruction of the Spanish Armada.

As she lay dying, the Council of England approached Elizabeth, wishing to know her wishes for the succession, for the Queen had no direct heir. 'I will that a king succeed me,' she replied, 'and who but my kinsman the king of Scots.' She died on 24 March 1603. A few hours later, Sir Robert Carey rode out of London, post haste for Edinburgh with the news.

During Edward VI's final illness, Lady Jane Grey (*opposite*) was forced to marry Lord Guildford Dudley (*right*), fourth son of the Lord Protector, John Dudley, Duke of Northumberland. His plan was that Jane should become Queen on Edward's death, thus ensuring a Protestant succession. Within ten days, Mary Tudor, the true heir to the throne had established her authority. Lady Jane was executed on Tower Hill on 12 February 1554 (*below*).

Northumberland tried to raise an army to back his foolish plan. It was a desperate throw, flying in the face of the law and Mary's popularity. When Northumberland left London to do battle, his friends rapidly deserted him. He surrendered to Mary and was led to the Tower amid the jeers and stones of bystanders. Mary's entry into London a few days later was triumphant. She was received with cheering, music and gunfire. For his part, Northumberland was led to the scaffold where he insisted that he had always supported the Catholic cause. An enormous crowd watched him die (*left*).

Edward VI (*opposite, bottom right*) was only ten when he came to the throne. For much of his reign, England was effectively ruled by Edward Seymour, Duke of Somerset (*opposite, bottom centre*). In 1549 Seymour was indicted for 'over-ambition', and power passed to Northumberland. Edward died in 1553, and was succeeded by his half-sister, Mary Tudor (*right*). Unhappy in love, unlucky in war, Mary had little but her faith for support during her sad life. Her marriage to Philip II of Spain (*opposite, bottom left*) was loveless, and she had the misfortune to suffer the loss of England's last French possession when Calais fell to the French in January 1558 (*opposite, top*).

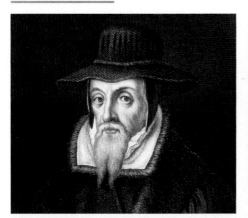

Protestants and Catholics alike found it hard to keep pace with the see-sawing of religious fashions in the 16th century. Henry VIII was first a Catholic, then a Protestant. Mary Tudor was devoutly Catholic, Elizabeth an avowed Protestant. Men and women of faith suffered in all their reigns, but those Protestants who were martyred in Mary's reign had their champion in John Foxe (*opposite, top left*), whose *Book of Martyrs* was first published in Strasbourg in 1554. Among those who died for the Protestant cause were Nicholas Ridley (*opposite, top right*) and Thomas Cranmer (*right*), both burnt at the stake for denouncing Mary. (*Opposite, below*) Robert Smith, George Tankerfield and others await their fate in Newgate Gaol.

When Shakespeare arrived in London, some time after the birth of his twins Hamnet and Juliet in 1585, there were three main acting companies. The two leading theatres where Shakespeare's plays were performed were the Swan and the Globe (*above*). Both were in Southwark, on the south bank of the river, for playhouses were frowned upon in the City of London (*left*). But the acting companies were often summoned to play at other venues – in stately homes, in the halls of livery companies or Inns of Court, and at the royal court itself. Perhaps it was as well that there was little scenery to move.

On 17 November 1558, Elizabeth succeeded her half-sister Mary and became Queen of England. She was twenty-five, 'comely rather than handsome', with fair hair, 'fine' eyes, and a delicate 'olive' complexion. Her Coronation (*right*) was an occasion of joy. 'After all the stormy, tempestuous, and blustering windy weather of Queen Mary was overblown,' wrote Holinshed in his *Chronicles*, 'the darksome clouds of discomfort dispersed, the palpable fogs and mist of the most intolerable misery consumed…it pleased God to send England a clear and lovely sunshine…and a world of blessings by good Queen Elizabeth.'

Elizabeth (*opposite*) had learnt her political lessons in the years of intrigue before she became Queen. Her mother was Anne Boleyn, executed for alleged adultery. Elizabeth herself had been imprisoned in the Tower, and had seen the tragedy that weakness and ambition could both bring. She was, however, a brilliant stateswoman, managing a succession of parliaments (*left*) so that she was loved as well as obeyed. She was also an accomplished sportswoman, one of whose chief delights was hunting (*above*).

LORD CHANCELLOR
HATTON 1589

TANDEM SI

Elizabeth chose her advisers with consummate care, and she was well served by them. The first and best was William Cecil, 1st Baron Burghley (*right*). Elizabeth appointed him at the beginning of her reign, saying 'This judgement I have of you, that you will not be corrupted with any manner of gift, and that you will be faithful to the state, and that without respect of my private will, you will give me that counsel that you think best.' It was a wise choice. Burghley stayed in office for forty years, building a fine estate at Burghley House (*above*). Sir Christopher Hatton (*left*) won the favour of Elizabeth by his dancing. He became Lord Chancellor in 1587, but lacked Burghley's perspicacity and statesmanship.

The contemporary print of Drake's ship, the *Golden Hind*, in 1587 (*left*) is a fairly accurate portrayal of the vessel in which he sailed round the world and from which he fought the Spanish Armada. Such ships were heavily armed, but quick to respond to wind and rudder, and, in capable hands, dartingly manoeuvrable. During his voyages of the 1570s and 1580s, Drake had dealings with several native peoples in Central and South America. Here (*above*), he meets a chief accompanied by a sceptre-bearer.

rake (*right*) was an
plorer, a navigator and a
rate. He was also a
triot around whom
any legends gathered.
hen the Spanish
mada was sighted in
ly 1588, Drake was
aying bowls on
ymouth Hoe. He is
lieved to have greeted
e news with the remark:
here is plenty of time to
in this game, and to
rash the Spanish too.'
the people of
ymouth he had no
ults; to the people of
ngland, few faults; and
his Queen, the only
ult was that of being
und out.

Habes Lector candide fortiß, ac inuictiß, Ducis Draeck ad viuum Imaginem qui toto terrarum orbe, duorum annorum, et mensium decem spatio, Zephyris fauentibus, circumducto, Angliam sedes proprias. 4. Cal Octobr. anno á partu Virginis 1580 reuisit cum antea portu soluisset Id. Decem: anni 1577.

IONIS NAVTICÆ.
um orbis ambitum circumnavigans, unica tantum navi, ingenti cum gloria
ITA est etiam viva delineatio navigationis Thomæ Caundish nobilis
temporis spacio, vigesimo prima omni huius 1686 navem conscendit, & decimo
em omnium admiratione reversus est.   Iudocus Hondius

In 1577, Sir Francis Drake (*opposite*) sailed from Plymouth in the *Pelican*, a ship of 100 tons. Ostensibly, he was not seeking plunder, but to found an English colony on the Pacific coast of North America. In reality, the likelihood is that Elizabeth had set one of her sea-dogs loose to strike a blow at Catholic Spain. After passing through the Straits of Magellan, Drake changed the name of his ship to the *Golden Hind* and sailed north along the coast of America as far as Vancouver. He then turned towards Asia, reaching the island of Java after sixty-eight days without sight of land. He returned to England by way of the Cape of Good Hope, becoming the first Englishman to circumnavigate the world. When he arrived back in Plymouth, he unloaded £1.5 million of Spanish gold. Elizabeth later visited Drake at Deptford and knighted him. The map (*left*) illustrates his adventurous route.

Sir Walter Raleigh (*left*) was an explorer, adventurer, poet and one of Elizabeth's many favourites. In 1586 he sailed to North America (*opposite, right*) where he made unsuccessful attempts to establish a colony in Virginia (*opposite, far right*), but from which he brought potatoes and tobacco back to England. He became a confirmed smoker, though there is a story that when his servant first saw Raleigh smoking, he thought his master was on fire, and threw a pitcher of water over him (*opposite, bottom*). From hereon, it was all downhill. Raleigh dabbled in intrigue, was sentenced to death, but had his sentence commuted to life imprisonment. He was released, sailed to the Orinoco in search of gold, failed to find any, and returned home where his suspended death sentence was invoked.

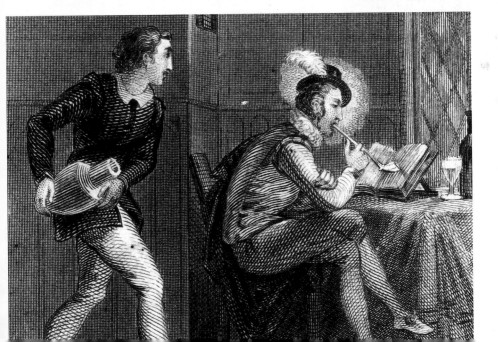

The battle between the ships of Howard of Effingham and the Spanish Armada (*left*) lasted ten days, from 21 to 30 July 1588. It was a running battle, as the Armada slowly fought its way up the Channel, with the English ships 'plucking their feathers' all the time. On 27 July, the Armada arrived off Calais, bruised but not seriously damaged. 'This is the greatest and strongest combination that ever was in Christendom,' wrote Howard, frustrated at his relative lack of success. That was to come, as were the gold medals struck to commemorate England's victory (*above*).

In the spring of 1588, Philip of Spain amassed a vast Armada of ships in the port of Lisbon. Its purpose was to establish a base for a military invasion of England by the Duke of Parma, whose all-conquering army was waiting in Flanders. It was the responsibility of Charles Howard of Effingham, High Admiral of England (*left*), to see that this did not happen. He wanted to attack the Armada in open sea, but the Council of England would not sanction this. Their worry was that the Spanish fleet might slip past Howard's ships and have the Channel at their mercy. It was not until July that Howard heard definite news of the approach of the Armada. The country prepared for invasion. Elizabeth rode to Tilbury (*opposite*) to encourage her people and deliver her most famous speech: 'I know I have the body of a weak and feeble woman, but I have the heart and stomach of a king, and a king of England, too.'

On the night of 28 July 1588, Howard sent eight fireships, blazing with pitch, into the massed squadrons of the Armada. They created panic. The Armada was too tightly packed together, there was little room for manoeuvre, and, once alight, several of the larger ships exploded. A south-west wind drove the ships further up the Channel and out into the North Sea. Medina Sidonia, the Spanish admiral, hoped to escape back to Spain by sailing right round the British Isles. No definite news of the fate of the Armada reached Spain until September, when Sidonia himself limped into Santander, with the first battered remnant of the fleet. In all, the Spanish lost sixty-three ships; the English none.

Mary Stuart (*opposite*) became Queen of Scotland when she was one week old. She was promised in marriage to Edward VI but the Scottish Parliament declared the promise null. At the age of six, Mary was offered in marriage to the son of Henry II of France and Catherine de Medici. Twelve years later, on the death of her young husband, Mary returned to Scotland, where she angered many by marrying Henry Stewart, Lord Darnley (*right*). Darnley was an ambitious man who disapproved of Mary's fondness for her Italian secretary and musician, David Rizzio (*above*). On 9 March 1566, Rizzio was hacked to death in the Queen's antechamber at the palace of Holyroodhouse, Edinburgh.

John Knox (*opposite*) was born and raised a Roman Catholic. Not until he was thirty did he come into contact with Lutheran ideas, but he immediately embraced them. He joined the murderers of Cardinal David Beaton in St Andrew's Castle in 1547, but was captured by the French when the castle fell, and made to serve eighteen months in the galleys. He regained his liberty, went to London and became chaplain to Edward VI, but fled to the Continent when Mary Tudor came to the throne. Here he wrote his *First Blast Against the Monstrous Regiment of Women*. He returned to Scotland where he became a powerful preacher (*above*), condemning all those who did not share his views. Some have described him as a borderline fanatic. Others feel he went all the way.

In quo quis peccat
In eo punitur.

Mary's affection for Darnley revived enough for them to produce an heir to the throne – the future James VI of Scotland and James I of England – though Darnley refused to attend the baptism of their son. It is possible that Mary was party to Darnley's murder a few weeks later: certainly she married the murderer, the Earl of Bothwell, on 15 May 1567. Scottish nobles took arms against her and she fled to England. Here she was imprisoned by Elizabeth, who rightly feared Catholic plots to place Mary on the throne. The most famous of these plots was led by Anthony Babington in 1586 (*left*). Mary was guilty of complicity and Elizabeth prepared her death warrant in October 1587 (*above*).

FAC-SIMILE OF AN OFFICIAL COPY OF THE WARRANT FOR THE EXECUTION OF MARY QUEEN OF SCOTS.

It took Elizabeth five months to reach the decision to sign Mary's death warrant (*left*). Even after she had signed it, she was loathe to despatch it, and it took all Burghley's boldness to take matters into his own hands. Three days after it had been signed, Burghley sent the warrant to Fotheringhay Castle, where Mary was imprisoned.

It arrived on the night of 7 February 1587, and Mary was told to prepare for death the following morning at eight o'clock. She was ready for martyrdom and received the news calmly. She dined, wrote letters, slept a little, and was then led to the great hall of the castle where she was beheaded (*right*).

Robert Dudley, Earl of Leicester (*left*), was the younger brother of Lord Guildford Dudley, and son of the Duke of Northumberland, both of whom had been executed at the beginning of Mary's reign. Leicester spent much of his life flirting – with Elizabeth, with his various wives, and with Fate. He became a privy councillor, high steward of Cambridge University and military commander. But his incapability reached its high point in 1588 when he died of poison, rumoured to have been intended for his wife. Robert Devereux, Earl of Essex (*opposite*), was a successful soldier, courtier and poet. Elizabeth loved him for his 'goodly person, his urbanity, and his innate courtesy', though she boxed his ears when he once turned his back on her. But Essex had too much ambition. In 1601, near the end of her reign, he attempted to raise the City of London against her Council, and he was beheaded for treason.

Elizabeth made frequent 'progresses' round England. She liked to be seen by her people and she liked to be entertained by her gentlemen. In 1575 she visited the Earl of Leicester at Kenilworth Castle (*right*), one of the 'wonder houses' of the time. It was 'all of hard stone, every room so spacious, so well-lighted, and so high-roofed within: so seemly to sight, so glittering of glass a-nights by continual brightness of candle-fire and torchlight, transparent through the lightsome winds…' Elizabeth was treated to a banquet served on a thousand dishes of glass or silver by two hundred gentlemen.

When Elizabeth came to the throne, learning was in a sad way. The universities were in a state of much decay, and there was a shortage of schools. By the end of her reign, however, things had improved (*opposite, top*); almost every corporate town had at least one grammar school, such as that at Louth (*opposite, bottom left*). Gresham College (*top*) had been built in 1596, and Sir Thomas Bodley (*above*) had built an extension to the Bodleian Library at Oxford. Both Oxford and Cambridge universities were equipped with printing presses. And the Scottish mathematician John Napier (*opposite, bottom right*) had developed the study of logarithms.

William Shakespeare (*opposite, below*) was born in his father's house in Stratford-on-Avon (*above*), probably on 26 April 1564. His father was John Shakespeare, a glover and wool dealer, and the house was comfortable and well-furnished (*opposite, above*). William spent the early part of his life in Stratford, where he was educated, grew up, married and had three children. He returned to Stratford for the last few years of his life and died in 1616, but his creative life was spent almost entirely in London.

His writing and acting career lasted some twenty-five years. In that time he wrote some of the finest poetry in the English language and a series of incomparable plays. As a professional actor, Shakespeare knew the limitations of the Elizabethan theatre – no women on stage, little by way of scenery or lighting, patrons and crowds alike whose tastes had to be taken into account. His genius lay in overcoming these restrictions and producing masterpieces.

From the time that they were first staged, both *A Midsummer Night's Dream* (*left*) and *Romeo and Juliet* (*opposite*) were among Shakespeare's most popular plays. The groundlings (those in the cheapest seats) were especially fond of the buffoonery of the comedy where Bottom is transformed into an ass and yet captures the heart of Titania, Queen of the Fairies. The fate of the 'star-crossed lovers', from the moment they first meet, touched all hearts. Both plays were written between 1594 and 1596, a period in which Shakespeare also wrote four other comedies and three histories.

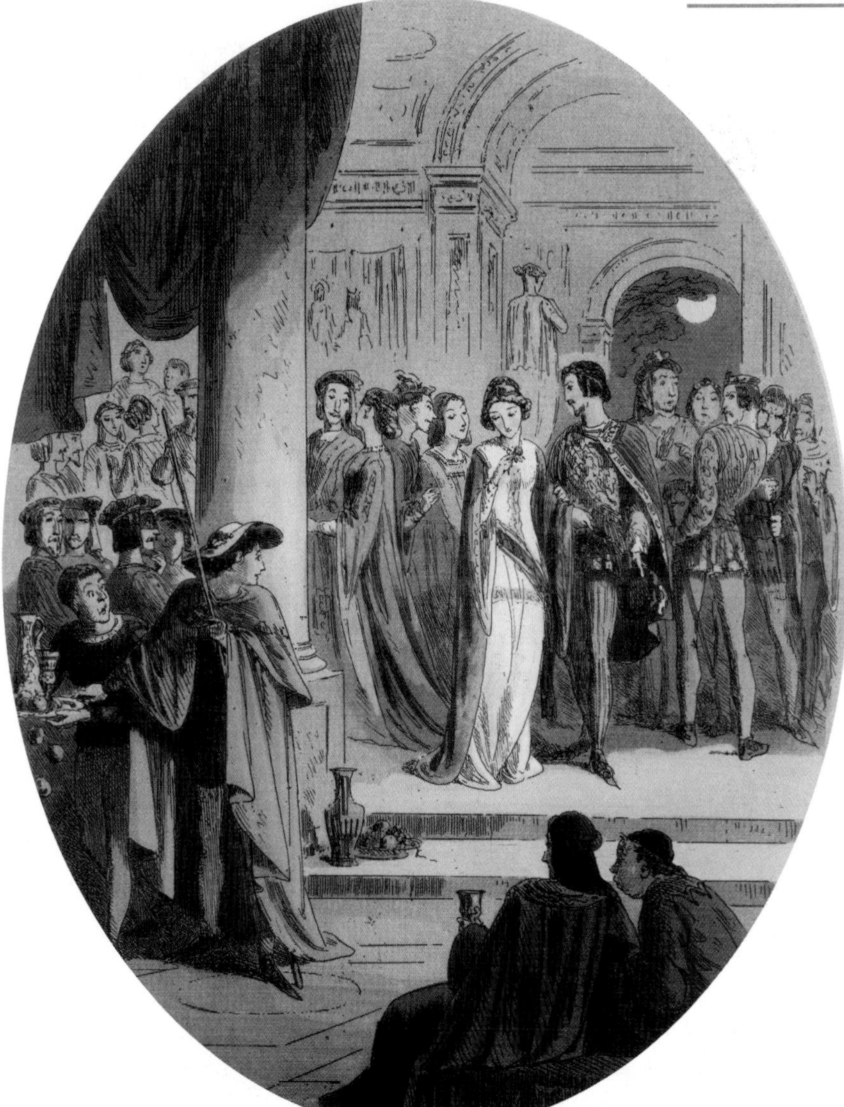

Thomas Tallis (1510–85), composer known as the 'father of English cathedral music'.

Title page of *Parthenia*, a first book of music for the virginals, composed by William Byrd, Dr John Bull and Orlando Gibbons.

Title page of the 1616 edition of *The Tragicall History of the Life and Death of Doctor Faustus* by Ch. Marklin, better known as Christopher Marlowe.

The only known portrait of Christopher Marlowe (1564–93), playwright and secret agent.

Thomas Heywood (1570–1641), dramatist and actor, author of *A Woman Filled with Kindness*.

Thomas Middleton (1580–1627), dramatist and author of *A Mad World, My Masters*.

Philip Sidney (1554–86), soldier and poet, who died at the Battle of Zutphen.

Edmund Spenser (1552–99), poet and author of *The Shepherd's Calendar* and the *Faerie Queene*.

Francis Bacon (*opposite*) was a contemporary of Shakespeare. He was also a writer, which has led many to suggest that Bacon was the true author of 'Shakespeare's' plays. There is no sound evidence of this, despite the suggestion made in the picture of 1610 (*top, left*) showing Shakespeare lifting the crown of fame from Bacon's head. Bacon was a politician and lawyer, who became Attorney-General and Lord Chancellor to James I. The arms and crest of the Bacon family (*left, below*) include the family motto – 'steady and constant' – a fair description of an obsequious man.

In 1618 Bacon was created Lord Verulam, a title taken from the Roman name for St Albans. He is best remembered for his writing on history (*History of Henry VII*), law (*Elements of the Common Law of England*) and philosophy (*The Advancement of Learning*). He was also an experimental scientist, and in March 1626 he caught cold while stuffing a fowl with snow to observe the effect of cold in preserving flesh. He died a few days later.

Hon.ᵐᵒ Franciscᵒ Baconᵒ, Baro de Verulam. Vice-Comes Sᶜᵗⁱ Albani. Mortuus 9 Aprilis,
Anno Dñi . 1626. Annoᵍᵘᵉ Aetat 66.

8
KING AND PARLIAMENT
1600–1650

30 January 1649 – a king becomes a martyr. When Charles I was executed, Cromwell's troops were clustered so densely round the scaffold that it was impossible for the crowd to hear the King's last speech: 'Truly I desire the people's liberty and freedom as much as anybody whatsoever, but I must tell you their liberty and freedom consists in having those laws by which their life and their goods may be most their own. It is not for having a share in government.' When the axe fell, an eyewitness reported, 'there was such a groan by the thousands present, as I never heard before and desire I may never hear again'.

Introduction

Charles I gave Britain little save some enduring images of his reign: the proud monarch on his splendid horse in the vast portrait by Van Dyck; the exasperated tyrant arriving too late to arrest those leading members of Parliament who opposed him ('I see the birds have flown...'); the heroic warrior raising his standard at Nottingham when he had brought his country to civil war; and the saint and martyr stepping on to the balcony of the Banqueting Hall in Whitehall on that last cold January morning.

There were other heroes and anti-heroes in the reigns of the first two Stuart kings – Guy Fawkes (father of British fireworks), John Hampden (who led the fight against illegal taxation), Oliver Cromwell, Inigo Jones (founder of English classical architecture and the man responsible for rebuilding the Banqueting Hall), Orlando Gibbons, William Harvey, and John Smith (pioneer of the first British settlements in North America.

John Lilburne was a Puritan who suffered beatings and imprisonment for his revolutionary views: 'The poorest man in England is not all bound to that government that he hath not a voice to put himself under.' Less admirable was a fellow Puritan, Matthew Hopkins, the English witchfinder-general. He was appointed in 1644, and within three years had sent hundreds of innocent women to their deaths. In 1647 Hopkins himself came under suspicion, and, being found guilty of witchcraft by his own test – he floated, bound, in water – was hanged.

Mercifully, there was progress in educating people's minds. *Mercurius Civicus*, the first British newspaper, was published. Ben Jonson acknowledged his own debt to the Master of Westminster School, under whom he had studied:

Camden, most revered head to whom I owe
All that I am in arts, all that I know.

Francis Bacon bridged the age; he published *The Advancement of Learning* in 1605, a review of the state of knowledge at that time, and went on to revolutionise the study of logic, philosophy and science itself.

And, for many, life steadily improved. Even the miseries of the Civil War passed most people by. When the opposing armies of Prince Rupert and Cromwell began to assemble on what was to be the battlefield of Marston Moor, a local farmer had to be told to stop work and get out of the way. 'Why?' he asked. The soldiers explained. 'What!' said the farmer. 'Are King and Parliament at war?' The war was already two years old.

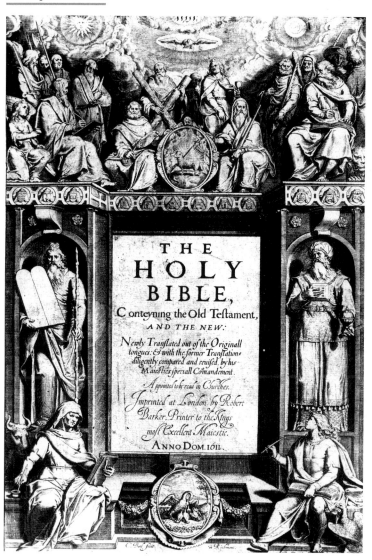

(*Left*) The frontispiece of the King James Authorised Version of the Bible, first published in 1611. It was a work of poetry and devotion, and shaped English literature as well as the faith of the English for four hundred years. The language was simple by the standards of the day, with a vocabulary of some 6,000 words, 90 per cent of them of English derivation.

The first of the Stuart kings. (*Above, right*) James VI of Scotland rides south to London to become James I of England. (*Left*) James I attends Parliament. (*Above, left*) Four Puritans seeking religious toleration at the Hampton Court Conference of 1604. James's reply was that they were to conform, or he would 'harry them out of the land'.

In 1605 a group of Catholics *(opposite, above)* hatched a plot to blow up the Houses of Parliament while King, lords, bishops and Commons were assembled there. In the ensuing chaos they hoped to seize power. The man they selected to do the deed was Guido (or Guy) Fawkes *(right)*, a Roman Catholic soldier of fortune. Fawkes placed the barrels of gunpowder in the cellars of the House, and covered them with straw. It is not certain whether the conspirators were betrayed or whether a watchman *(opposite, below)* stumbled on the barrels on the night before they were to be ignited. Punishment was swift and ferocious. The conspirators were dragged through the streets *(above)* and hanged, drawn and quartered.

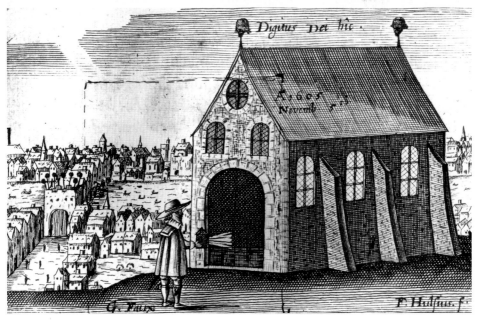

Inigo Jones was commissioned by James I to rebuild the Banqueting Hall of Whitehall Palace (*left*), and was employed to stage the masques of the poet Ben Jonson (*opposite*), who succeeded Shakespeare as the finest English dramatist in James's reign. Jonson was a modest man who acknowledged his debt to his old teacher, William Camden (*below, left*), and to Shakespeare himself. (*Below*) Jonson's dedication to Shakespeare, printed in the First Folio edition of 1623.

To the Reader.

This Figure, that thou here seeft put,
    It was for gentle Shakespeare cut;
Wherein the Graver had a ftrife
    VVith Nature, to out-doo the life:
O, could he but have drawne his VVit
    As well in Braffe, as he hath hit
His Face; the Print vvould then furpaffe
    All, that vvas ever vvrit in Braffe.
But, fince he cannot, Reader, looke
    Not on his Picture, but his Booke.

                                    B. I.

John Donne (*left*) led a rich and adventurous life. He was raised as a Roman Catholic, studied law and entered Lincoln's Inn at the age of twenty. In 1597 and 1598 he served as a soldier in two campaigns against the Spanish, and then became secretary to Sir Thomas Egerton, whose niece he secretly married. For this he was imprisoned. He became a Protestant and a poet, and his sonnets are still considered among the finest in English poetry. Donne was forty-two when he entered the Church at the behest of James I, and became Dean of St Paul's. The Cathedral (*opposite, below*) dominated the City of London (*opposite, above*), though the steeple was not replaced after being destroyed by lightning in 1561.

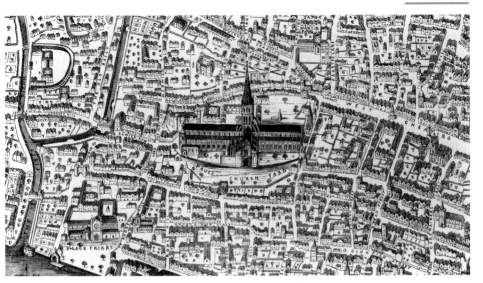

On 16 September 1620, the *Mayflower* (*left*) sailed from Plymouth Harbour. On board were one hundred and forty-nine people, forty-seven of them officers and crew. The rest were Separatists, Puritans who had been persecuted for their religious beliefs and who wished to start a new life in the New World. Sixty-five days later they landed at Cape Cod in Massachusetts. Among their number was Myles Standish (*right, above*, leading the column in white stockings), who became the military captain of their first settlement. The Pilgrim fathers, as they became known, were later joined by others, including John Eliot (*right, below*), one of the first Europeans to preach Christianity to Native Americans, and translator of the Bible into the their language.

John Smith – with pike planted upright – lands in Virginia, April 1607. The picture is a later representation of what was not so grand a moment. Smith had sailed with one hundred and forty-three others in ships financed by the London Company. Their aim was to harvest the riches of the New World and send them back to England. They christened their new colony Jamestown, after their King. Smith was almost immediately expelled from the colony for his mutinous attitude, but was pardoned and within a few weeks became its leader. He was a wise choice, for he was a practical man who saw the dangers that surrounded them. He forced all to work, threatening 'He that will not work, neither shall he eat.' It was a tough code, but it kept the colony together in the early, desperate days.

For all his faults and weaknesses as a king, Charles has long been seen as a good family man. With Henrietta Maria and their children, Charles was painted many times by the court artist Van Dyck *(right and below)*. In reality he was initially cold to his wife but, after the death of the Duke of Buckingham, Charles transferred his devotion to her.

Henrietta Maria (*right*) was only fifteen when she married. She was a young woman with a lively spirit and a great love of dancing. By contrast, Charles (*below*, in the Van Dyck triptych) was withdrawn, humourless and ascetic.

William Harvey (*left*) was one of the greatest English physicians. He studied medicine at Cambridge, and then at Padua under Hieronymus Fabricus. He was appointed physician to St Bartholemew's Hospital (*right*) and in 1615 he became Lumleian lecturer at the College of Physicians. In 1628 he published his treatise *Exercitatio Anatomica de Motu Cordis et Sanguinis*, in which he explained his theories on the circulation of the blood through the human body, theories that he demonstrated to Charles I (*below, right*). Harvey became Charles I's private physician and attended him at the Battle of Edgehill in 1642. Harvey died in 1657.

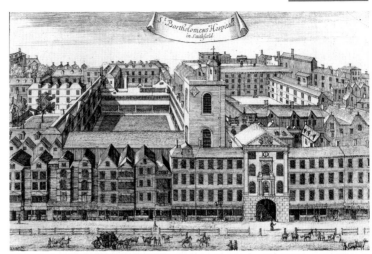

In his twenty-four-year reign, Charles managed to offend most sections of society. His unconstitutional demands to extend Ship Tax to inland towns infuriated John Hampden MP (*opposite*). His support for Laud led to political lampooning – here (*above, top*) Laud is depicted dining off the ears of Puritans. His restriction of free speech outraged the English Leveller, Colonel John Lilburne (*right*), who was described as 'our first democrat'. On 4 January 1642, Charles entered Parliament to arrest five MPs (*above*). He was too late: 'the birds' had flown. Three months later, the Civil War began.

Charles I believed in the Divine Right of Kings – that he ruled by the will of God, and that he could do no wrong. Such a man needed good advisers. Charles had two, but he showed them little loyalty. The first was William Laud, Archbishop of Canterbury (*opposite, top right, and below*, in a contemporary cartoon). The second was Thomas Wentworth, Earl of Strafford (*right*). Laud's aim was to purge the Church of Calvinists and Presbyterians. In 1640, he was impeached by Parliament, tried (*opposite, top left*), and imprisoned in the Tower. Strafford soon followed him there. He had aimed to make Charles the 'most absolute prince in Christendom', but now Charles denied him help. Strafford was beheaded on Tower Hill in 1641 (*below*). Laud languished in prison for four more years before he, too, was executed

A. Doctor Vsher Lord Primate of Ireland,
B the Sheriffes of London,
C the Earle of Strafford;
D his kindred and friends.

At first the Civil War was evenly matched. Both sides had generals of considerable skill and undaunted courage. The Parliamentary commander-in-chief was Thomas Fairfax, a professional soldier (*above*). The most famous Parliamentary officer was Oliver Cromwell himself, seen here (*right*) leading the cavalry charge that decided the Battle of Marston Moor, despite being wounded in the arm, on 2 July 1644.

The rival tactics of Oliver Cromwell (*opposite, far left*) and Prince Rupert (*opposite, right*) mirrored the characters of the Roundheads and Royalists themselves. Cromwell was dour, canny, well-disciplined. Rupert was dashing, hot-headed and careless. The troops on both sides, whether mounted dragoons (*above*) or musketeers (*right*) were seldom professional soldiers. They believed in the causes for which they fought, but they longed to return to their farms and their homes.

The trial of Charles I began on 20 January 1649 at Westminster (*opposite, far left*). Three times Charles refused to respond to the charge of treason, denying that an earthly court was competent to try a king. But the regicides, as they were later known, were determined men with the power of a victorious army behind them. On Thursday 25 January, Charles was condemned and two days later sentence was passed – 'that Charles Stuart, as a Tyrant, Traitor, Murderer, and public Enemy to the good people of this Nation shall be put to death by severing of his Head from his Body'. Charles was executed on 30 January. This contemporary portrait of the execution (*left*) is surmounted by portraits of Thomas Fairfax, Charles and Oliver Cromwell. Charles's last words were 'I go from a corruptible to an incorruptible Crown, where no disturbance can be.'

Cromwell (*opposite and above, right*) was forty-three when the war began. Although he had no military experience, he formed and moulded the New Model Army into a superbly trained force, without which Parliament may well have lost the war. The thorn in Cromwell's side was Robert Devereux, 3rd Earl of Essex. Devereux was personally a brave man, but a poor general. He was hesitant in battle and a poor strategist whose unwise invasion of Cornwall in 1645 could well have cost Parliament dear. Cromwell's problems did not end with the death of Charles. In this contemporary picture (*below, right*) he is shown grappling with his many opponents. His right foot tramples on a struggling Scotsman. A Frenchman is squeezed under his left arm. An Irishman is grasped by the neck between Cromwell's knees, and a Hollander lies prostrate on a table.

Cromwell was not a man to hesitate when faced with opposition. After Charles's death, the Royalist cause was dead in England and Wales. There remained resistance in Ireland, which Cromwell crushed with the massacres of the garrisons of Wexford and Drogheda (*opposite, below*). He then turned his attack to Scotland, defeating a Royalist army at Dunbar in 1650 before moving south to overwhelm Charles II's untrained troops at the Battle of Worcester in 1651. Parliament posed the next problem. There were those who favoured too much democracy, and Cromwell contemptuously dismissed what was left of the Long Parliament, replacing it with what amounted to a Puritan Convention (*opposite, above*). Contemporaries portrayed him as a rat catcher (*right*).

Old London Bridge (*opposite, top and bottom*) was a busy place in the early 17th century. It was still the custom to display the heads of traitors on the gates at either end (*left*, on the tower at the Southwark end of the Bridge), though this was discontinued after the Restoration in 1660. In severe winters, the Thames froze, and huge Frost Fairs were held on the ice (*below*) with dancing, the roasting of oxen, cock-fighting and bear-baiting.

Immediately after his execution, Charles I's body was brought to Windsor Castle (*right*) where it was taken for burial in the Chapel Royal – seen on the far right of the castle. Windsor was put to an unlikely use. It became a prisoner-of-war camp for officers from the Royalist army. Common soldiers were less well treated. Most of them were sent in barges down the river to be transported and sold into slavery in the Americas. During the Interregnum of 1649 to 1660, poor people were allowed to make their homes in the castle, but they were all evicted when Charles II returned in 1660.

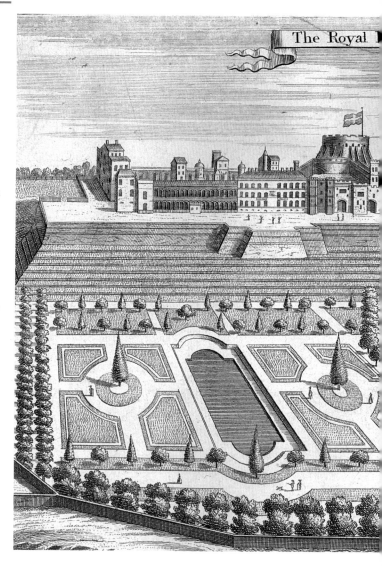

The Royal

of WINDSOR CASTLE.

River Thames

OFFERING MOST
Excellent fruites by Planting in VIRGINIA.
Exciting all such as be well affected to further the same.

LONDON
Printed for SAMVEL MACHAM, and are to be sold at his Shop in Pauls Church-yard, at the Signe of the Bul-head.

James I personally loathed smoking and wrote a book against it, but the early colonists of Virginia soon found a market for tobacco (*top and above*) in England. A sign from Samuel Manan's shop offered 'the most excellent fruits' imported from Virginia – snuff and tobacco – as early as 1609 (*right*). Opinion was divided as to the joys and dangers of smoking. The puffing cross-dresser (*opposite*) was a warning that it was possible to waste 'names, fames. Goods, strengths, healths and lives…in practising the apish art of [tobacco] tasting'.

9
PLAGUE AND FIRE
1650–1700

Early on Sunday morning, 2 September 1666, a baker and his wife in Pudding Lane were awakened by the sound of crackling flames. At first there was little alarm. When the Lord Mayor of London was aroused from his bed at three in the morning, he decided the fire was not serious and returned to his slumber. At the same time, Samuel Pepys's maid awoke her master: 'So I rose and went to the window…I thought the fire far enough off and so went back to bed and to sleep.' But it was a hot, dry September, a wind fanned the flames, and the fire rapidly spread. Taverns, houses, churches and even Old St Paul's were soon alight. Five hours later, Pepys recorded, 'above 300 houses have been burned down to-night by the fire we saw, and it is now burning down all Fish Street, by London Bridge'. People scrambled from their homes while the Great Fire of London raged around them (*right*).

Introduction

Britain's brief flirtation with republicanism came to an end in 1660, when army commanders invited Charles II to return from continental exile. The Merry Monarch was happy to oblige. Theatres reopened. Nell Gwyn trod the boards of Thomas Killigrew's fine new Drury Lane playhouse. Henry Purcell wrote the first English opera. Samuel Pepys wrote his secret diary in a childish code and invented the glazed bookcase. Izaak Walton wrote *The Compleat Angler*, a celebration of rod and line. Isaac Newton, and other members of the newly formed Royal Society, placed England in the forefront of scientific study.

From the ashes of the Great Fire of London, Sir Christopher Wren planned to build a city to rival any in the world. Petty minds and vested interests scotched his plans, but he lived long enough to see the completion of his masterwork – St Paul's Cathedral. Grinling Gibbons delicately decorated the choir stalls and organ screen within. The churches of Wren and Nicholas Hawksmoor stood proud above the foetid streets of the capital.

There was still trouble to come. Twelve hundred Scottish Covenanters, opposed to the reintroduction of episcopacy, were held throughout the winter of 1679 in the yard of Greyfriar's Church, Edinburgh. The Dutch sailed up the Medway and threatened London. In the awesome Weeping Valley of Glencoe, at five o'clock on a snowy morning, a company of soldiers under a Campbell commander massacred thirty-eight Macdonalds who had been their hosts for twelve days. When Charles died in 1685, his illegitimate son James, Duke of Monmouth, made a bid for the British throne. This sad and bungled rebellion came to a soggy and sorry halt at Sedgemoor, the last battle to be fought on English soil. There followed the full horrors of hanging Judge Jeffreys and the Bloody Assizes, whence many a misled Englishman was lucky to be transported to the new colonies, rather than hanged from a West Country gallows.

Horse racing began on Newmarket Heath and Epsom Downs. Coffee houses opened in the City of London. Mr Punch made his first British appearance behind Inigo Jones's beautiful church of St Paul, Covent Garden. It was built for the 4th Earl of Bedford, who told Jones he would have the church 'not much better than a barn'. Well, then,' replied Jones, 'you shall have the handsomest barn in England.'

James II lasted less than three years before he fled from London, dropping the Great Seal of England into the Thames as he went. The Glorious Revolution of 1688 ushered in William of Orange under terms that the Stuart kings would never have countenanced. But Britain had not heard the last of the Stuarts.

Two years after his father's execution, Charles II attempted to overthrow Cromwell's republic. The royal army was crushed at the Battle of Worcester in 1651, which Cromwell described as 'the crowning mercy'. The would-be king was forced to flee (*left*). He was pursued, but escaped by hiding in an oak tree (*above*) in the grounds of Boscobel House (*above, top*). The oak tree became famous, and gave its name to many 'Royal Oak' public houses in England.

By 1660 people had tired of the strict laws of the Puritan republic, and there were many politicians who favoured a return to monarchy – but on their terms. Charles II (*right*) was invited to come back to England. His arrival was greeted with wild enthusiasm, and cheering crowds lined the roads from Dover to London. His entry into the capital (*opposite*) was unopposed and lavishly spectacular. 'Divers maidens' presented a petition to the Lord Mayor, begging to be allowed to meet Charles. 'And if their petition be granted,' wrote Thomas Rugge in his *Journal*, 'they will all be clad in white waistcoats and crimson petticoats, and other ornaments of triumph and rejoicing.' It was a taste of things to come.

There were conflicting views of Charles. To most English people he was their deliverer from the grim days of the Commonwealth (*left*). To the Scots, he was the adventurer who had launched his bid to become King ten years earlier by plunging their own country into war (*opposite, below*). But the Restoration passed without trouble. It was time to settle old scores. The regicides (those who had condemned Charles I to death) were arrested and hanged, drawn and quartered at Charing Cross. The body of Oliver Cromwell was disinterred, and his remains were hung from a scaffold (*opposite, above*).

THE SCOTS HOLDING THEIR YOVNG KINGES NOSE TO Y GRINSTŌᴺᴱ

Come to the Grinstone Charles tis now to late:
To Recolect tis presbiterian fate:.

You Counant pretenders must Ibee
The Subiect of Youer Tradgie Comedie

Jockie

Stoupe Charles

One of the joys of the Restoration was the reopening of theatres throughout England and a lifting of the Puritan censorship. New theatres were built, among them the fine Theatre Royal in Drury Lane (*below*). Here one of the many attractions was Nell Gwyn (*left*). She was a capable actress and a renowned beauty, who soon became one of Charles's many mistresses. She certainly caught the attention of Samuel Pepys: 'I saw pretty Nelly standing at her lodgings in Drury Lane in her smock-sleeves and bodice, looking upon one – she seemed a mighty pretty creature.'

New theatres and new audiences attracted new playwrights. The plays of John Dryden (*above*) – *All For Love*, *The Indian Emperor*, *The Mayden Queene* – were at the time as popular as those of William Shakespeare. William Wycherley (*above, right*) was a dramatist and soldier best known for *The Country Wife* – a coarse delight of a play – *The Gentleman Dancing-Master* and *The Plain Dealer*. William Congreve (*right*) developed his love of the theatre as a young man during the late 17th century. His best works include *The Old Bachelor*, *The Double Dealer* and *The Way of the World*.

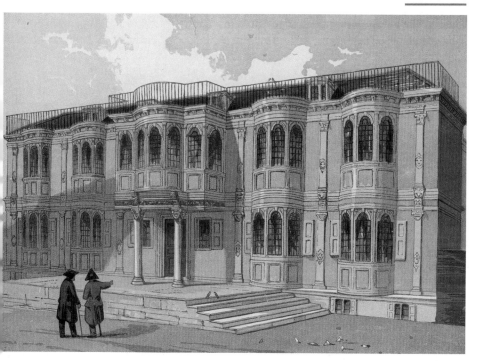

Greenwich was one of Charles II's favourite haunts. For many years it had been the site of royal pleasure. The Old Palace (*above*) was built by Humphrey, Duke of Gloucester, in the 15th century, to protect the eastern river entrance to London. Henry VIII, Mary Tudor and Elizabeth were all born there. Charles demolished the palace and commissioned John Webb to build a new one on the river front (*opposite, above*). The view of London from the top of Greenwich Park (*opposite, below*) was one of the finest in London. With his worthy Secretary to the Navy, Samuel Pepys, Charles was keen to increase the strength of England's fleet, and Greenwich became home to the Royal Dockyards.

VERSUS LONDINUM.

Charles was interested in art and science, as well as music and the theatre. In 1662 he became patron of the Royal Society, and in 1676 he established the Royal Observatory at Greenwich (*above and left*). Better and more powerful telescopes gave astronomers the chance to study the heavens in far greater detail.

John Flamsteed (*right, below*) was appointed the first Astronomer Royal. He compiled the first accurate catalogue of the fixed stars and prepared the way for much of the work of Isaac Newton. The Royal Observatory was built at Greenwich so that it would be sufficiently far away from the City to escape the smoke from coal and wood fires, thereby allowing users of telescope and quadrant (*right, above*) clear skies for their observations.

The Royal Society included many of the greatest names of the age. *(Left)* Charles II as patron is crowned with fame, and supported by Francis Bacon and William Brouncker, Irish mathematician and first President of the Society. Among the members were John Aubrey *(opposite, top left)*; John Locke, the philosopher *(opposite, top right)*; John Evelyn, diarist and author *(opposite, bottom left)*; and Sir William Petty, physician, mathematician, political economist and Surveyor General of Ireland *(opposite, bottom right)*.

CAROLVS II. SOCIETATIS REGALIS AVTHOR & PATRONVS

ARTIVM INSTAVRATOR

Robert Boyle (*left*) was an Irish physicist and chemist. He was one of the founder members of the 'invisible college', an association of Oxford intellectuals which was the forerunner of the Royal Society. As well as his scientific work, he was a director of the East India Company and worked for the propagation of Christianity in the East. He was also one of the first scientists to formulate an atomic theory.

Boyle worked for several years in his Oxford laboratory investigating the relation between the pressure and volume of gasses. Eventually he had assembled enough evidence to produce what has become known as Boyle's Law – that the pressure and volume of gas are inversely proportional. Boyle presented the air pump that he used in his experiments (*right*) to the newly formed Royal Society in 1660.

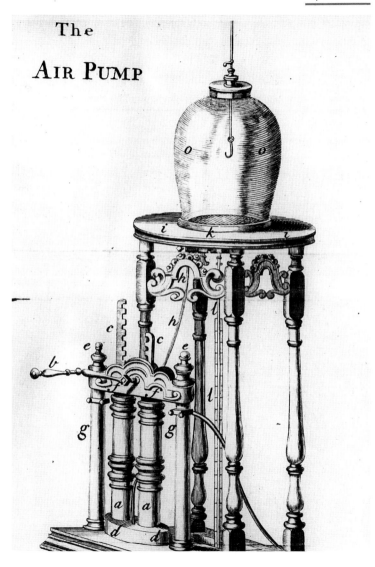

The

AIR PUMP

Sir Isaac Newton (*opposite, above left*) was a scientist and mathematician. He was born in 1642 and spent most of his life at his house in Woolsthorpe, Lincolnshire *(left)*. As well as formulating the Law of Gravity, he studied the nature of light and the construction of telescopes. He built his own observatory *(below)*, which was derided by others who referred to it as Newton's 'so-called' observatory.

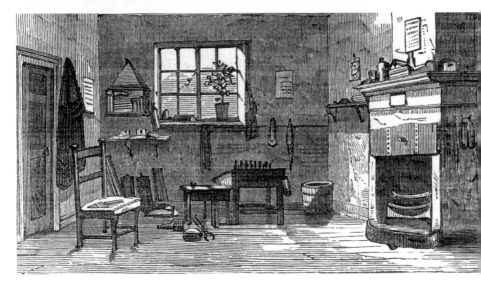

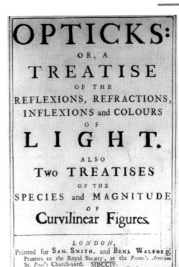

OPTICKS:
OR, A
TREATISE
OF THE
REFLEXIONS, REFRACTIONS,
INFLEXIONS and COLOURS
OF
LIGHT.

ALSO

Two TREATISES
OF THE
SPECIES and MAGNITUDE
OF
Curvilinear Figures.

LONDON,
Printed for SAM. SMITH, and BENJ. WALFORD,
Printers to the Royal Society, at the *Prince's Arms* in
St. *Paul's* Church-yard. MDCCIV.

His most famous written works were the *Principia Mathematica* of 1687, and *Opticks* (*above right*, title page). He was also a member of the Royal Society, and his signature is on the summons to a Meeting of the Society (*right*), at which the Council and Officers were to be elected on 1 December 1712. Like Robert Boyle, Newton straddled the change from medieval to modern science, for both were also alchemists.

SIR,

THESE are to give Notice, That on *Monday* the First Day of *December* 1712, (being the next after St. *ANDREW's DAY*) the Council and Officers of the ROYAL SOCIETY are to be Elected for the Year ensuing; at which ELECTION your Presence is expected, at Nine of the Clock in the Forenoon, at the House of the ROYAL SOCIETY, in *Crane Court*, *Fleet Street*.

To
Thomas Jesed Esq;

Is. Newton P.R.S.

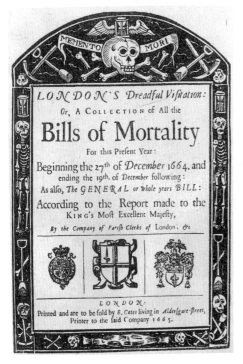

LONDON'S Dreadful Visitation:
Or, A COLLECTION of All the

Bills of Mortality

For this Present Year:

Beginning the 27th of December 1664. and
ending the 19th. of December following:

As also, The GENERAL or whole years BILL:

According to the Report made to the
KING's Most Excellent Majesty,

By the Company of Parish Clerks of London, &c

LONDON:
Printed and are to be sold by E. Cotes living in Aldersgate-street,
Printer to the said Company 1665.

Nothing prepared Britain for the epidemic of 1665. London (*opposite, top left*) was worst hit. The first deaths were noted early in June. By the middle of August, Bills of Mortality (*opposite, bottom left*) were recording well over three hundred deaths per week in a single parish. Bodies were collected nightly in carts and taken to pits were they were unceremoniously dumped (*below*). Bonfires were lit at street corners to purify the air (*right*). Doctors wore protective clothing when they treated patients (*opposite, right*).

For five days the Great Fire raged through the City of London (*above*). Fire fighting equipment was rudimentary, and the City was packed with inflammable material – straw, pitch, timber, brandy and cloth. One by one the great buildings caught fire – Old St Paul's, the halls and offices of the City Livery Companies, churches and fine houses. The entire City could have been destroyed, but after three days Charles II gave orders that entire streets in the path of the flames should be blown up, to create fire-breaks. From the Thames (*opposite, below*) the spectacle must have been terrifying.

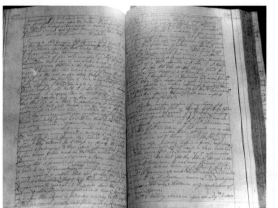

The greatest chronicler of the age was Samuel Pepys (*right*), a quiet, industrious, energetic man who lived life to the full. He was devoted to his wife, Elizabeth, though this did not prevent his gaze fastening on other women. In 1660 he recorded in his *Diary*: 'My wife this day put on first her French gown, called a sac, which became her very well' (*opposite, below*). Pepys is also credited as the inventor of the glazed bookcase, of which this Hepplewhite mahogany 'breakfront' (*opposite, above right*) is a fine example. The *Diary* itself (*opposite, above left*) was left undiscovered for many years in a linen press.

When the Great Fire was finally extinguished, plans were made for the rebuilding of the City. The man entrusted with this task was Sir Christopher Wren (*opposite, top right*). Wren's design for a new London included broad streets, handsome piazzas and an opulent new cathedral (*opposite, top left*). But most of those whose property had been destroyed were loath to part with a single square centimetre of the site. The old narrow lanes and alleys were reinstated. Little of Wren's bold dream survived, but the new St Paul's Cathedral (*above*) was magnificent. (*Opposite, below*) Charles II, hand on paper, visits Wren (fourth from left) at St Paul's. Grinling Gibbons (extreme left) and John Evelyn (third from left) are also in attendance.

The interior of the new St Paul's (*below*) was as impressive as the exterior. Ornate friezes embellished the arches, rich mouldings crowned the pillars, elaborate wrought-iron screens and gates separated the nave from the side aisles. But perhaps the greatest glory was the wood carving on pews and pulpit, choir stalls and organ screen. This was the work of Grinling Gibbons (*opposite*), a sculptor and wood carver who was born in 1648. At first his talent was little recognised, but he was 'discovered' by John Evelyn in 1671 (*right*) while carving a crucifix.

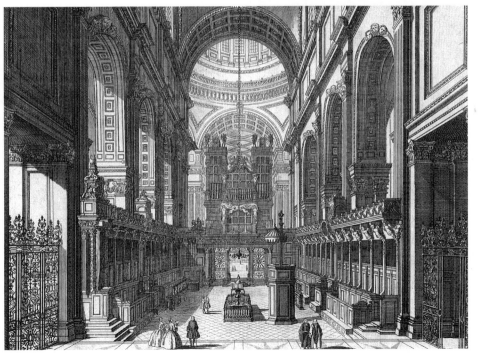

Wren's output as an architect was prolific. As well as St Paul's, he designed the chapel at Pembroke College and the library at Trinity College, Cambridge; the Ashmolean Museum and the Sheldonian Theatre at Oxford (*opposite, above right*); and in London the Royal Exchange, Temple Bar, the Royal Observatory, Chelsea Hospital and Marlborough House. Also in London he rebuilt and redesigned more than fifty churches destroyed in the Great Fire, among them St Clement's, Eastcheap (*opposite, above left*); St Stephen's Walbrook (*opposite, below*); and Christ Church, Spitalfields (*right*).

Printed & Sold
by Christopher Browne
at the Globe at the West
end of S.t Pauls Church
LONDON

J. Kip inventor et Sculptor London f. 1690.

The Chelsea Hospital (*left*) was founded by Charles II in 1682 as a home for veteran soldiers of the British army, and as a companion to the Royal Naval Hospital in Greenwich. The site had been originally occupied by a College of Theology (*above*) established by the Dean of Exeter some sixty-five years earlier. The College had never been popular – it was described by Archbishop Laud as 'Controversy College' – and it was pulled down to make way for Wren's new design. The Hospital was completed in 1692 and four hundred and seventy-six army pensioners were admitted.

Francis Russell, 4th Earl of Bedford, was a businessman who was anxious to make money as a building speculator in the mid-17th century. He commissioned Inigo Jones to design a number of houses 'fitt for the habitacions of *Gentlemen* and men of ability'. Jones produced his fine Palladian piazza (*above*), with St Paul's Church and neo-classical arcades (*far left*). To many Londoners, Covent Garden came as a shock, for they were unused to the concept of such spaciousness. Here on 23 May 1662, Samuel Pepys saw one of the first performances of Mr Punch (*left*) in Britain.

New trade routes
brought new products. In
17th-century London,
coffee was more popular
than tea as a hot and
stimulating beverage.
Coffee houses, such as
that at Bride Lane, Fleet
Street (*far right*), opened
in the City, where men of
business met to discuss
their affairs, to read
newsheets and to debate
the latest issues (*right*).
But coffee drinking had
its opponents. In 1674
*The Womens Petition
against Coffee (below)* was
published.

THE

WOMENS

PETITION

AGAINST

COFFEE

REPRESENTING
TO
PUBLICK CONSIDERATION
THE
Grand INCONVENIENCIES accruing
to their SEX from the Excefsive
Ufe of that Drying, Enfeebling
LIQUOR.
Prefented to the Right Honorable the
Keepers of the Liberty of *VENUS*.

By a Well-willer——

London, Printed 1674.

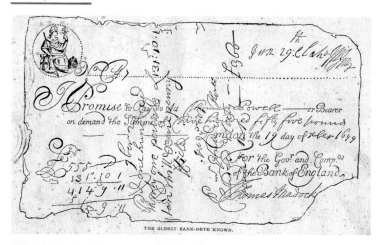

THE OLDEST BANK-NOTE KNOWN.

The idea of a Bank of England had been discussed since the 1650s. It was founded in 1694 at Mercers' Hall, Cheapside, but was moved to the Grocers' Hall in Princes Street a few months later *(below)*. The aim was to raise money for the war with France. The first Governor was Sir John Houblon *(opposite)*, a former member of the Grocers' Company. (*Left*) An early banknote issued by the Bank of England in 1699.

The Four Days' Fight between the English and Dutch fleets (*left*) took place from 1 to 4 June 1666 over a wide area of the North Sea, from the mouth of the Thames to the Dutch coast. Pepys was astonished at the outcome: 'we are beaten – lost many ships and good commanders – have not taken one ship of the enemy's…'

PARADISE
LOST.

BOOK I.

F Mans firſt Diſobedience, an
the Fruit
Of that Forbidden Tree, whoſ
mortal taſt
Brought Death into the World
and all our woe,
/ith loſs of *Eden*, till one greater Man
eſtore us, and regain the bliſsful Seat,
ng Heav'nly Muſe, that on the ſecret top
f *Oreb*, or of *Sinai*, didſt inſpire
hat Shepherd,who firſt taught the choſen Seed,
1 the Beginning how the Heav'ns and Earth
oſe out of *Chaos :* Or if *Sion* Hill
elight thee more, and *Siloa's* Brook that flow'
aſt by the Oracle of God ; I thence
voke thy aid to my adventrous Song,
hat with no middle flight intends to ſoar
A   Abov

In his youth, John Milton (*opposite, far left*) was no saint, but after six years of study he set out to produce a work of poetry 'or drama which would be doctrinal and exemplary for a nation'. This project was delayed by the Civil War. Though struck by blindness in 1652, Milton's greatest work was written in the later part of his life. *Paradise Lost* (*opposite, above right*) was first published in 1667. It is the story of man's disobedience and fall, and the fight between Good and Evil. Evil is represented by Satan and Beelzebub (*opposite, below right*). (*Right*) Satan in threatening mode in the background.

THE
Pilgrim's Progress.
FROM
THIS WORLD
TO
That which is to come.
The Second Part.

Delivered under the Similitude of a

DREAM,

Wherein is set forth
The manner of the setting out of *Chri-
stian's* Wife and Children, their
Dangerous JOURNEY,
AND
Safe Arrival at the Desired Country.

By *JOHN BUNYAN*,

I have used Similitudes, Hos. 12. 10.

LONDON,
Printed for *Nathaniel Ponder* at the *Peacock*,
in the *Poultry*, near the Church, 1684.

John Bunyan (*opposite*) was the son of a tinker. He became a soldier in 1644 at the age of sixteen, and shortly after began to think seriously about religion, seeing life as a struggle towards eventual salvation. After the Civil War, Bunyan became a non-Conformist preacher, whose sermons led him into trouble. In November 1660 he was arrested and imprisoned for twelve years. He was released under the Declaration of Indulgence of 1672, but was arrested again one year later. During six months in Bedford Gaol he wrote his masterpiece, *The Pilgrim's Progress* (*above, right*), which presented his vision of Christian's journey from the City of Destruction to the Desired Country.

Izaak Walton (*above*) was born in Stafford in 1593. He made just enough money as an ironmonger in London to retire at the age of fifty, and spent most of the rest of his life in Winchester. His passion was fishing, though he was not a great fisherman. In 1653 he published *The Compleat Angler*, a handbook with observations on rivers, lakes, how to make artificial fishing flies, and how to prepare fish for the table. The book was revised by Charles Cotton in 1672 and published as *The Experienc'd Angler* (*right*). Both works were charmingly illustrated (*opposite*).

George Fox (preaching in a tavern, *opposite, top*) founded the Society of Friends – or Quakers – in 1646. He was a religious rebel who objected to state control of religion, priests, lawyers and soldiers. The early Quakers were often unruly in their behaviour and always outspoken in their views. James Nayler, Fox's co-founder, was one of many persecuted for this, being whipped by the Hangman at the cart's tail (*opposite, below left*), and having his tongue burnt through with a hot iron (*opposite, below right*). Despite torture and punishment, the Quaker movement continued to grow. (*Above, left*) Quakers meet in Synod Hall. (*Above, right*) An early 18th-century view of a Quaker meeting.

When Charles I attempted to introduce the Book of Common Prayer in Scotland, he met with fierce resistance. At a meeting held in Greyfriar's churchyard, Edinburgh, in 1638 (*below, right*), a Covenant was drafted pledging a struggle to the death against Charles's wishes. James Graham, 1st Marquis of Montrose, fought against the Covenanters until betrayed and hanged (*right*). John Graham, 1st Viscount Dundee (*opposite*), later led William II's armies against the Covenanters.

In 1691 William III was concerned about unrest in Scotland. There were rumours of a possible French invasion. He decided that all clan chiefs must take an oath of allegiance before New Year's Day 1692. One chief, Macdonald of Glencoe, was late in taking the oath. William's adviser, the master of Stair, insisted an example should be made of the Macdonalds. More than a hundred soldiers were billeted on the Macdonalds. After a week of apparent friendship, the soldiers massacred the chief and thirty-seven others, including two women and two children (*opposite, above and below*). The atrocity did much to increase support for William's enemies, the Jacobites, among them Rob Roy MacGregor (*right*). 'Red Robert' spent much of his life as an outlaw, but managed to escape the gallows.

James, Duke of Monmouth (*opposite*), was half-brother to James II. In 1685 Monmouth led a rebellion, championing the Protestant cause against the Roman Catholic King. He struck too soon, for James had not yet become unpopular. Monmouth and his rebels were defeated at the Battle of Sedgemoor. There followed the Bloody Assizes, presided over by Sir George Jeffreys (*right, below*), a cruel and vindictive man who sent hundreds to the gallows or into semi-slavery. When James II fled from England, Jeffreys became a fugitive. He disguised himself as a sailor, but was recognised and seized by the mob in Wapping (*above*). He was imprisoned in the Tower of London, where he died.

William of Orange and his wife Mary (*right*) accepted the invitation of leading English politicians to replace James on the throne. William landed at Torbay in November 1688, having promised to approve the Bill of Rights limiting royal power (*opposite, below*). The flight of James allowed William to impose his authority on England, but he was faced with Catholic opposition in Ireland. The decisive battle between supporters of William and supporters of James was fought at the Boyne on 11 July 1690 (*opposite, above*). William's return to London after the conquest of Ireland was greeted with fireworks in Covent Garden (*below*).

James II (*opposite, top left*) succeeded his brother Charles in 1685. His Coronation was celebrated with a dazzling fireworks display on the River Thames (*above*). His popularity, however, did not last long, for James was a Roman Catholic and out of step with the vast majority of his subjects.

As King, James did almost everything wrong. He attempted to raise taxes without Parliament's consent, he publicly attended Mass and became a pensioner of the French King. By 1688, he was so unpopular that leading members of his government invited William of Orange to replace him. James fled by river (*right*), dropping the Great Seal of England into the Thames as he left. He sailed to France, where he was greeted ceremoniously, but guardedly, by Louis XIV (*above, right*). He never returned to England.

10
POLITICAL SOLUTIONS
1700–1750

as it will appear at
London on July. 14. 1748.
by Jos.ª Walker.

End

In 1721 Edmund Halley succeeded John Flamsteed as
Astronomer Royal. Halley did invaluable work in mapping
the stars and in predicting the arrival of comets – the most
famous of which was named after him. He, in turn, was
succeeded by James Bradley in 1742. Bradley was an
excellent scientist and 'the founder of modern observational
astronomy'. He was also an irresistible campaigner for more
funds, enabling him to improve the instruments in the Royal
Observatory at Greenwich just in time for the eclipse of
1748. (*Right*) Two men observe the eclipse over London as it
was expected to occur on 14 July 1748.

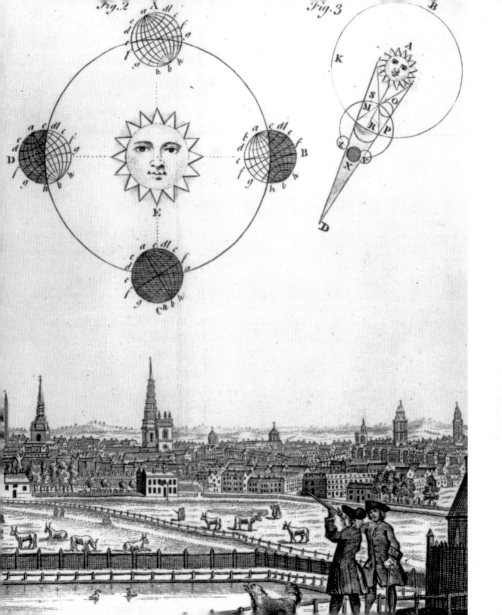

Introduction

In 1707 the Act of Union dissolved the Scottish Parliament. It was to be almost three hundred years before it reassembled. But Scotland was an uneasy and restless land. When Queen Anne died in 1714, there were many north (and south) of the border who shook their heads and their fists at the accession to the British throne of the Elector of Hanover. George was an unattractive man whose greatest achievement was to bring the composer George Frideric Handel with him to Britain.

So the first half of the 18th century witnessed two armed risings that sought to restore the Stuart line. The first, in 1715, was easily defeated, for its figurehead (James, the Old Pretender – son of King James II) was as unattractive as George and did not even bother to make an appearance. The second, in 1745, was far more serious. Its leader was the Old Pretender's son, Bonnie Prince Charlie, who was handsome and cocky, and the British government was caught napping. Charles led his army to within three days' march of London. King and court prepared to flee. But Charles was an adventurer, not a strategist, and he turned back. The Highlanders were pursued and detroyed by 'Butcher' Cumberland at Culloden Moor. Charles fled to France, leaving behind broken dreams, broken hearts, wistful songs and a vengeful British government.

Thomas Arne wrote *Rule, Britannia* to celebrate a much earlier British success. Daniel Defoe broke new literary ground with *Robinson Crusoe*, and Henry Fielding produced what many still consider one of the finest English novels – *Tom Jones*. William Hogarth recorded the joys and squalor of life with such paintings as *The Idle Apprentice*, *Beer Street* and *Gin Lane*. Country houses became ever more lavish and turned into stately homes, prime among them Sir John Vanbrugh's Blenheim Palace (for the 1st Duke of Marlborough) and Castle Howard (for the 3rd Earl of Carlisle). 'Capability' Brown designed sumptuous parks in which to set such palaces. Thomas Chippendale filled them with some of the finest furniture of all time.

Highwaymen became an ever-increasing menace to travellers throughout Britain, but especially on the heaths and in the woods that surrounded major towns. In London, law-abiding citizens turned to the Bow Street Runners, or to Jonathan Wild, the self-styled 'Thief-taker General of Great Britain and Ireland'. The Wesleys struggled to save people's souls and to ameliorate the lot of the poor. The rich sauntered beside the Thames in London's Vauxhall Gardens, admiring the fountains, the entertainment and the illuminations. The destitute sat in workhouses and picked oakum.

In 1707 the Scottish Parliament signed its own death warrant when it approved the Act of Union. In return, Scotland received just under £400,000, 'full freedom and intercourse of trade and navigation', and the right to send fifteen peers and forty-five elected members to the Parliament at Westminster. The Marquis of Queensberry presented Scotland's acceptance to Queen Anne (*opposite, below*). When Anne died, many Scots refused to accept George I as King, preferring James Stuart, the old Pretender (*opposite, top left*). The Earl of Mar (*opposite, top right*) raised a Jacobite army, but the rising was short-lived and unsuccessful. Thirty years later, the Young Pretender won a great victory at Prestonpans (*left*), but this was the last victory for the Stuarts.

In 1700 Louis XIV of France accepted the bequest of the Spanish empire to his grandson, banned English imports to France, and gave formal recognition of James Stuart's right to the English throne. This provoked the War of the Spanish Succession. British troops, and those of the Grand Alliance against Louis, were led by John Churchill, Duke of Marlborough *(right,* accompanied by his Negro page). In 1704, at the Battle of Blenheim *(opposite, above),* more than 100,000 troops took part. After the battle Marshal Tallard, the French commander, surrendered to Marlborough *(opposite, below).*

A grateful nation and government richly rewarded Marlborough after the Battle of Blenheim. A palatial residence was built for him near Woodstock in Oxfordshire (*opposite, above*), designed by Sir John Vanbrugh (*right*), though later completed by Nicholas Hawksmoor, after Vanbrugh had lost the favour of Queen Anne. The two men also shared the credit for Castle Howard in Yorkshire (*above*), built for the Earl of Carlisle. (*Opposite, below*) The Mausoleum in the grounds of Castle Howard, near New Malton, Yorkshire.

Five years after Blenheim, Marlborough's army again clashed with the French, this time at Malplaquet. The result was a stalemate, both sides suffering heavy casualties in the bloodiest battle of the war *(below)*. Fighting continued for a further six years before peace negotiations were opened in Utrecht in 1715. *(Left)* A broadsheet depicting the Treaty of Utrecht and promising 'Plenty Peace and Traffick (Trade)'.

(*Right*) A French illustration of 'Marlbrouck' (Marlborough) to accompany the song *'Marlbrouck va à ton guerre'*, still sung by French schoolchildren two hundred and fifty years later.

William III was succeeded by his sister-in-law, Anne (*below, right*). Anne was a staunch Protestant who, unlike earlier Stuarts, listened to her ministers (*below, left*). Anne's particular favourite was Sarah Jennings, later Duchess of Marlborough (*opposite*), until their quarrel in 1711, which led to the fall of Marlborough and the return of power to the Tories.

Long before Anne's death, British politicians were concerned as to who should succeed her. The Act of Settlement of 1701 blocked Catholic succession, so the right now passed to the descendant of Charles I's sister, Elizabeth of Bohemia. Elizabeth's daughter was Sophia, Electress of Hanover (*above, left*), who in turn was the mother of George, Elector of Hanover (*opposite*). Sophia died a few months before Anne, so on Anne's death the crown passed to George. (*Above, right*) Sophia Dorothea of Zolle, wife of George – a woman who bore a striking resemblance to her mother-in-law.

Robert Harley, 1st Earl of Oxford (*above*), was Anne's chief
minister when the South Sea Company was created in 1711,
though the company did not begin trading from its headquarters in
Threadneedle Street (*opposite, below*) until after the Treaty of
Utrecht in 1715. In January 1720 the South Sea Company offered
to take over the majority of the British National Debt. Expecting
to make vast profits out of trade in the South Seas, it attracted a
huge amount of financial speculation and its shares soared in value
by over 1000 per cent in a few months. In September 1720, the
Bubble burst. Share values plunged and a scandal implicated two of
the King's mistresses, the Chancellor of the Exchequer, the Post-
master and the First Lord of the Treasury. (*Opposite, above*)
Hogarth's view of the South Sea speculation.

Daniel Defoe (*opposite*), Jonathan Swift (*right*) and Henry Fielding (*far right*) have all been hailed as the Father of the English Novel – Defoe for *Robinson Crusoe* and *Moll Flanders*, Swift for *Gulliver's Travels*, and Fielding for *Tom Jones*. Defoe's early life was eventful. He was placed in the pillory (*below*) for satirising the Church, and was for several years a double agent.

George II (*right and opposite, bottom left*) was a man of considerable physical courage, but little strategic skill. As his seal showed (*opposite, bottom right*), he claimed to be King of Great Britain, Scotland and France, though Britain had lost her last French possession two hundred years earlier. Like his father, George fancied himself as a soldier. During the War of the Austrian Succession, he became the last British monarch to fight on the battlefield, at Dettingen in 1743 (*opposite, above*). At the height of the battle, he dismounted, and, 'sword in hand', led his troops against the French infantry.

Despite the failure of his father to win back the British crown in 1715, Charles Edward Stuart (*opposite*) set out to rekindle the fire of rebellion. He was a handsome youth, dashing and charming, brave and bonnie. When he landed at Eriskay in the Hebrides on 23 July 1745 he had only seven followers, though others quickly joined him, some while he was still on board the *Elizabeth* (*above*). There were many who openly told him to 'Go home', to which he replied 'I am come home…and I am persuaded that my faithful Highlanders will stand by me.'

At first the Jacobite cause prospered. The English were caught unawares and surprised by the extent of support for Bonnie Prince Charlie. After the Battle of Prestonpans, the Prince entered Edinburgh in triumph (*opposite*). He marched into England and reached Derby, then fatally turned back. The Highlanders were pursued by the Duke of Cumberland (*right*) and forced to give battle at Culloden Moor (*above*) in April 1746, where Charles and his men were routed.

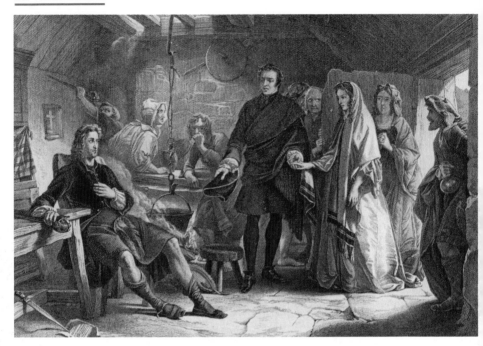

After Culloden the rising was brutally suppressed by 'Butcher' Cumberland. Charles fled with a price of £30,000 on his head, hiding in caves or seeking shelter among the few still bold enough to support him. In June 1747 Charles met Flora MacDonald (*above*). Disguised as Betty Burke, her maid, Charles managed to cross from the mainland to the Isle of Skye, and thence to France. Apart from two secret visits to London between 1750 and 1760, Charles spent the rest of his life in France and Italy. (*Opposite*) The monument to the Forty-Five at Glenfinnan, Loch Shiel, Inverness-shire, marking the spot where Charles first raised his father's standard.

Those who had followed Bonnie Prince Charlie paid a high price. At least eighty leading Jacobites were executed, some in Carlisle (*left, centre*) but most in London. (*Bottom left*) 'A View of the Manner of Beheading the Rebel Lords on Tower Hill, London 1747.' (*Top left*) The execution of Lords Kilmarnock and Balmerino. (*Opposite, bottom left*) Jacobite medals struck for those who had followed the Prince. (*Opposite, bottom right*) The execution of Lord Lovat, an old campaigner who had not fought against England, but had sent his son to do so.

(*Left*) Bonnie Prince Charlie leaves Scotland in the summer of 1747. Songs, romances and legends were all created once he had gone, and loyal Jacobites still drank their toasts to 'the King across the water' for many years afterwards.

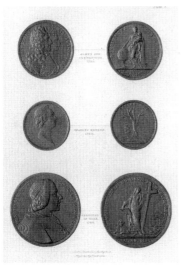

Sir Robert Walpole, Earl of Oxford (*opposite*), was destined for the Church but turned to politics after the deaths of his two older brothers. He entered Parliament at the age of twenty-five in 1701, and rose rapidly through the ranks to become First Lord of the Treasury and Chancellor of the Exchequer before he reached forty. George I spoke no English, and was uninterested in the workings of British political institutions. This gave Walpole a far freer hand in shaping policy than he would otherwise have had. Walpole established the system of cabinet government and became the first British Prime Minister. In this post, with his mastery of the Commons (*right*) he was virtually unassailable, and he remained in office until 1742. After George I's death in 1727, Walpole maintained excellent relations with George II, who presented him with the house at 10 Downing Street.

In 1700 Louis XIV of France accepted the title 'King of Spain' (*opposite, above*) on behalf of his grandson. The war that followed was fought on land and sea. (*Above*) The British bombardment of Port Royal in Acadia. (*Left*) Admiral Benbow in command at the Battle of Cartagena, 1702. (*Opposite, below*) The British fleet breaks the French and Spanish blockade of Gibraltar, 1705.

George Anson (*opposite*) was one of the best British seamen in the 18th century. In 1740, during the war with Spain, he set sail with six undermanned and ill-equipped ships to harass Spanish ships and settlements in the East Indies. He was highly successful. In the Philippines his ship *Centurion* captured a Spanish galleon off Manila (*below*) to add to his other prizes. Almost four years after leaving England, Anson returned to London in a triumphant procession (*right*).

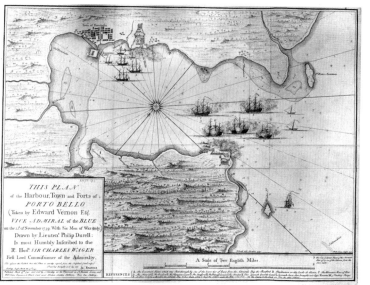

THIS PLAN
of the Harbour, Town and Forts of
PORTO BELLO
(Taken by Edward Vernon Esq.
VICE ADMIRAL of the BLUE
on the 22 of November 1739 With Six Men of War only)
Drawn by Lieuten' Philip Durell :
Is most Humbly Inscribed to the
R'. Hon'. SIR CHARLES WAGER
First Lord Commissioner of the Admiralty

A Scale of Two English Miles.

The war with Spain from 1739 to 1745 was a trade war. Ostensibly, it was caused by the mistreatment of Captain Jenkins, who claimed Spanish authorities had cut off his ear – the ear was passed round the House of Commons for examination. It was a war fought across the globe, by Anson in the east, by Vernon in the west. Admiral Edward Vernon (*opposite*) studied the plans of the Spanish settlement at Porto Bello in Panama (*left*) before attacking and capturing it on 22 November 1739 (*below*).

Vernon was a captain in the navy at the age of twenty-one, and a rear admiral three years later. When he captured Porto Bello he became a national hero. To his sailors he was known affectionately as 'Old Grog', a name given him because he wore a grogram coat. When he ordered that the daily ration of rum should be diluted with water, this mixture became known as 'grog'. Vernon was a thorn in the side of the authorities. He published many pamphlets criticising Admiralty organisation and calling for change. As a result he was cashiered from the navy in 1746.

Sir Henry Morgan (*left*) was a mixture of pirate and privateer. Most of his raids were on Spanish possessions in the Caribbean, and these unofficial services to Britain were rewarded with a knighthood and the Governorship of Jamaica. Ned Low (*opposite, top left*) was a true pirate, owing allegiance to no one. William Kidd (*opposite, top right*) was a privateer who protected the Anglo-American trade routes and was allowed to shelter in New York Harbour (*opposite, below*), where he welcomed ladies on board his vessel in style. Kidd turned to piracy later in life and was eventually hanged in Execution Dock, London.

John Wesley (*left*) was a tireless traveller (he covered over 250,000 miles in his life), and an inexhaustible preacher – he preached over 40,000 sermons, including one at his father's tomb in Epworth churchyard (*below*). With his brother Charles and George Whitefield, John was the founder of the Methodist Church, bringing hope of comfort and salvation to miners, labourers, the poor and the sick. As a preacher he is perhaps un-rivalled in history. Crowds of 30,000 to 40,000 gathered outdoors to hear him speak. He was not, however, an easy man to live with, and his wife deserted him after twenty-five years of marriage.

In 1735 Charles and John Wesley sailed to America (*above*) as missionaries. Here John preached to a variety of congregations, including groups of Native Americans (*left*). Unfortunately, he aroused the hostility of the colonists and embarked on an unhappy love affair. He returned to England two years later.

A wealth of elegant houses were built in London in the mid-18th century. Leicester Square (*opposite, above*) was the fashionable address of earls, writers and artists alike. Albany in Piccadilly (*opposite, below*) was built by Sir William Chambers for the 1st Viscount Melbourne in the 1770s. Holland House (*above*) was older, but became the home of Joseph Addison, who wrote many of his *Spectator* articles pacing the 30 metre long gallery with a glass of wine at either end. All this valuable property needed protection. That was the job of men like John Townsend (*right*), a Bow Street runner at the end of the 18th century.

The revival of English music owed much to Germans and Italians. From Germany came George Frideric Handel (*opposite, far right*), whose masque *Acis and Galatea* (*opposite, below left*) was composed for the Duke of Chandos. From Italy came the famous castrati singers (*left*) in a performance of Handel's *Julius Caesar*. (*Below*) The arrival of Francesco Bernadi in London. (*Opposite, above left*) Dr Arne, composer of *Rule, Britannia*.

Palaces, mansions and stately homes all required the appropriate setting. In the mid-18th century, Lancelot 'Capability' Brown (*right*) and others developed a new type of park and garden. Instead of the elaborately formal French style, the accent was on simple concepts that produced a more natural effect. Brown designed the grounds for Warwick Castle and Blenheim Palace, and two of the best examples of his work are to be seen at Kew Gardens (*opposite, top*) and Chatsworth in Derbyshire (*opposite, bottom*).

There was a grand revival of British painting in the 18th century. Richard Wilson, Gainsborough, Reynolds, Cotman and later Constable and Turner all produced works that matched the greatest in the world. William Hogarth was a painter who concentrated on what he called his 'modern moral subjects', pointing up the virtues and vices of the society in which he lived. His paintings of the vices of the age have achieved more lasting fame – such as that of a theatre dressing room (*above, left*), and a crowd of men watching a cockfight at the Cock-Pit Royal (1759) (*below, left*). One of the most famous is *Gin Lane* (*opposite, top left*), a terrifying indictment of times when anyone could be 'drunk for a penny, dead drunk for twopence'.

Hogarth (*bottom left*) did much to liberate the art of portraiture, and one of his best works is his own *Self-Portrait* (*above*) with his dog, painted in 1749. Hogarth hated foreigners, and condemned British art experts for their neglect of British talent.

Travel could be a dangerous occupation in the 18th century. Highwaymen lurked on the outskirts of most towns, prepared to rob rich and poor alike. London was beset by Gentlemen of the Road – on Hampstead Heath (*below, left*), Blackheath, Hounslow Heath, the Dover Road, and in Epping Forest. The most famous highwayman was Dick Turpin – butcher, rustler, housebreaker and horse thief. Turpin was hanged at York, but his legendary ride on Black Bess (*above*) was probably made fifty years before Turpin was born, by Swift Jack Nevison, who robbed a sailor in Kent and established an alibi by proving he was in York only sixteen hours later. (*Opposite*) 'Colonel Jack', daring highwayman, robs poor Mary Smith. Some of the 'Gentlemen' just weren't gentlemen.

11
IMPERIAL FOUNDATIONS
1750–1770

Beating Up for Recruits by Robert Dighton. Unlike the navy, there was no press gang to provide recruits for the army, so would-be soldiers came from debtors' prisons, local work-houses, and straight from the fields. The series of wars between 1739 and 1785 lured others to enlist in what amounted to a rush of patriotic fervour. Medical and sanitary conditions greatly improved in the army, thanks to the work of John Pringle; pay was increased, and some of the old barrack square stiffness eased.

Introduction

The world seemed to shrink. Merchant ships and men-of-war sailed into Bristol and London, Dublin and Plymouth, Glasgow and Liverpool, bringing the fruits of the earth and news of momentous happenings far, far away. Within a few aggressive years, Britain captured an empire. General Wolfe and his troops scaled the Heights of Abraham, and established the British hold on Canada. Across the globe, in the heat and dust of Bengal, an East India Company officer named Robert Clive, with a force of 2,200 native Sepoys and 800 Europeans, defeated Siraj-ud-Daula's army of 50,000. India fell to Britain.

These and other victories (Minden and Quiberon Bay) were celebrated in William Boyce's rousingly patriotic song *Heart of Oak* (not *Hearts*), written for David Garrick's *Harlequin's Invasion* in 1759. Less happy that year about imperial progress was John Byng, an English admiral who failed to relieve the Mediterranean island of Minorca from a French blockade. He was found guilty of neglect of duty and shot on board the *Monarque* in Portsmouth Harbour – *'pour encourager les autres'*, was Voltaire's cynical comment.

By 1770, James Cook had already sailed to the Baltic, surveyed the St Lawrence and the shores of Nova Scotia, and commanded the *Endeavour* on a voyage to the Pacific to observe the transit of Venus. His most famous achievement, and his death, lay only a few years ahead.

Francis Egerton, 3rd Duke of Bridgewater, employed James Brindley to design and construct one of the first English canals. Hundreds of navvies sweated to dig the forty-two miles from Worsely to Manchester. Young artists and young aristocrats took the Grand Tour of Europe. Huge livery stables in every town provided teams of horses to pull less ambitious travellers in stagecoaches from inn to inn across the British Isles.

Towns grew in size and wealth. For the wealthy and the fashionable there were the attractions of the spa – in Tunbridge Wells, Epsom, Harrogate, Leamington, Cheltenham, Buxton, Bath and a dozen more towns. Dublin had become one of the finest cities in Britain. Edinburgh had blossomed into a leading European centre of culture, and boasted a fine university designed by Robert Adam. Swansea had been ruined by the intense development of its copper and other metal industries. Cardiff had yet to know prosperity.

All seemed well, but a member of the notorious Hell Fire Club had raised the spectre of Liberty. John Wilkes was the MP for Aylesbury. In an issue of his own paper – *The New Briton* – he accused the government of putting lies into the mouth of the King. Across the Channel, there was worse to come.

Not every episode in the Seven Years' War was crowned with British success. In 1756 Pitt the Elder (*left*) sent Admiral John Byng (*below, left*) with an ill-equipped squadron to relieve Minorca, then blockaded by the French. Byng failed, and was brought home under arrest charged with cowardice and neglect of duty. Though acquitted of the former, he was found guilty of the latter and condemned to death. He was shot by a firing squad on board the *Monarque* in Portsmouth Harbour *(opposite, above)*. The event caused considerable concern. Satirists had a field day, portraying Britain as a *Lion Dismember'd* (*opposite, below*).

James Wolfe (*far left*, in caricature, *and left*, more formally depicted) spent much of his short life on the battlefield. The Duke of Newcastle (*opposite, above*) thought him mad, prompting George II to declare: 'Mad is he? Then I wish he would bite some other of my generals.' Wolfe's greatest achievement was the conquest of Canada. On 13 September 1759 he led his troops up the St Lawrence to the Heights of Abraham (*opposite, below*), overlooking Quebec. Wolfe was killed in the battle that ensued (*below*).

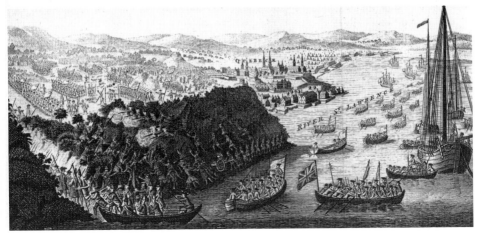

Robert Clive *(left)* was a former clerk with the East India Company who masterminded a series of campaigns that drove the French from Madras, Arcot and ultimately the entire Indian sub-continent. His greatest victory was at Plassey *(opposite, above)*, where his mixed European and Sepoy troops defeated an army seventeen their number. *(Below)* Clive greets his Indian ally, Mir Jaffir, after the battle. *(Opposite, below)* Clive receives a decree from Shah Alum, Mughal Emperor of India, transferring administration to the East India Company.

The British ruled India through the local princes, kings, rajahs and maharajahs. Holding together this ramshackle empire was no easy matter. The old capital was Delhi (*below*) where the Mughal Emperor had his palace (*left*), but the Mughal Emperor was no longer in control. Policing the subcontinent was the work of the private army of the East India Company, whose troops drilled on Bombay Green (*opposite, above*) and manned Fort St George in Madras (*opposite, below*).

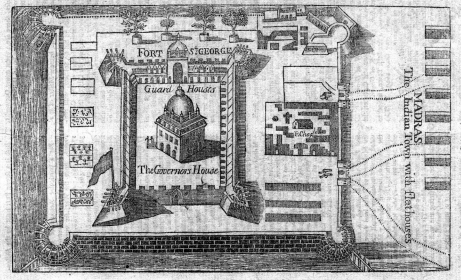

PLAN *of* FORT S<small>T</small>. GEORGE *and* MADRASS.

FORT S<small>T</small> GEORGE

Guard Houses

The Governors House

F. Chapel

MADRAS
The Indian Town with flat houses

At the height of British triumph in the Seven Years' War, George III (*above, left*) replaced Pitt the Elder, the Whig Prime Minister, with his former tutor, the Earl of Bute (*above, right*). Bute was unpopular, unskilled and inexperienced. It was an action typical of the King, whose political ineptitude often lost him public confidence. Usually, on such occasions, the best the King could hope for was some gentle lampooning, as in *Affability*, a cartoon of King George and Queen Charlotte by Thomas Gillray (*opposite*).

George III was at his best in the domestic setting. He was a loyal husband and an attentive father. His passion was for farming – he was known personally to reward those he saw practising good husbandry, as in the case of the 'industrious haymaker of Weymouth' (*above*). George was less at ease when it came to state occasions, such as in St Paul's Cathedral (*right*). Politically he was eager to have a hand in government, but was always clumsy in his attempts to control and manipulate the situation. His long reign was thus a mixture of great successes and miserable failures.

In 1762 George III bought Buckingham House (*opposite, below*) as a London residence for himself, Queen Charlotte and his family (*opposite, above*). He also employed the Scottish architect Sir William Chambers (*left*) to add a new wing to Windsor Castle (*below,* with Nell Gwyn's house on the extreme left). Windsor had been neglected during the reigns of George I and II, and was almost uninhabitable.

John Wilkes (*opposite*) was a rake, a profligate, an MP and a publisher. In 1763 he was charged with libel after suggesting in Issue No. 45 of *The New Briton* that government ministers had put lies into the King's mouth. He was acquitted, but remained an outspoken advocate of free speech, to the delight of his supporters, who took to the streets on his behalf (*above*).

Gibraltar had long been the key to the Mediterranean, a rocky fortress commanding the narrow straits through which all trade between southern Europe and the New World must pass. It had been ceded to the British at the Treaty of Utrecht in 1715, but with Britain heavily engaged in the American War of Independence, the Spanish blockaded the port by land and sea in an attempt to recapture it. The defence of Gibraltar was led by George Augustus Eliott (*above*, on horseback).

The defence was heroic, for the siege lasted four years, with some interruptions. One of these was the arrival of a British fleet commanded by Admiral Darby on 12 April 1781 (*above*). His ships broke through the Spanish blockade, bringing much needed supplies to the beleaguered garrison.

Warren Hastings (*far right*) was governor general of Bombay. (*Opposite, above*) Dundas, Pitt and Sydney are accused of nepotism in the administration of Company affairs. Hastings returned from India in 1784 and was immediately impeached, the attack on him being led by Burke, Fox and North (*opposite, below*). His trial in Westminster Hall (*below*) lasted seven years and cost him some £750,000 before he was acquitted. (*Right*) An entrance ticket to the seventh day of the trial.

The coming of the canals changed the face of Britain and revolutionised the carriage of heavy goods. Raw materials and finished goods were carried from port to factory, from factory to market at a fraction of the previous cost. In 1759 Francis Egerton, 3rd Duke of Bridgewater (*left*), commissioned James Brindley to build the first English canal. It was forty-two miles long and linked Manchester with Runcorn, among other places. At Barton, an aquaduct carried the canal over the River Mersey (*opposite, below*). The later Grand Junction Canal (*opposite, above*) linked London with Oxford and the Midlands.

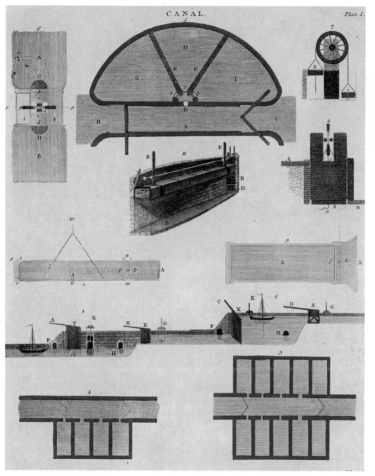

The true father of British inland navigation was James Brindley (*above*), a remarkable engineer who was responsible for the construction of three hundred and sixty-five miles of canals between 1759 and 1772. Despite the degree of sophistication involved (*left and opposite*), Brindley was totally illiterate, and most of the problems he encountered were solved without recourse to writing or even drawing. When faced with a particular difficulty, Brindley simply went to bed and lay there until he had thought of a solution.

As roads improved, travel by coach became more reliable and slightly more comfortable. Journeys not only started and finished at inns (*left, and opposite, top left*) but involved frequent stops at inns to change horses (*opposite, top right*). Gradients posed problems, as in this picture of *A Sunday Trip up Richmond Hill* (*above*), and passengers were often asked to dismount. The group on their way to Bury Fair (*opposite, below*) may well have been required to do exactly this.

Bath was the most elegant city in England in the late 18th century. Its graceful crescents and terraces were largely the work of John Wood Senior, and his son, John Wood the Second. John Wood Senior designed the Circus (*below*). John Wood the Second designed the Royal Crescent (*opposite, above*) and the Pump Room (*opposite, below*). Beau Nash (*left*) was the talented dandy who brought the elite of London to Bath.

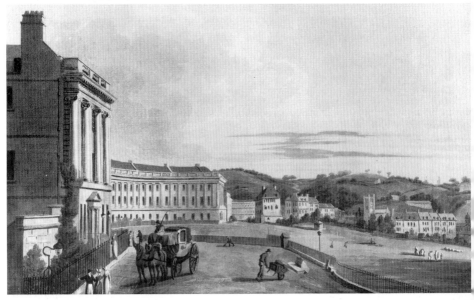

Sarah Siddons (*above, left*) was the daughter of the actor Richard Kemble and the wife of actor Richard Siddons. At the age of nineteen she was spotted by David Garrick (*below, left*, with Sarah) who took her to Drury Lane. At first audiences were not impressed, but in 1782 she triumphed in a variety of roles. From then on, she was the darling of the London stage, appearing as Lady Macbeth, the Queen in *Hamlet* (*opposite*), Volumnia in *Coriolanus* and Hermione in *A Winter's Tale*. She gave her farewell performance in 1812, at the age of fifty-seven.

'Up the Warren Hill, East of the Town of Newmarket 1790' – the figure standing on the coach (centre) is the Prince of Wales, later George IV. Newmarket Heath was the heart of the horse racing world in the late 18th century, and the gentry flocked to see the finest four-legged bloodstock put through its training. This was the age of the English sporting gentleman, typified by Squire Western in Henry Fielding's *The History of Tom Jones, A Foundling*. A man who could ride straight, put his horse at every gate, hedge, wall or fence, drink bumpers of ale with his fellows, and shake the rafters with his singing, was as fine a chap as could be found anywhere in the world – or so it was believed.

Introduction

The foundations of 20th-century Britain were established in the late 18th century. Steam power changed the economy, the geography and even the fertility of the British people – for industrialisation facilitated marriages at a younger age and led to a steady increase in a population which had remained static at some eight million for the last hundred years.

It all happened so quickly. In less than a single lifetime – and life expectancy was cruelly short at the time – Britain became the most advanced industrial nation in the world. John Kay, William Hargreaves, Richard Arkwright, Henry Cort, Samuel Crompton, James Watt, Matthew Boulton and Josiah Wedgwood created a new society. Factory replaced field or cottage as the workplace. Wages replaced crops or products as the reward. Slums replaced hovels as homes.

Press gangs roamed the ports of seaside

towns and emptied the gaols of their prisoners – snatching the unlikely and the unlucky to serve on board the warships that protected 'perfidious Albion' from the Corsican tyrant across the water. Other sad souls left the land and made their way to Stoke, Newport, Birmingham, Manchester, Bradford or any one of a hundred more swelling towns. And there they toiled in what William Blake called the 'dark Satanic mills', for members of the industrial aristocracy cared no more for their workers' comfort than the landed gentry ever had.

Those not confined in mine or factory, furnace or workshop discerned the dawn of a wonderful and exciting new age. The delights of the seaside, with its bathing machines and its invigorating air, were patronised by King George III himself. There was a new daily paper to inform one and all of Britain's latest successes. It was called *The Times*. There were more and more theatres to attend – Goldsmith's *She Stoops to Conquer* was first performed at Covent Garden in 1773, Sheridan's *The Rivals* two years later. Cricket was born on Hampshire's Broadhalfpenny Down. Fine new poetry by Keats, Shelley, Wordsworth and Coleridge, and the paintings of Constable and Gainsborough, helped to keep alive the notion of England as a 'green and pleasant land'.

In 1796, in the little Gloucestershire town of Berkeley, Edward Jenner vaccinated an eight-year-old boy with cowpox matter taken from the hands of a local milkmaid. It took a year for his fellow physicians to accept its protective efficacy in the battle against smallpox.

Meanwhile, there was a far more important battle to be fought – against the Godless, shameless and corrupting ideas of the French Revolution...

COMMON SENSE;

ADDRESSED TO THE

INHABITANTS

O F

A M E R I C A,

On the following interesting

S U B J E C T S.

I. Of the Origin and Design of Government in general, with concise Remarks on the English Constitution.

II. Of Monarchy and Hereditary Succession.

III. Thoughts on the present State of American Affairs.

IV. Of the present Ability of America, with some miscellaneous Reflections.

Man knows no Master save creating Heaven,
Or those whom choice and common good ordain.
THOMSON.

PHILADELPHIA;
Printed, and Sold, by R. BELL, in Third-Street.
MDCCLXXVI.

The American War of Independence and the French Revolution unleashed a torrent of philosophical debate and new ideas. Thomas Paine (*above, right, and below, right*) was a radical. In 1774 Benjamin Franklin persuaded him to visit America. Here Paine quickly espoused the American cause. His pamphlet *Common Sense* (*above*) sold over 100,000 copies in three months, with its appealing message to the new nation: 'We have it in our power to begin the world over again'. Adam Smith (*opposite*) was a Scottish economist and philosopher, best known for his *Wealth of Nations*, a masterpiece which presented a revolutionary view of market forces and modern economics, and which is still highly regarded today. At a public dinner, Pitt insisted that Smith be seated first, saying 'we are all your scholars'.

(*Right*) *The Times Anno 1783*, James Gillray's cartoon showing European reaction to Britain's loss of her American colonies. On the far left, a Dutchman says 'The Devil take you, Monsieur, I think I have paid the Piper.' A Spaniard sees this as revenge for the British capture of Gibraltar, 'You have made me the laughing stock of Europe.' The Frenchman sarcastically offers a pinch of snuff, 'for we'll not give you back America', while John Bull throws up his hands in despair: 'Tis lost, irrevocably lost.'

One of the most effective innovations in arable farming was the seed drill, invented by Jethro Tull (*opposite*) earlier in the 18th century. It was followed by a host of other machines, some of which were primitive in design. McDowgale's Hoe (*above*) was an improvement for the small farmer in that it needed no draught animals, and yet provided a more powerful machine. Baird's Turnip Slicer (*right*) tackled the crop newly introduced to provide winter fodder for animals.

The rise in the population of Britain in the reign of George III was caused by three things – more work, more money and more food. The factory system, an essential component in the Industrial Revolution, became part of the Agricultural Revolution. Cows were milked in large new sheds (*left*), rather than in the open farmyard. Selective breeding produced larger beasts (*below, left*), just as it appeared to produce larger noblemen in James Gillray's caricature of the 6th Duke of Bedford – *Fat Cattle*.

Robert Bakewell (*below*) of Dishley Grange, Leicestershire, was one of the new breed of farmers. He applied selective breeding to sheep, cattle and horses, establishing new breeds such as the Leicester sheep and longhorn cows. Oil cake was introduced as a new feed for cattle, though this cartoon of 1802 (*left*) suggests that there were those who were suspicious of the quality of the meat this might produce.

In 1787, Captain William Bligh (*opposite*) was chosen to command HMS *Bounty* on a voyage to Tahiti, where he was to collect breadfruit trees with the object of introducing them to the Caribbean. When the ship sailed after a six-month stay on the island, Bligh's men mutinied, casting him and a handful of loyal crew members adrift (*left*) with scant provisions and no chart. Bligh's incredible seamanship brought them safely to Timor after a voyage of 4,000 miles. Fletcher Christian and the other mutineers sailed on to the island of Pitcairn (*below*).

THE LANDING OF CAPTAIN COOK AT BOTANY BAY 1770

AUSTR

The British were not the first to land in Australia. The Dutch had been there long before them, but the British were the first to set up a permanent colony. Captain James Cook of HMS *Endeavour* surveyed the east coast of Australia in 1770, claiming the land for Britain (*left*). Cook was a highly skilled navigator, but he owed at least some of his success to the work of John Harrison, an English clockmaker who spent much of his life seeking a way of determining longitude accurately. In 1762 Harrison finally produced a chronometer which did this to within eighteen miles, and Cook made good use of Harrison's invention.

ALIA

Accompanying James Cook (*opposite, bottom right*) on his voyage to the Pacific from 1768 to 1771 was the botanist and zoologist Sir Joseph Banks (*opposite, bottom left*). Banks played a considerable part in the establishment of the colony at Botany Bay (*above*), later to become the destination for many shiploads of transported British convicts and debtors. The main purpose of the 1768–71 expedition was to observe the transit of Venus, but Cook sailed on to explore the coast of Australia and New Zealand. Four years later, he returned, anchoring in Queen Charlotte Sound, on the south island of New Zealand in February 1775, and meeting Maori chiefs (*left*), before sailing on to his tragic death on Hawaii in 1779 (*opposite, top*).

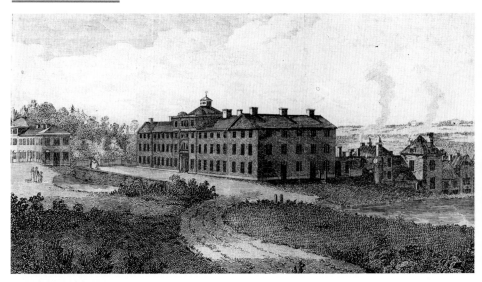

James Watt (*opposite, top left*) established his workshop in Heathfield, Birmingham, in 1790 (*left*). Here he developed his plans for the use of steam power which he used at the nearby Soho manufactory (*above*). Joseph Black (*opposite, top right*) discovered the properties of latent heat. John Rennie (*opposite, bottom right*) was one of Watt's pupils who later became a brilliant engineer. William Murdock (*opposite, bottom left*, central figure) improved Watt's steam engine and pioneered coal-gas lighting.

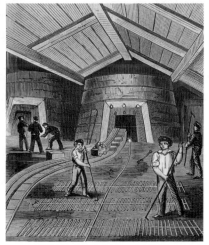

The Age of Iron marched from triumph to triumph. New techniques were developed for its production, new uses were found for it. Vast new smelting houses were built, like the one at Broseley in Shropshire (*above*). Such was the demand, Britain had to import 50,000 tons a year.

Quality as well as quantity were needed. In the 1780s Henry Cort (*above*) took out a series of patents for a process known as 'puddling', which produced a high quality wrought iron. It used a 'reverberatory' furnace (*opposite, below left*), and raw coal and low-carbon iron were kept separate to reduce impurities in the finished product. Another of Cort's patents was for the use of 'grooved rolls' (*opposite, below right*). Cort's inventions were widely used, but he was ruined by a prosecution for debt, and died comparatively poor.

Sir Richard Arkwright (*right*) patented his spinning frame (*opposite*) in 1767. It revolutionised the production of cotton cloth, as it produced for the first time a thread strong enough to be used as a warp. Like the master in Hogarth's *Honest Apprentice (above)*, Arkwright was an ardent taskmaster, who became unpopular with his workforce. His factories were attacked and wrecked, but Arkwright made a considerable fortune.

Josiah Wedgwood (*above, top*, with typical Wedgwood vase, *and above*, in his workshop) was a potter from Burslem. His styles and designs borrowed heavily from Ancient Greek and Roman pottery, and he renamed his large factory, near Hanley, 'Etruria'. With his partner Byerley, Wedgwood opened a set of smart showrooms in St James's Street, London (*right*), even then one of the most fashionable addresses in town.

Travelling by stagecoach was slow, uncomfortable and dangerous in the late 18th century. The coaches themselves had improved over the centuries, but little had been done to make road surfaces better. In wet weather, deep ruts formed in which coaches frequently became stuck. Passengers were then asked to alight (*left*). If they were lucky, they had to wait till the coach was able to proceed. If they were unlucky, they had to push it. John Loudon McAdam (*above, top*) was a Scottish engineer who developed a greatly improved method of road construction, though not all regarded the change with approval (*above*).

TREVITHICKS,
PORTABLE STEAM ENGINE.

Catch me who can.

Mechanical Power Subduing
Animal Speed.

Long before the days of George Stephenson's *Rocket*, animals were hauling coal trucks along 'railways' (*bottom left*). Richard Trevithick (*top left*) was a Cornish engineer and inventor who adapted Watt's steam engine into the first steam locomotive, or 'portable steam engine' (*above*). Trevithick did not know how to exploit his invention. Its use was largely confined to being a tourist attraction in London, where his London Locomotive merely completed many circuits of a special track at Euston Square, London (*opposite*).

In 1784, Viscount Torrington recorded in his diary that the new iron bridge at Coalbrookdale, Shropshire, 'must be the admiration of all as it is one of the wonders of the world'. It was built by John Wilkinson and Abraham Darby III, using iron produced at their nearby foundry (*below*).

It was a staggering achievement, constructed entirely of iron and assembled from what amounted to a kit (*right*). It had a central span of 30 metres and a rise of 15 metres. 'Though it seems like a network wrought in iron,' wrote Charles Dibdin, 'it will apparently be uninjured for ages.'

BRIDGE.

Thomas Telford (*opposite*) was a shepherd's son from Westerkirk, near Langholm, who became an architect and engineer of the highest ability. He was apprenticed to a stonemason at fourteen, and then worked in both Edinburgh and London. Among his greatest creations were the Pont Cysylte aquaduct in Wales (in background of portrait), the Caledonian Canal, the road from London to Holyhead, and the suspension bridge over the Menai Straits at Conway (*above*).

The English liked to depict themselves as hearty eaters and drinkers, and good ale was seen as a joy and a tonic combined. Drunkenness was no sin to those who drank for pleasure (*left*), though condemned in the poor. Increasingly, beer and ale were commercially produced in large brewhouses (*above and top*), rather than in cottage or local inn.

George III set the fashion for seaside holidays. He was a frequent visitor to Weymouth, where he would change into his royal swimwear in a bathing machine, from which His Royal Highness would bravely emerge, once it had been wheeled into the shallows. Within a short time bathing machines were to be seen at Scarborough (*opposite, below*), Brighton, Bournemouth, Sidmouth and a dozen other resorts (*opposite, above*). Many visitors were content merely to breathe the good sea air (*above, right*), lacking the courage to face either the waves or the formidable attendant (*above, left*) who stood guard over the bathing machines

There were 'no go' areas in most cities in the late 18th century. 'Jack Ketch's Warren' in London sheltered gangs of up to a hundred thieves. Blackmailers patrolled 'Sodomites' Walk' looking for likely victims. Prostitutes and pickpockets (*above*) worked together in fashionable quarters. The 'Mohocks' (*opposite, above*) were posses of often well-to-do young blades, who taunted and attacked the elderly nightwatchmen. In the country, the commonest crime was poaching (*opposite, below*), which might add a pheasant or a rabbit to the pot, but could result in hanging or transportation for the poachers.

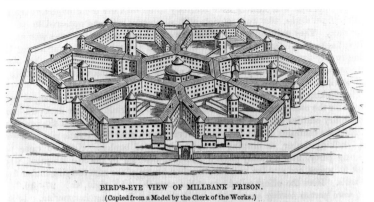

BIRD'S-EYE VIEW OF MILLBANK PRISON.
(Copied from a Model by the Clerk of the Works.)

Punishments were harsh in the reign of George III. There were more than two hundred capital crimes, and flogging was inflicted frequently and publicly (*opposite*). The chapel of the old Newgate Gaol (*below, left*) was often the scene for the funeral of one of the hundreds who died in prison each year. To house the growing prison population, large new prisons were built such as that at Millbank, London (*above, left*).

Scientific knowledge steadily increased during the late 18th
century, and mercifully doctors and surgeons became far more
skilled, particularly in the art of examination (*below, left*), though
this contemporary cartoon suggests that they were not always
more respected (*below, right*). Alexander Monro (*right*) was a
Scottish anatomist who was born in London. He founded the
Edinburgh Royal Infirmary, and was the father of Monro
'Secundus', an early expert on the nervous system and the brain,
ear and eye.

One life-saving discovery was made by Dr Edward Jenner (*above*) of Berkeley, Gloucestershire, in 1796. Others had already noticed that sufferers from cowpox were often spared the worst effects of smallpox – George III had had experience of this as a young man. But when Jenner deliberately infected a young boy with cowpox (*right*), he was risking a charge of manslaughter in the pursuit of medical science. The boy recovered and was later successfully inoculated with smallpox by Jenner. A year later, vaccination became generally accepted as a life-saver.

The ailment that crippled many Englishmen (and a few Englishwomen) was gout. Although often regarded as a source of humour, there was nothing funny about the suffering that gout imposed. Victims commonly rested the swollen and inflamed foot on a stool, but the pain remained (*below*). This cartoon of 1799 graphically depicts gout as a little devil, sinking claws and fangs into a big toe (*right*).

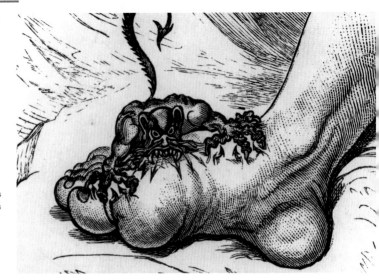

The connection between gout and diet was poorly understood. (*Above*) James Gillray's cartoon shows three sufferers from gout, colic and 'tisic' (consumption) each toasting punch, though punch was quite likely to be the cause of rather than the cure for their respective diseases. Those that could afford to went to spas such as Cheltenham, Tunbridge Wells, Harrogate, Buxton or Bath (*right*) to 'take the waters' and purge their systems of the poisons inherent in their diets.

Sir Joshua Reynolds (*left*) took a leading role in the formation of the Royal Academy of Arts in 1768. Its object was to raise professional standards, and fine premises were erected at Burlington House, in Piccadilly (*opposite, top*). Reynolds was a portrait painter of taste and skill, placing his sitters in classical poses, and producing works that were considered the finest of the English school. His painting of Lavinia, Countess Spencer (*opposite, bottom left*), dates from 1785. The leading portrait painter of the age, however, was Thomas Gainsborough (*opposite, bottom right*).

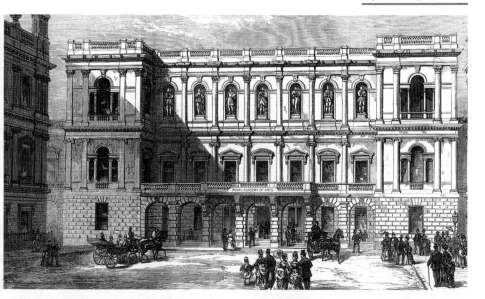

Samuel Johnson (*right*) was a giant of a man – by turn surly and delightful, kind and irascible, pompous and witty. He spent much of his life compiling a *Dictionary*, a monumental work which was many years ahead of its time for scholarship and thoroughness. His constant companion from 16 May 1763, when they first met, was James Boswell (*opposite*, seated centre). Boswell's great work was his *Life of Johnson*, an appealingly honest account of his adventures with his formidable companion. The third figure in the picture of Johnson and Boswell at the Mitre Tavern in London (seated left) is Oliver Goldsmith.

Like his friend Keats, Shelley (*opposite, top left*) died young. Shelley was a radical and an avowed atheist, and a savage critic of the government. He published a clutch of superb poems, but was drowned in a boating accident in 1822. His second wife, Mary Wollstonecraft Godwin (*opposite, top right*), eloped with him at the age of seventeen. She is chiefly remembered today as the creator of *Frankenstein*, which she wrote while staying at Byron's house on Lake Geneva (*opposite, below*). Lord George Byron (*left, in Greek costume*) was a friend of Shelley, a devout believer in the cause of Greek Independence and a libertine whose short life was at least considerably more exuberant than those of his fellow poets.

Robert Burns (*opposite*) was a humble farmer who became Scotland's Poet Laureate. He was born in 1759, and received much of his education from John Murdoch. Among Burns's most famous poems is 'Tam O'Shanter', the story of a drunken farmer who one night stumbles upon a 'hellish legion' of devils and witches (*right, above*) in the Kirk of Alloway. Tam flees from them, but they pursue him, led by 'Cutty Sark' (*right, below*). Tam is within a whisker of being caught, when his faithful horse, Meg, reaches the Bridge of Doon, over which the witches cannot follow. But Cutty Sark grabs Meg's tail and pulls it from the horse's body

The Romantic Age bred a generation of the finest poets, diarists, novelists and men and women of letters. They included Keats (*opposite, top right*), Wordsworth (*opposite, bottom left*), and Coleridge (*above, left*), whose *'Rime of the Ancient Mariner'* was later illustrated by Gustave Doré (*above, right*). Fanny Burney (*opposite, top left*) recorded the gossip, fashion and great events of the day in her *Diary*. Thomas de Quincy (*below, right*) evaluated the literary outpourings of his contemporaries. Many died young. Wordsworth was an exception, living to a ripe old age in the peace of Dove Cottage, Grasmere, in the Lake District (*opposite, below right*).

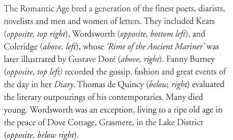

The late 18th century was a golden age for the London theatre. A host of fine new venues were built, from the humbler King's Theatre in the Haymarket (*opposite, bottom right*) to the grander His Majesty's Theatre (formerly the Italian Opera House) (*opposite, above*) and Her Majesty's Theatre (*opposite, bottom left*). Sheridan, Goldsmith and Dibdin produced fine new plays, and Samuel Foote kept audiences happy with a series of farces. Sheridan was also a theatrical impresario, who supported professional actors against what he regarded as aristocratic dilettantes – those who 'played' at being on the stage. (*Left*) Sheridan as harlequin leads (from left) Mrs Billington, Charles Kemble and Mrs Siddons against the 'Pic Nics' in James Gillray's cartoon.

The Noble Art of Self-Defence had not yet been invented. Pugilism in the 18th century was a bare-knuckle affair, and fights continued until there was a knockout or until one or both of the contenders (or the crowd) was exhausted. Bouts sometimes lasted for hours, with blood-spattered bodies scarcely able to stand. But the fighters were heroes, and hundreds would turn up at open air venues to see the likes of Humphreys and Mendoza (*opposite, above*), or Tom Johnson and Isaac Perrins (*left*), whose bitter contest took place at Banbury on 22 October 1789.

Class played a big part in 18th-century sport. Young aristocrats enjoyed a game of racket fives at the tennis court in Leicester Square, London (*right*). Less than aristocratic youngsters found their delight in the open air of a city street, where a game of football involved dozens in each team and covered a pitch often more than a mile long (*opposite*). In a brutal and dangerous world, rich and poor alike had to learn to use their fists, even if it was in a game of football (*below*).

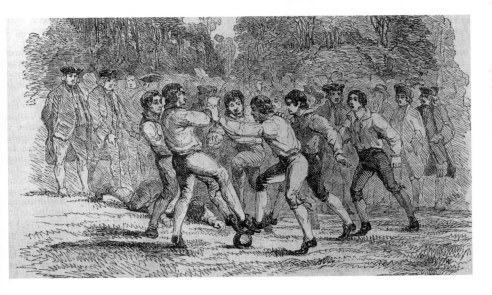

Not perhaps as exciting as falconry was 'owling'. The sport was based on the knowledge that owls are often mobbed by flocks of smaller birds, which see them as predators. The owl was held on a long leash until the small birds appeared, and then released to fly among them and wreak what havoc it could. The passion for sport among English gentlemen was exceeded only by their inventiveness.

In the 1790s Wolfe Tone (*opposite, bottom right*) and others founded the Society of United Irishmen, whose aim was to join Protestant and Catholic together. This posed a threat to the British government, then at war with Revolutionary France. Robert Emmet (*right*) joined the United Irishmen at the age of eleven, and later plotted to seize Dublin Castle (*above*). Lord Edward Fitzgerald (*opposite, bottom left*) joined the United Irishmen in 1796, and arranged for the French to invade Ireland. The United Irishmen, however, were unable to synchronise their own movements with those of the French, and at the Battle of Vinegar Hill (*opposite, above*) in June 1796 they were routed. All three men died violently. Emmet was hanged, Tone cut his throat while in prison, and Fitzgerald was mortally wounded while being arrested.

James Gillray and Thomas Rowlandson were the leading British satirists and caricaturists of the late 18th and early 19th centuries. In a blistering series of cartoons they lampooned the famous and the fashionable, and wickedly exposed the shortcomings of the age. Gillray was the son of a Lanark trooper. His work, such as the cartoon showing Pitt and Napoleon dividing the world (*below*) was more political than that of Rowlandson, though he was also happy to comment on the follies of fashion in the 1790s (*left*). Rowlandson was a portrait painter and his cartoons had a gentler touch. (*Opposite, above*) *A Scientific Demonstration in Front of an Audience*, and (*opposite, below*) *Dr Syntax in Paris*, one of a series entitled *Dr Syntax in Search of the Picturesque*.

13
YEARS OF STRUGGLE
1800–1815

The end of a 'damned close run thing' – the Duke of Wellington (*left*, with sword) greets Marshal Blücher on the field of Waterloo, 18 June 1815. The battle had raged all day, and Napoleon had come within a whisker of winning, but the arrival of Britain's Prussian allies decided events. The French Imperial Guard made one last heroic charge, but failed to break the British lines. Napoleon left the field in disgust, hastening in his carriage back to Paris, and on to St Helena and obscurity. It was the only time Wellington and Napoleon faced each other in battle.

Introduction

Britain was saved from foreign invasion by the Battle of Trafalgar in 1805. Europe was 'liberated' by the Battle of Waterloo in 1815. Bonaparte was safely marooned on the island of St Helena. Britain could breathe again.

Not that the war had in any way curtailed the pleasures offered by London. Even when the struggle against Bonaparte was at its most desperate, there was much to enjoy. There was Madame Tussaud's famous waxworks – the villains of the French Revolution so gruesomely reproduced, the poor family of Louis XVI so pathetically recreated. There was Astley's Amphitheatre in Westminster Bridge Road, where the great clown Grimaldi appeared every night, with acrobats, conjurors and jugglers, and where horses raced round the sawdust ring. There was the new headquarters of the Zoological Society in Regent's Park, the National Gallery, The Quadrant in Regent Street, and Thomas Lord's fine new cricket ground.

For the cerebrally inclined, there were the new novels of Jane Austen and Sir Walter Scott, to be purchased from Lackington Allen and Company's bookshop in Finsbury Square or Hatchard's in Piccadilly. There was the Exhibition Room in Somerset House, Bullock's Museum, Vauxhall Bridge, and the marvels of the gas lighting in Pall Mall. Further afield there were Longleat House, Prinny's wonderfully exotic Royal Pavilion at Brighton, Holland House in Middlesex, and Eaton Hall in Cheshire.

Women's dresses underwent an astounding romantic revival. One fashion journal applauded an opera dress that had a Circassian bodice made of American velvet and trimmed with Chinese cord – to be worn with an Armenian headdress and an eastern mantle. Beau Nash himself would have found it hard to produce a male outfit to rival that. Wigs disappeared, after a flour famine in 1800 during which pastry making was forbidden even in the royal household.

Robert Raikes introduced Sunday Schools to the children of the poor. Bell and Lancaster introduced their 'mechanical system of education', by which a schoolmaster taught a lesson to his brightest pupils, who in turn taught it to the less able children. Sir Humphrey Davy introduced his safety lamp to coal miners. With the support of Thomas Clarkson and the Quakers, William Wilberforce was in the thick of his lifelong fight against slavery and the slave trade. And in 1802 a benevolent House of Commons limited a child's working day to twelve hours in a factory and thirteen hours in a mine. Sixteen years later the law was still being ignored.

William Pitt the Younger (*opposite*) was the second son of the Earl of Chatham. By the age of twenty-four he had become the youngest ever Prime Minister. He was known as 'the Great Commoner', for he had an outstanding ability to influence and manipulate the House of Commons (*above*). His great opponent was Charles James Fox, who predicted that Pitt's ministry would last but a few weeks. It lasted twenty-four years. (*Left*) Horne Tooke sits at his easel and paints portraits of Fox, on the left, and Pitt.

Crowds thronged the streets of London to watch Nelson's funeral cortège as it passed on its way to St Paul's Cathedral (*above*). His victory at Trafalgar had saved England from invasion, and he was mourned by the entire population. In some ways he was an unlikely hero – small in stature, the son of a humble parson, somewhat cold, and an acknowledged adulterer. For more than ten years he had been having an affair with Lady Emma Hamilton (*left*, in costume as Thalia, the comic Muse). She was a courtesan, the wife of Sir William Hamilton, and the mother of Nelson's daughter Horatia.

While Nelson (*right*) always had public sympathy and approval, poor Emma was regularly the object of scorn and derision. In an unflattering cartoon of 1798 she is depicted as Dido in Despair, bemoaning the departure of her lover on his way to defeat the French at the Battle of the Nile. 'Ah where, ah where is my gallant sailor gone?' she cries. 'He's gone to fight the Frenchmen for George upon the throne…' Nelson lost the sight of his right eye during an attack on Bastia in 1794, but he often wore his eye-patch over his left eye in order to protect it. This was how he could justifiably claim that he saw no signal to withdraw.

Copenhagen, Aboukir
Bay, the Battle of the Nile
and Trafalgar, as shown
here (*left*), are all seen as
Nelson's victories, the
products of his skill,
tactical brilliance and
daring. His own sailors
spoke of 'the Nelson
touch', his ability to strike
at the enemy in an
original and shattering
way.

ENGLAND EXPECTS EVERY MAN WILL DO HIS D U T Y

(*Above*) Nelson briefs his officers before the Battle of Trafalgar. (*Left*) The famous battle signal flown from Nelson's flagship *Victory* before the battle – 'England expects that every man will do his duty.' The last word had to be spelt out letter by letter, for there was no flag in the navy signalling code for 'duty'.

At the height of the battle Nelson was mortally wounded by a musket ball fired by a French sniper from the rigging of the *Redoubtable*. The sniper had identified Nelson by the badges of the four orders of knighthood that he wore on his uniform. In the picture (*above*) Nelson lies on deck, while Captain Hardy of the *Victory* hurries towards him. An English ensign is returning the French fire. Nelson was one of 1,690 British sailors killed in the battle. The French and Spanish lost 5,860. A hundred years were to pass before a sea battle of comparable size and destruction was to take place.

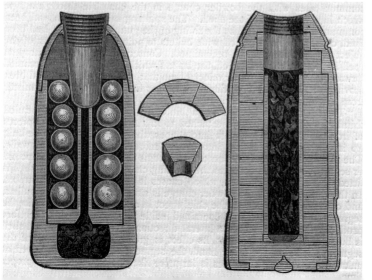

Britain's armed struggle against Revolutionary France and Napoleon lasted for almost twenty years. During that time new weapons were introduced to the British army. There was the rifle, used by the Rifle Brigade, and the innovatory Shrapnel Shell (*left*), invented by the English artillery officer Henry Shrapnel (*opposite*). The shell was fired in the conventional way, but exploded on impact, releasing a cluster of shot and fragments of metal. (*Above*) Members of the Honourable Artillery Company parade in their uniforms.

The afternoon of 18 June 1815. In the background French cavalry regiments attack the British squares, which the infantry defend with their Brown Bess muskets. The farmhouse in the centre is La Haye Sainte, where some of the bitterest fighting took place. Napoleon saw it as the key to the battle, and launched Ney's light cavalry against it at four o'clock. The British were given the order 'Prepare to receive cavalry!' but, in the words of Victor Hugo, 'the cold infantry remained impassive.' Wellington gave orders for his cavalry to counter-attack. A few minutes later, the first Prussian guns were heard firing from the fringe of the Paris Wood.

After his final victory over Napoleon at Waterloo, Arthur Wellesley, 1st Duke of Wellington (*opposite*), was regarded as the saviour of the nation. He stayed in France for a year after the battle, dazzling the ladies – who included Fanny Burney, Lady Caroline Lamb, Lady Shelley and Madame de Staël – and attempting to sort out the problems created by the restoration of the Bourbon dynasty. But his popularity was not to last. Later his support for Catholic emancipation resulted in his portrayal (*left*) as eclipsing the glory of the King himself.

Henry 'Orator' Hunt was a well-to-do farmer whose quick temper landed him in gaol in 1800. He came out a vehement radical, dedicated to Parliamentary reform. The campaign to change the qualifications for the right to vote grew rapidly, and large crowds gathered all over the country to urge reform. Hunt was one of the most popular speakers at such meetings, and in 1819 more than 50,000 people met in St Peter's Square, Manchester, to hear him speak. The protest was orderly, but the magistrates ordered troops to disperse the crowd. Eleven people were killed and more than four hundred injured in what became known as the Peterloo Massacre.

(*Above*) The Chamber of Horrors in the early days of Madame Tussaud's Waxwork Museum. The figures on display are authentic villains of the first half of the 19th century. James Blomfield Rush shot his landlord. John Nichols Thom (or Tom) was a madman who called himself the King of Jerusalem and shot a policeman. James Greenacre manufactured 'amalgamated candy' and was hanged for murdering his fifth wife.

Marie Grosholtz Tussaud (*right*, in waxwork form) learned the skills of wax-sculpting in Paris in the 1770s. She became a favourite at the Court in Versailles, which led to her being imprisoned during the French Revolution. She opened her waxwork museum in London in 1802, with thirty-five figures that she had inherited from her uncle. The collection grew rapidly and no expense was spared in buying authentic costumes for the figures. Madame paid £18,000 for George IV's Coronation and state robes.

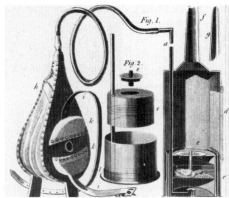

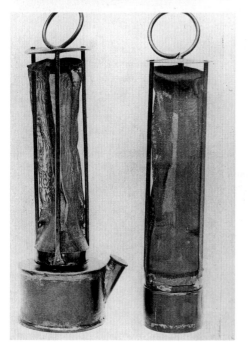

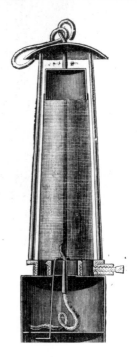

Sir Humphry Davy (*above*) was a chemist and scientific pioneer who specialised in the study of gases. He discovered the anaesthetic qualities of laughing gas, but his most valuable work was to invent the miners' safety lamp (*opposite, below*). This enabled coal to be worked from deep shafts (*opposite, top left*) with minimal danger of igniting the deadly firedamp, a gas that caused horrific underground explosions. (*Opposite, top right*) An early diagram showing how the safety lamp worked.

The first public display of gas lighting took place in 1807 in Pall Mall, London, as part of the birthday celebrations of the Prince of Wales. The Prince was delighted, and lent his weighty patronage to the development of gas lighting. In 1812, the Gas-Light and Coke Company received a charter to supply gas to the City of London, Westminster and Southwark, and the first gas-fuelled street lamps were erected on Westminster Bridge (*above*). Gas lamps were seen as a powerful weapon in the fight against street crime which had reached high levels at the beginning of the 19th century.

Not everyone supported gas lighting, however. A cartoon (*above, left*) published just after the Pall Mall display, was ironically entitled *The Good Effects of Carbonic Gas*. It shows a man leaning from a top window gasping 'Murder, murder! Oh, my Breath', while the woman below cries 'I can't breathe'. Across the way another complains 'What the Devil! Are you funking [smoking] us all with your stinking smoke?' (*Above, right*) The handsome gas lamps, known as Bude lights, in Trafalgar Square.

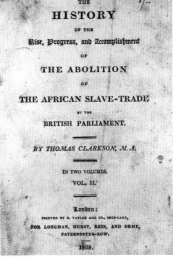

THE

HISTORY

OF THE

Rise, Progress, and Accomplishment

OF

THE ABOLITION

OF

THE AFRICAN SLAVE-TRADE

BY THE

BRITISH PARLIAMENT.

BY THOMAS CLARKSON, M.A.

IN TWO VOLUMES.

VOL. II.

London:

PRINTED BY R. TAYLOR AND CO., SHOE-LANE,

FOR LONGMAN, HURST, REES, AND ORME,

PATERNOSTER-ROW.

1808.

The campaign to end the slave trade was strongly supported by the Quakers and by Thomas Clarkson, seen here addressing a meeting of the Anti Slavery Society in Freemasons' Hall (*above*). With Granville Sharp, Clarkson helped Wilberforce found the Society. (*Left*) The title page of Clarkson's *History of the Rise, Progress, and Accomplishment of the Abolition of the African Slave-Trade by the British Parliament* 1808. (*Far left*) An acerbic comment on Lord Brougham's failure to chair an anti-slavery meeting.

William Wilberforce (*right*) was the radical MP for Hull. At the age of twenty-five he became an evangelical Christian whose life's work was the abolition of slavery. It took him nineteen years to end Britain's part in the slave trade, an immense achievement considering the weight of commercial opposition. Wilberforce wanted to proceed to the abolition of all trade in slaves and slavery itself, but ill-health forced him to retire from Parliament in 1825.

John Nash (*left*) was one of the finest English architects of all time. As a relatively young man he retired to Wales, but he lost most of his money through financial speculation before he was forty, and he returned to practise in London. Here his flair and talent came to the notice of the Prince of Wales, and Nash was commissioned to plan the layout of the new Regent's Park and the streets to the south. The masterpieces of this development were Regent Street itself and The Quadrant (*opposite, below*) near Piccadilly Circus, and Waterloo Place (*opposite, above*) at the bottom of Lower Regent Street.

When George, Prince of Wales, came of age in 1783, he was given Carlton House as his personal residence. Over the next twenty years he spent a small fortune on its restoration and enlargement. Henry Holland designed an elaborate new east wing (*opposite, below*), and the Regency interior (*opposite, above*) was 'bold in outline, rich and chaste in ornaments'. Among habitués of the new Carlton House were the playwright Richard Brinsley Sheridan (*above, left*), the politician Charles James Fox (*above, right*) and the man who was at once the terror and delight of the Prince, George Bryan Brummell (*left*).

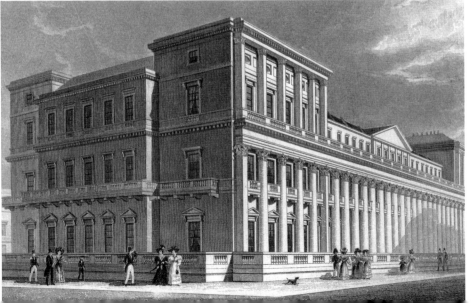

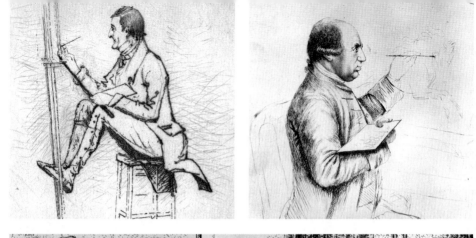

was perhaps the first
golden age of English
painting. The outstanding
talents were those of
Thomas Gainsborough,
John Constable (*right*)
and Joseph Mallord
William Turner (*opposite,
above left*). The most
famous animal painter of
the time was George
Stubbs (*opposite, above
right*). The appreciation
and acquisition of works
of art became part of the
social scene, with crowds
gathering at galleries and
auction houses. (*Opposite,
below*) George Cruik-
shank's cartoon depicts *A
Day of Fashion – the
Morning Drop-in at
Christies.*

The National Gallery (*above and opposite*) was founded after the English landscape painter and connoisseur Sir George Beaumont (*right*) had persuaded the government to buy thirty-eight paintings, among them works by Raphael, Rembrandt and Van Dyck, previously belonging to the Russian-born merchant and philanthropist John Julius Augerstein. The government paid £57,000 for this collection, and Beaumont added a further sixteen pictures – including two Rembrandts. The collection was first housed in Pall Mall, before being moved to its splendid new premises in Trafalgar Square.

The Covent Garden Theatre in Bow Street, London, was originally built by Edmund Shepherd in
1732. In 1763 much of the auditorium was wrecked when the audience rioted against price
increases, and the theatre itself was destroyed by fire in 1808. It was believed that the leader of the
orchestra had set fire to the building as he had a grudge against the manager. The New Covent
Garden Theatre, or Royal Opera House (*above*), was designed by Robert Smirke and opened in
1810, with more expensive seats, and more riots.

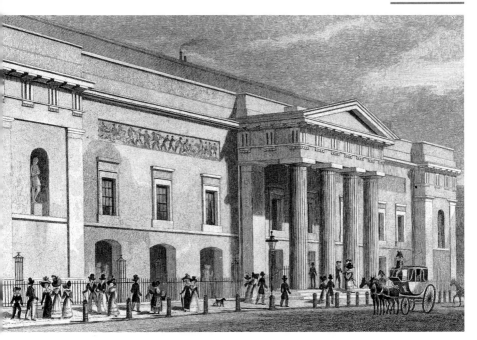

The east front of the Royal Opera House (*above*) was modelled on the Temple of Minerva in Athens. Its calm was shattered on opening night when not a word of the play was audible. The audience kept shouting 'Old prices! Old prices!', until the military were called in and the Riot Act was read from the stage. Two months later the old prices were restored. Public opinion had triumphed. It is surprising how often this happened in early 19th-century England.

In peace and war crowds flocked to centres of entertainment. There was Philip Astley's Amphitheatre in Surrey Road, London (*opposite, below*), where horsemen and women showed their incredible riding skills, where mock sea and land battles were fought, and where the contests of the old Roman arenas were recreated. Charles Hughes, one of Astley's former horsemen, opened a rival establishment at the Royal Circus in St George's Fields (*opposite, above*). For those who fancied knockabout fun, there were the clowns, of whom the greatest was Joseph Grimaldi ('Joey'). (*Above, right*) Grimaldi sings *All the World's in Paris* from the pantomime *Harlequin Whittington*. (*Above, left*) Grimaldi as 'Hock' in *The Sixes* at his farewell benefit performance at the Sadler's Wells Theatre.

The Zoological Society of London was founded by Sir Thomas Stamford Raffles (*opposite, top left*), whose other main claim to fame was as the founder of the colony of Singapore. The Society opened its Zoological Gardens in Regent's Park (*above*). It was an immediate success. More than 1,000 visitors a day came to see the monkeys, bears, emus, kangaroos, llamas, zebras and turtles. Gentlemen were requested to leave their whips at the gate, though ladies were permitted to keep their parasols. A rival establishment opened at the Surrey Zoological Gardens (*left*) where residents and visitors were much the same.

The most popular and most successful literary figures of the age were Sir Walter Scott (*above*) and Jane Austen (*above, right*). Scott was first known for his poetry – *The Border Minstrelsy* and *The Lay of the Last Minstrel*. One of his most popular works was *The Lady of the Lake (opposite)*. Later he wrote the Waverley novels, producing almost one a year to pay off his debts. Jane Austen produced six great novels, the first of which was *Sense and Sensibility*, first published in 1811 and illustrated with a series of engravings (*right*). *Pride and Prejudice* followed in 1812, *Mansfield Park* in 1814, *Emma* and *Persuasion* in 1815, and *Northanger Abbey* in 1816.

For the rich there was Eton College. Here education was a rough and tumble, depicted by *The Oppidans Museum or the Eton Court of Claims* (*left*), and *First Absence, or Etonians Answering Morning Muster* (*below*). For the poor, there were only the Sunday Schools of Robert Raikes (*opposite, far right*). Even these provoked opposition from religious objectors (*opposite, top left*) and reluctant attenders (*opposite, bottom left*).

Introduction to
Period 3 – 1815–2000

A description of the events of two mornings may serve to chart Britain's progress through the 19th and 20th centuries.

On Monday, 10 October 1825, George Stephenson's *Locomotion* pulled out of Stockton station, hauling a mixed train of coal and passenger wagons bound for Darlington, some ten miles away. It was the first run on the first regular passenger railway in the world and it ushered in an age of unparalleled prosperity for Britain. Within twenty years a further 6,000 miles of track were in operation: Britain had been gripped by railway mania. 'Though Britain will never be in chains,' commented the satirical magazine *Punch*, 'she will pretty soon be in irons', accompanying the pun with a cartoon map that suggested a rail link between Ramsgate and Calais, and a floating line between Dungeness and Boulogne.

The railways became the arteries of Britain's industrial body, a body that was for many years the fittest and the finest in the world. Coal mining, iron and steel production, shipbuilding, machine tool-making, arms and armaments and railways themselves became the staple industries of a new, sprawling, ugly, merciless but hugely profitable economy.

For almost three-quarters of a century it seemed that Britain was an enchanted land – poisoned by pollution, riddled with exploitation but unmatchable in the creation of wealth. Like some vast commercial kitchen, Britain took in the raw materials of the world and cooked them into goods that tempted and nourished its customers in every continent. Britain grew relentlessly, in population, influence, power and prestige.

The *chef d'oeuvre* of this gargantuan feast was Queen Victoria's Diamond Jubilee, on 22 June 1897. The citizens of London gathered on that morning to cheer the Old Lady of Windsor on her way from Buckingham Palace to St Paul's Cathedral. They were conscious that their city was at the heart of the largest empire in the history of the world, covering a quarter of the Earth's surface, and ruling a quarter of its people. At eleven o'clock, the Queen went to the telegraph room in the Palace and sent a simple message: 'Thank my beloved people. May God bless them' – all 372 million of them. The message was flashed by Morse code to the lonely island of Pitcairn in the Pacific, to the Cape Province (where Her Majesty's troops would soon be struggling to reassert her authority), to Borneo,

Bermuda, Australia, the Channel Islands, and a hundred other outposts of the Empire on which the sun never set. It was also sent to Ireland, still a thorn in the imperial flesh, and destined to remain so for another century or more.

The British fleet sailed unchallenged through the Seven Seas, though there were rumours that Germany was a threatening rival. The newly reformed British army was currently resting between wars, though in the last twenty years it had inflicted military defeats on Afghanistan, Egypt, the Zulus, the Boers, the Mahdi in the Sudan, and Upper Burma. The British people believed they were invincible, their own yearly reference books being unable to keep up with the expansion of empire, markets, companies and profits. The Conservatives were in office, and seemed likely to hold power for many years to come. All was right with the world.

Little over a hundred years later, Britain woke late on the morning of 1 January 2000, after a night of millennial celebration that had an air of the grin-and-bear-it, make-do-and-mend approach that had been adopted on the Home Front during the darkest days of the Second World War. The partying of the night before had been good-humoured, peaceful, impressive in some places. In London, the river of fire had failed to ignite, the giant wheel opposite the Houses of Parliament had failed to revolve and the Dome had been subjected to such adverse publicity that a crisis threatened. Britain was dithering about joining the European single currency, England had only just qualified for football's World Cup, and train drivers were proposing strike action against their French-owned rail companies. The Labour Party was in office, and seemed likely to hold office for many years to come. It was impossible to say how much of the world was all right.

A hundred years of decline had succeeded a hundred years of staggering success. Why? The simple answer is that the rest of the world had caught up. Early in the 20th century German levels of production overtook those of Britain. By the 1930s, the United States had become an economic power of hitherto unimaginable proportions. The Revolution of 1917 had unleashed a massive military and economic force in the Soviet Union. Since the Second World War, Japan and Korea had hijacked most the British car and shipbuilding industries. The Empire itself had been blown away by the winds of change and the

determination of nationalists in India, South Africa, Canada, Kenya, the Caribbean, Burma – almost everywhere save the loyal Falkland Islands. A political paralysis had gripped Britain. The Irish problem was still unresolved. Nobody was quite sure what to do with the monarchy: in Australia republicans had only just lost a referendum that sought to free them from ties to the Queen.

It had not all been Britain's fault. Two desperately destructive world wars had cost the best that Britain had, in human and material resources. In the second half of the 20th century, international capitalism had put its money where there were richer pickings to be had than in a country that had earlier come to terms with the trade unions and Britain's gentle form of socialism. The British had lost the bravura self-confidence that had made their country so successful and so unattractive in late Victorian times. Gone was the air of certainty, the belief that all the evil in the world could be defeated by the speedy despatch of a gunboat, a crate of Bibles, or both. Britannia no longer ruled the waves, or the global stock exchange, or the cricket fields, football pitches, coaling stations, docksides, rubber and tea plantations, diamond mines or railroads of the world. It was not easy to come to terms with such a change in fortune.

But British inventiveness still had much to give – and sell – the world: the turbine and jet engines, the hovercraft, television, radar, penicillin, the Flying Bedstead, the Beatles and the Rolling Stones, the first test tube baby, and Dolly the Cloned Sheep.

14
RURAL CHANGE
1815–1845

The Hall of Infamy, alias the Oyster Saloon in Bridge Street, or New Covent Garden. George Cruikshank's lively drawing is a comment on the political behaviour of both Whigs and Tories in the period leading up to the introduction of the Great Reform Bill in 1832, for Bridge Street connects Westminster Bridge and Parliament Street. Passions for and against the Bill, which aimed to extend the franchise to some of the middle class, were high. 'The Bill, the whole Bill, and nothing but the Bill,' cried the Whigs, while the Tory Duke of Wellington sourly warned 'Beginning reform is beginning revolution.'

Introduction

In a couple of generations the English countryside changed forever. It was not simply that fields and meadows were slashed apart by the network of railways, or that the old rhythms of life were superseded by the impatient pounding of the locomotives. It was where the iron way came from and where it went, what it promised and what it could deliver. Farms and farm workers bowed to the inevitable – steam and the machines it powered blew their lives apart. In the country, steam revolutionised agriculture. There were Ransome Sims' and Jeffries' threshing machines, Patrick Bell's reaper in 1826, Fowler's steam ploughing system, and Darby's Pedestrian Broadside Digger. Fewer hands were needed to plough, sow, reap and mow. There was little employment to be found on the land.

Railways led to towns and cities where there were factories. Whole families left the cottages in which they had grown up. One last time they passed the village churchyard where their ancestors lay buried, and shuffled on to the nearest railway station. A ticket to Manchester, Leeds, Middlesborough, New Lanark, Bradford (nicknamed Worstedopolis), or Birmingham bought new hope.

Some hardy souls stayed on the land to fight for their livelihoods. In February 1834, six farm labourers from Tolpuddle in Dorset encouraged others to take illegal oaths, promising joint action against their employers. Local land owners were quick to stamp on this threat from organised labour. The Tolpuddle Martyrs, as the six labourers came to be known, were transported as convicts to Australia. Two years later the remainder of their sentences was remitted, though nobody bothered to inform the authorities in Australia. Other rebels took more direct action. In 1830 a wave of rick-burning and machine destruction in several parts of Britain was labelled the 'Riots of Captain Swing'. It was the last labourers' revolt. In the savage repression that followed, nineteen rioters were executed, four hundred and eighty-one were transported.

And worse things happened in Ireland. There the rural economy had been so ill-managed that much of the country relied for subsistence on a single crop – the potato. In the 1840s, fungus struck. Whole fields of potatoes rotted overnight. There was nothing for the people to eat. Starving people seldom have the strength to protest, let alone riot. Villages died.

Those who took to the towns never came back. Life in factories, mills and mines was hard, mean, damaging, but at least it was life.

The Prince Regent (*opposite*) was fifty-eight when he succeeded his father as King in 1820. His Coronation took place in Westminster Abbey in July 1821 (*above*). It was a magnificent affair, though somewhat marred by the arrival of George's wife, Caroline of Brunswick, demanding that she be crowned Queen. George had married her in 1795 (*far right*), but had tired of her by 1820, and persuaded Parliament to draw up a Bill to dissolve the marriage (*right*) on the grounds of her adultery with her servant, Bartolomo Pergami. The process was opposed by many, and subsequently abandoned. Caroline did not find her way into the Abbey, however, and had to be content with an annual pension of £50,000.

A

BILL

To deprive Her MAJESTY Caroline Amelia Elizabeth of the Title, Prerogatives, Rights, Privileges, and Pretensions of Queen Consort of this Realm, and to dissolve the Marriage between His MAJESTY and the said Queen.

Note.—The first column contains a Copy of the Bill—The second column contains the CLAUSES THAT DROP OUT, and which are now proposed to be restored.

The Royal Pavilion at Brighton was originally designed by Henry
Holland and was first occupied by the Prince of Wales in 1787. It
was small and cramped, but in 1807 'Prinny' had the idea of
enlarging it in the style of an Indian palace (*right*). Eventually it
was John Nash who combined the strange blend of Indian,
Chinese and Moorish styles. By 1822 it was completed. The
interior was sumptuous. The saloons (*below*) were richly
decorated, but the *pièce de resistance* was the Banqueting Hall
(*opposite, below*) with its green and turquoise ceiling, its immense
crystal chandeliers, its painted panels and its brilliant yellow
carpet.

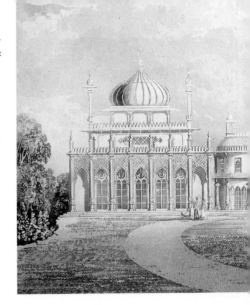

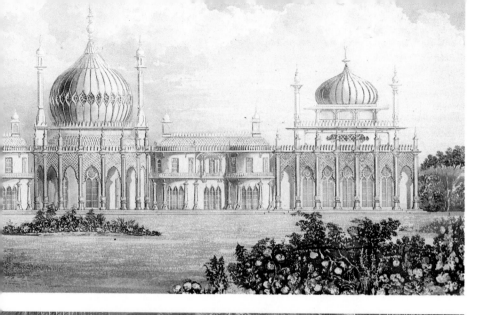

Copenhagen Fields in Islington, London, had for many years been the venue for marches and protest meetings on a wide variety of issues. Dissenters, radicals and revolutionaries regularly gathered there. On 21 April 1834 many thousands of Trade Unionists met in support of a petition to the King on behalf of the Tolpuddle Martyrs. The Martyrs were six farm labourers from the Dorset village of Tolpuddle who had been sentenced to seven years transportation for administering illegal oaths to those wishing to join their Union. The wheels of justice slowly turned, and in 1836 the remainder of their sentences was remitted and all six returned to England.

The Great Reform Bill reached Parliament in 1831 (*above, left*). Its main provisions were to give the vote to town-dwellers who paid £10 rent or more a year, and to countrymen (no women were enfranchised) who paid forty shillings a year as free-holders. The Bill was backed by the Whigs and bitterly opposed by the Tories, who saw it as removing political power from those with the biggest stake in the country – the great landowners. (*Below, left*) Wellington and Peel throw up their hands in horror as William IV announces his support for the Bill.

The Bill was twice defeated in the House of Lords in 1831. Rioting broke out in many parts of the country. William IV promised to create as many new (Whig) members of the Lords as were necessary to pass the Bill. In 1832 it was passed in triumph. (*Right*) The Lion of Reform is surmounted by William and the Whigs, while Britannia slays the Snake of Reaction.

Agricultural workers all over Britain struggled through poverty in the early 19th century. (*Below, left*) Lord Melbourne turns his back on a starving family. (*Below, right*) The words 'Anti Corn Law' are scrubbed from the floor of the Covent Garden Theatre after an Anti Corn Law meeting there. (*Opposite*) Death appears as the Poor Man's Friend in a country hovel. (*Left*) Farm workers, dressed as women, take part in the Rebecca Riots of 1843, sparked by economic recession.

F.SMYTH

Daniel O'Connell (*above*) was an Irish land owner who supported Peel's Catholic Emancipation Act. (*Right*) O'Connell is depicted whipping Peel along the road of emancipation. After calling a mass meeting at Clontarf, O'Connell was arrested. (*Opposite, above*) O'Connell arrives at the Four Courts in Dublin for his trial in January 1844. He was imprisoned but released in September (*opposite, below*).

The famine that struck Ireland in the 1840s was sudden and terrible. Through neglect and exploitation, the population of Ireland had been reduced virtually to living off a single crop – the potato. The fungus that struck plants and crops already harvested caused fields to rot overnight, and a million people died. Some scrabbled in fields for what might be saved (*left*). Riots broke out in potato stores that had not succumbed to the blight (*opposite, below*). A few philanthropists established soup kitchens to feed the starving (*opposite, above*). Failure of the crop meant that tenants were unable to pay their rent. Landlords showed little sympathy, and thousands of families were evicted from their cottages. The turf roofs were removed to prevent others finding shelter within (*above*).

For many Irish families, the only hope of building a new life was to emigrate to the United States. From Cork and Killarney, from Queenstown and Sligo, they set off in ships that were barely seaworthy, crammed like cattle below decks (*left*). In many instances, the captains of emigrant ships were instructed by their owners to sail into the Atlantic, and then scuttle the ship, leaving the passengers to drown. The crew would escape in lifeboats and the owners would collect the insurance money. For the Irish it seemed there was no escape but death from the misery that surrounded them.

English opinion was divided on the problems raised by the Irish Famine. Some were genuinely appalled and sought to do what they could to help the starving people. Others, as in this contemporary cartoon (*above, right*), where the fat landlord likens Irish emigration to sending hogs to market, saw the Irish as little better than animals. After the perilous journey, and with their few belongings, lucky emigrants survived to experience the moment of hope when they sighted America (*below, right*).

After the repeal of the Corn Laws, comparative peace returned to the countryside, broken only by the sound of the new machines that were replacing manual labour. Not every wild idea was realised – the relaxing-looking steam plough (*opposite, above*) remained a dream – but there was a machine for almost every task. (*Opposite, below*) John Heathcott's steam plough of 1837, a fixed traction engine that pulled the plough along the furrow. (*Top, right*) Crosskill's Archimedian root washer. (*Centre, right*) A steam-powered threshing machine of the 1840s. (*Bottom, right*) An improved steam plough on trial at the estate of Lord Willoughby d'Evesby.

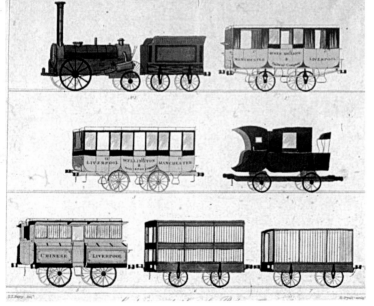

The coming of the railways in the 1820s and 1830s revolutionised transport in Britain. One of the earliest lines to be opened ran from Liverpool to Manchester (*above*). The task that confronted George Stephenson, the engineer, was staggering. He had to plan the construction of thirty-one miles of double track through difficult country, with tunnels and viaducts, floating it across the notorious bog at Chat Moss. Early rolling stock (*left*) still owed much to the design of the stage-coach.

William Huskisson (*right*) played an important and tragic part in the early days of Britain's railways. As President of the Board of Trade and MP for Morpeth, he was well aware of the part railways could play in furthering the industrial revolution in the north of England. So he was among the dignitaries present on 16 September 1830 when the Liverpool and Manchester Railway was formally opened. Unfortunately, Huskisson was confused by the working of the railway, stepped on to the track and was fatally injured by a shunting locomotive.

In 1823 work began to extend the British Museum. The new architect was Robert Smirke, who planned a great classical façade in Great Russell Street (*above*). The interior, too, was built on the grand scale, from the staircase by the North Entrance (*left*) to the circular Reading Room – later to be used by Karl Marx as a place of study when writing *Das Kapital*. The new building was opened on 19 April 1847.

The Reading Room proved inadequate to house the Museum's vast collection of books – 100,000 volumes from George III's library; 20,000 volumes from Thomas Grenville; 16,000 volumes on natural history alone. An additional library was opened in the main building (*right*), but most visitors were more interested in the other exhibits – coins and medals from the Bank of England; zoological specimens from Africa and the Far East, and, of course, the Elgin Marbles.

Fashionable London clubs were centres of the dreadful vices of gambling and smoking (*opposite above left*) in the early 19th century. In the gaming rooms of The Albany, in White's and Boodle's, and especially in the Great Subscription Room at Brook's (*above*), fortunes were won or more usually lost every night. Charles James Fox gambled away £200,000. General Scott, who drank only water and kept a clear head, won £200,000. Edward Gibbon, author of *Decline and Fall of the Roman Empire*, (*opposite above right*) once gambled for twenty-two hours at a stretch, and lost £500 for each hour. As well as providing comfort and excitement, the great London clubs employed some of the world's finest chefs. Escoffier himself worked in the kitchens of the Reform Club (*opposite, below*).

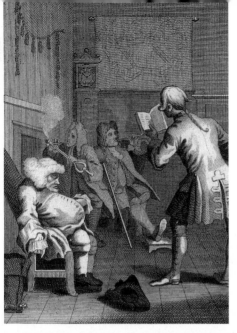

In 1834 the Palace of Westminster was destroyed by fire (*above*). The cause of the fire was soon established. It had been the practice to keep records of the old Court of Exchequer by a system of wooden tallies, notched elm sticks that were split in half – one for the Exchequer, one as a receipt for the payer. 'The sticks were housed at Westminster,' Charles Dickens told an audience at Drury Lane. 'It would naturally occur to any intelligent person that nothing could be easier than to allow them to be carried away for firewood by the miserable people who live in that neighbourhood. However, they had never been useful…and so the order went forth that they should be privately and confidentially burned.'

It was decided to burn the Exchequer sticks in the big furnace beneath the Chamber of the House of Lords, in the Old Palace (*above*). The furnace overheated. A faint glow was discernible that evening, but no action was taken until it was too late. By morning the House of Lords, the Commons and almost all the buildings that constituted the Palace of Westminster lay in smoking ruins. A Parliament house that had stood for centuries had been destroyed in a few hours.

(*Above*) Prisoners in the Brixton House of Correction exercising on a treadmill, 1840. (*Left*) The racket court in the Fleet Prison, 1774. The prison was used mainly for debtors, who were unable to earn money while they were there, and unable to get out until they had earned money.

(*Above, left*) Elizabeth Lenning in the condemned cell of Newgate, July 1815. She was hanged for a murder that she probably did not commit. The law was a most imprecise instrument in those days, and, in a case of murder, even if found 'not guilty', an accused could be retried. (*Above, right*) Elizabeth Fry, Quaker and prison reformer. Fry visited Newgate for the first time in 1813 and found three hundred women and children imprisoned there in appalling conditions. She devoted the rest of her life to prison and to asylum reform.

The Brontë sisters – Charlotte (*above, left*), Emily (*above, right*) and Anne (*left*) – produced some of the most powerful novels in English literature. In their short lives, (none of them lived to be forty) they created a handful of masterpieces. All three adopted pseudonyms. Charlotte wrote *Jane Eyre*, *Villette* and *Shirley* under the name Currer Bell; Emily's only novel was *Wuthering Heights*, published as the work of Ellis Bell; and as Acton Bell, Anne wrote *Agnes Grey* and *The Tenant of Wildfell Hall*. (*Opposite*) The parsonage at Haworth, Yorkshire, where the Brontë sisters lived with their father and their brother, Bramwell.

Dr Thomas Arnold (*right*) has been credited as the principal force behind the reform of the British public school system in the early 19th century. He was appointed headmaster of Rugby School (*opposite, above*) in 1828. Here he introduced mathematics, modern history and modern languages to the curriculum; established the system of forms and classes; and appointed prefects to maintain discipline when no masters were present. From being a bear pit, the School Room at Rugby (*opposite, below*) became a place of order, where ushers and masters could teach several classes within one room. Arnold's methods were described as 'Muscular Christianity'.

Second only to the love of horse racing was the British love for pugilism. A man who was 'a game chick – a proper man with his fists' was regarded as a hero. One of the greatest was Tom Spring (*left*). His real name was Thomas Winter, and he was a butcher by profession. In 1821 Spring claimed the championship of England after the death of Tom Cribb, and two years later he was called upon to defend that title. His challenger was an Irishman named Jack Langan, and the fight took place at Worcester on 7 January 1824 (*above*). It was a brutal and bloody affair (*opposite*) in which Spring eventually emerged the winner. Spring retired four years later and became landlord of the Castle Tavern in Holborn.

Pleasures were public and private in Regency England. There was the formal fun to be had at a fancy dress ball (*opposite, top*), and in the Royal Salon in Piccadilly (*above*). Here the great and the not-so-good could kick the waiters if they were too slow, and 'quiz' friends and enemies alike. Two of the more private pleasures were smoking (*opposite, below right*) and snuff taking (*opposite, below left*). Both tobacco and snuff came from many sources – Virginia, Egypt, Turkey, the East Indies and South America.

15
STEAM 1830–1850

William Frith's glorious painting of the hurly-burly that greeted arrivals at and departures from London's Paddington Station. Within a few years of the opening of the first passenger railway, Britain was gripped by a railway fever. Rival companies fought each other to produce the fastest and most comfortable trains, the finest stations and the greatest profits. Paddington was the headquarters of Brunel's Great Western Railway, the only broad gauge track in the country. In constructing it, Brunel was behind the times. The standard gauge of Stephenson had already been accepted by every other company, but not until 1892 did the GWR admit its mistake.

Introduction

Soon shall they arm,
UNCONQUER'D STEAM! Afar
Drag the slow barge, or drive the rapid car;
Or a wide-waving wings expanded bear
The flying-chariot through the fields of air.
Erasmus Darwin – *Botanic Garden*

There was nothing to rival steam. It drove pumps, locomotives, hammers, buses, looms, ships and all manner of machines. It never tired. It asked no wages save the coal that fired its boilers. It worked wherever it was placed. It inspired poets, artists, even composers. And, best of all, it made fortunes.

It delighted monarchs and masses. Queen Victoria much enjoyed her first journey by train from Slough to Paddington in 1842. Some were contemptuous. The Duke of Wellington remarked that he saw 'no reason to suppose that these machines will ever force themselves into general se'. A few abhorred the railway. George Charles Brantley Fitzhardinge Berkeley, MP for West Gloucestershire, hated 'the echo of our hills reverberating with the noise of hissing railroad engines, running through the heart of our hunting country', thereby destroying the noble sport to which he had been accustomed from his childhood.

It was abused by some. There were factory owners who valued steam power a great deal more than the wellbeing or even the lives of their workers. Hands who collapsed through exhaustion, or were injured while at work, were fined for 'loss of steam' as their machines lay idle. It is, nonetheless, a mistake to see all employers as evil.

Those who harnessed the power of steam became heroes. George Stephenson was one of the earliest. 'He seemed,' wrote a friend, 'the impersonation of the moving, active spirit of the age.' Crowds lined the streets leading to Westminster Abbey for the funeral of Robert Stephenson in 1859. *The Engineer* sang the praises of Isambard Kingdom Brunel, creator of the Great Western Railway and the first giant transatlantic steamships – the *Great Eastern* and *Great Britain*: 'In all that constitutes an engineer in the highest, fullest and best sense, Brunel has no contemporary, no predecessor!'

And there were many others, less famous but equally heroic – James Nasmyth (who built a vast steam-hammer for his foundry near Manchester), Joseph Bramah, Richard Roberts (whose ingenious tools and machines enabled others to build bridges, viaducts and tunnels), David Napier (who manufactured many of the weapons that armed Britain in the 19th century), Henry Maudslay (who played a key role in the development of machine tools), and generations of the Darby family from Coalbrookdale.

Victoria was born at 04.15 on Monday 24 May 1819 – 'a pretty princess, as plump as a partridge'. Her doting father and mother loved her dearly, but by the time she was four (*opposite*) Victoria was already surrounded by men and women anxious to gain influence over the little heiress to the throne. At nineteen (*above*), Victoria was Queen, and two years later she met and married Prince Albert of Saxe-Coburg and Gotha (*right*).

The father of the railway in Britain was George Stephenson (*far left*). He was a brilliant engineer whose locomotive *Rocket* (*left*) beat all comers for speed and dependability at the Rainhill Trials in 1829 (*above*). The public were amazed, and not a little frightened, to discover *Rocket* could achieve a speed of 30 mph (40 kph).

Stephenson was very much a 'hands-on' engineer. He designed
all the tunnels, viaducts and bridges needed for his lines, and
personally supervised the navvies working for him (*right*). His
greatest early success was the construction of the Liverpool and
Manchester Railway, which opened in 1830. Its western
terminus was Edge Hill station in Liverpool (*below*). Stephenson
was something of an eccentric: he spent much of his time at his
house in Tapton, near Chesterfield, trying to persuade
cucumbers to grow straight. In the end he forced them to, by
growing them in glass tubes.

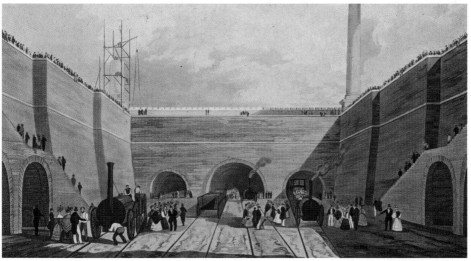

George Hudson (*opposite, top left*) was known as the Railway King, and grateful princes, passengers and shareholders were depicted paying homage at his court (*above*). For a while it seemed that the railways could do no wrong. They made travel so much easier, and they paid a handsome dividend on their shares. John Bull was to be seen steaming down the rails of progress (*opposite, top right*), but there were warning voices. *Punch* thought that railways were going too far, too fast, like some monstrous juggernaut (*opposite, below*). And when dividends occasionally disappointed, crowds of angry investors were quick to gather (*right*).

The early bridges and viaducts of the railway system were works of great beauty as well as outstanding engineering, though Wordsworth did complain of the Kendal and Windermere railway: 'Is there no nook of English ground secure, from rash assault?' At Ivy Bridge, the stone viaduct over the River Erne was elegant and graceful (*above*). The more utilitarian iron-built Crumlin viaduct (*opposite, above*) in Monmouthshire, was the work of Charles Liddell.

Liddell was also responsible for the Kilsby Tunnel near Rugby, on the main line from London to Birmingham – with its great ventilation shaft (*right*). Many engineers liked to decorate the entrances to their tunnels (*opposite, below*). On the London to Bristol line, Brunel created a medieval tower and gateway as the entrance to Box Tunnel. Though explosives were sometimes used to blast a passage through the rock, most tunnels were hacked out by hand.

Two great engineers were responsible for the two bridges across the Menai Straits, joining Anglesey to the mainland of Wales. The earlier bridge was Thomas Telford's road suspension bridge (foreground), built between 1819 and 1826. It was constructed of wrought iron, with a span of 300 metres and a total weight of 2,186 tons. The later bridge was the Britannia Tubular Bridge, with a span of 600 metres, built by Robert Stephenson, son of George Stephenson, in 1850 to carry the main line railway from London to Holyhead.

The development of railways was accompanied by changes in road transport for the public. On 4 July 1829, George Shillibeer began his bus service between Paddington and the Bank in London. His bus (*above*) carried twenty-two passengers for a fare of one shilling (5p). An attempt was made to bring steam power to the roads with the *New Favorite* (*left*) whose solid rubber tyres bounced over the cobblestones between Edinburgh and Leith.

The improvements in bus services were accompanied by a vast increase in the number of carts, coaches, drays and wagons on the roads of cities. London Bridge was regularly crammed with traffic (*above*) and the average horse-drawn speed across London was little better than walking pace. Many other buses followed in the wake of Shillibeer's pioneer model. One of the best was the 'knifeboard' omnibus with regular routes all over London, including this from the Bank to the Strand (*right*).

From 1834 onwards, the streets of British cities were plied by the hansom cabs *(opposite, above and below)*. They were the creation of Joseph Aloysius Hansom *(below, left)*, an architect responsible for Birmingham Town Hall and the Roman Catholic cathedral at Plymouth – the Victorians were nothing if not versatile people. Competing with the hansom was the Tribus *(left and below)*, a new 'patent cabriolet' with room for three passengers.

There were those who left the shores of Britain because they had to – convicts who were transported to the colonies, the starving Irish who sought new life in the United States, Scottish families cleared from their Highland homes and driven to taking ship for Canada. But there were also those who left of their own free will, for a variety of reasons. In California, the Yukon, South Africa and Australia there was always the hope of finding a fortune in the gold fields. In India and the Far East there were opportunities in tea and rubber plantations, or in the offices of some great trading company. Wherever the Union Jack flew, there were openings for ambitious young men. Throughout the 19th century, many sold all they had, and boarded a ship to seek a better future thousands of miles away (*above*).

The electric telegraph was one way that the far-flung could keep in touch with home. For Britain, the first of these cables was laid under the sea, to connect Wales with Ireland, and England with France. In 1843 the steam tug *Goliath* (*above*) became the first vessel to be used for this purpose. Sixteen years later, Brunel's *Great Eastern* accomplished the astonishing feat of laying a transatlantic cable from Liverpool to New York.

Mining techniques improved. Deeper shafts could be sunk, and pit-head gear increased in size and complexity, as at this Staffordshire colliery (*opposite, below*). The output of coal rose from 6.2 million tons in 1770 to 49.4 million tons in 1850. For miners themselves – such as these tin miners in Cornwall (*right*) – work was still rough and dangerous, whatever the underground harvest. To cope with the demand for new buildings, there was a great increase in the production of building materials – slate, stone, and for the grander developments, black marble from Red Wharf on the island of Anglesey (*opposite, above*).

Sir Rowland Hill (*left*) was one of the founders of the Society for the Diffusion of Useful Knowledge in 1826. His most useful act was the introduction of the Penny Post in 1840. For the uniform cost of one penny, letters could be sent to any destination in the British Isles, and the Penny Black (*opposite*) became the first postage stamp issued in the world. The innovation brought about a huge increase in the numbers of letters and packets posted. Hill himself superintended the main London sorting office (*below*).

The Corn Laws, which fixed the price of wheat – and therefore bread – protected land owners at the expense of the poor (*left*). By the 1840s a strong campaign was under way for their repeal. Some farm workers preferred direct action, and rick-burning was a common protest against the hated laws (*below*).

The leader of the Anti Corn Law League was Richard Cobden (*far right*), an economist and politician and 'the Apostle of Free Trade'. The League held meetings in many major cities, like this Anti Corn Law Bazaar at the Theatre Royal, Covent Garden (*below*). Robert Peel, the Prime Minister, eventually lent his support to the movement (*right*) and the Laws were repealed in 1846.

As Home Secretary, Peel (*opposite, top left*) organised London's police force in 1829, and the first police officers were nicknamed 'Bobbies', or 'Peelers', in his honour. (*Opposite, bottom left*) Peel raises his hat to a Peeler outside the House of Commons. Some officers, such as Tom Smith (*opposite, right*) continued to wear top hats right up to the 1860s, though beards and moustaches (*below*) were not *de rigueur*. The forerunners of the police were the night-watchmen, or Charley's, often regarded as figures of fun (*right*).

Factories and mills were grim places in the early days of the Industrial Revolution. In the cotton mills on Union Street, Manchester (*above, right*), little consideration was given to the working conditions of the hands. Factories housed machines, not people. Production was what mattered, and the health and well-being of the men, women and children who worked there was unimportant. (*Opposite*) An illustration from *The Life and Adventures of Michael Armstrong* by Frances Trollope, mother of Anthony Trollope. Furnaces and foundries offered more money, but greater hardship and tougher work. (*Below, right*) James Naysmith's giant steam hammer at his foundry near Manchester. The print is from a painting by Naysmith himself.

The Great Reform Bill of 1832 fuelled demands for further changes in the electoral system of Britain. William Lovett (*opposite, bottom right*) and Thomas Cooper (*opposite, bottom left*) led the Chartists. They were supported by some Members of Parliament, including Feargus O'Connor (*above*), MP for County Cork. On 10 April 1848 the Chartists held their last great meeting on Kennington Common (*opposite, above*). Police warned the Chartists that they would not be allowed to cross the Thames to lobby Parliament, but a monster petition was later delivered to Downing Street, where it was received by an anxious Lord John Russell (*right*).

After the old Palace of Westminster was destroyed by fire in 1834, a competition was held to choose an architect to design the new Houses of Parliament. The winner was Charles Barry (*opposite, far right*), who had already designed the Manchester Athenaeum and London's Reform Club. Barry's plan was for an immense Gothic palace fronting the Thames. Construction began in 1837 and was completed in 1858. The finished result (*above*, in Roger Fenton's photograph of 1860) did not please everyone.

Barry's partner in the project was Augustus Welby Northmore Pugin (*above, left*). Pugin was responsible for much of the embellishment of the Palace and for the carvings and decoration of the interior, including the ornate chamber of the House of Lords (*opposite, below*). The pair worked well together. Pugin spent his evenings producing elaborate drawings at his home in Margate, travelling to London by the new railway every morning to meet Barry and discuss progress. The bell named 'Big Ben' in the Clock Tower posed the biggest problem. It weighed 16 tons and its 650 kilogram clapper produced a crack in the bell during tests. The bell was described as 'porous, unhomogeneous, unsound and defective'. It has lasted since 1857.

/ Latticed Window
(with the Camera Obscura)
August 1835

When first made, the squares
of glass about 200 in number
could be counted, with help
of a lens.

William Henry Fox Talbot (*opposite, below right*) was a pioneer of photography. In August 1835 he produced the first negative image (*opposite, above*) of a latticed window at Lacock Abbey (*opposite, below left*). Later, Talbot opened a studio in Reading (*above*, with Talbot on extreme right). (*Right*) Three of Talbot's early box cameras.

Charles Dickens (*far right*) followed his unhappy childhood by becoming the most famous writer in the world in the 1850s and 1860s. He was an illustrator as well as a writer, contributing as a young man under the pseudonym 'Boz' to the *Morning Chronicle* (*below, right*). His first novel, *The Pickwick Papers* (*below, left*), was an immediate success, readers of the serial delighting in the adventures of Pickwick, Mrs Bardell and the Fat Boy (*opposite*). Of the hundreds of other characters, one of the most popular was Mrs Gamp, from *Martin Chuzzlewit* (*above, left*).

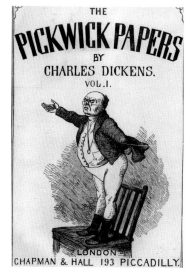

Colour and flounces were *à la mode* in the 1820s and 1830s. The ribbons, bows, bonnets, full skirts and elaborate sleeves that were the features of day dresses in January 1829 (*above*) were still the height of fashion in August 1832 (*opposite*). Gleaming ringlets and a coy smile added the final irresistible touches.

16

WORKSHOP OF THE WORLD
1850–1870

The Great Exhibition of the Works of Industry of All Nations, at the Crystal Palace, Hyde Park, 1851. 'The vast fabric may be seen as an Arabian Night's structure, full of light, and with a certain airy unsubstantial character about it, which belongs more to an enchanted land than to this gross material world of ours. The eye…wanders along those extended and transparent aisles…almost distrusting its own conclusions on the reality of what it sees, for the whole looks like a splendid phantasm…'
The Times, May 1851.

Introduction

In 1851 Britain celebrated its uncontested title of 'Workshop of the World' with the Great Exhibition, held in Hyde Park, London. The prime movers of the event were Prince Albert, Henry Cole and Joseph Paxton. Albert provided the inspiration and enthusiasm, Cole the bureaucratic expertise and Paxton the grand design. Indeed, the whole project was in danger of collapse before Paxton submitted his revolutionary ideas for a temple of iron and glass made in thousands of prefabricated sections.

It was a rush job. The Exhibition was due to open on 1 May 1851. Gangs of workmen began levelling the site in August 1850, and the first formal deed of contract to erect the building was not signed until 31 October 1850. Within the next one hundred and fifty days, however, 2,000 workmen assembled the entire Crystal Palace from over 4,000 tons of iron, 600,000 cubic feet of timber, 900,000 square feet of glass, thirty-two miles of guttering and two hundred and two miles of sash bar.

Crowds gathered to watch their progress. In a single day (25 February 1851) it was estimated that over 100,000 people paid five shillings (25p) each for admission to the site. 'All manner of operations seemed to be going on at once,' wrote an eye witness, 'sawing, planing, glazing, painting, hammering...'

When the building was finished, the area around it was landscaped and the exhibits placed in position. There were more than 100,000 of them, from vertical printing machines to steam breweries; from soda water machines to sportsmen's knives with eighty blades; from 'superior fertiliser' (guano) to the largest porcelain vase in the world; from the Koh-I-Noor diamond to Count Dunin's 'Man of Steel', a figure constructed of 7,000 pieces adjustable from dwarf-to giant-size.

It was the foretaste of a fast approaching boom. The value of British exports increased at a record rate in the 1850s. Cotton goods doubled, to almost two and a half million yards. Rates of profit touched 50 per cent. A second exhibition in London, eleven years after the Great Exhibition, had more than twice the number of exhibitors. The world's trade increased by 260 per cent between 1850 and 1870, and Britain had more than its share in this unprecedented bonanza. By 1875, £1,000 million of British money had been invested abroad, and the amount of gold coinage issued by Britain had increased by 700 per cent. For the first and only time in its history, the country believed itself strong enough to abandon protectionism and embark on a period of totally free trade.

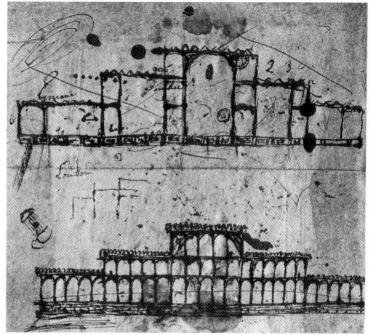

Three men planned the Crystal Palace and made the Great Exhibition possible. The first was Prince Albert, whose inspiration it was. The second was Henry Cole (*below, left*) who had the patience, resilience and drive to see the project through. The third was Joseph Paxton (*above, left*). Paxton saved the project. He had already been building glass structures for twenty years – notably the Lily House at Chatsworth – when he scribbled the first design for the Crystal Palace on a piece of blotting paper (*above*), a few months before the Exhibition was due to open.

The wisdom and benefit of prefabricating sections of the Crystal Palace may be seen from this early etching published in the *Illustrated London News* in December 1850. With a system of ropes and pulleys, workmen raise one of the ribs for the transept roof, 30 metres above ground. The public paid a shilling (5p) each to watch the construction. The money was placed in a fund to provide compensation for workmen injured on site.

The construction of the immense palace of glass was a breathtaking achievement. The ground was first levelled in August by a force of thirty-nine men. By September the number employed had risen to a thousand. The prefabricated pieces of iron that provided the skeleton were bolted together – 1,060 iron columns, 2,224 trellis girders, 358 trusses, 30 miles of guttering, 202 miles of sash bar. The edifice rapidly arose (*above*). On a visit to the site, Paxton himself noted that three columns and two girders were erected in sixteen minutes.

Workmen had their occasional rests (*above*). They needed them. Week after week through the winter and spring of 1851, they worked to prepare the building. Crowds gathered to watch their progress. On 25 February it was estimated that the site had over 100,000 visitors. Carpenters and glaziers followed the ironworkers, and five hundred painters followed them. Finally, fabric workers suspended unbleached calico from top to bottom of the south side to reduce the sun's glare and heat. Incredibly, the Palace was ready on time.

The Crystal Palace was a triumph of its time. A generation earlier such a building could not have been erected. It relied on standardised, interchangeable mass-produced components; on steam-driven machines; on division of labour; on the electric telegraph to communicate instructions swiftly. It relied also on cheap labour, on gangs of men with the courage to risk life and limb as they placed 200,000 sheets of glass on the roof, and on muscle power to haul the tons of components in special trolleys to and fro across the eighteen acres of site.

The opening ceremony took place on 1 May 1851. Beefeaters from the Tower of London guarded the gates (*opposite*) through which the royal party would pass on their way to the massive Hall for the inauguration. Half a million people assembled in the park. 'All London, and half the country, and a good part of the world, were wending their way to see the Queen pass in state to open the GREAT EXHIBITION OF ALL NATIONS,' wrote Henry Mayhew. (*Above*) The Medieval Court, designed by Pugin.

Inside the Palace more than 15,000 contributors exhibited 100,000 objects along a ten-mile frontage of gallery. The whole of the western half was taken up by British exhibits, but there was plenty of space left for the European nations, the Americas, Africa and, of course, the British Empire. The Canadian Gallery (*above*) included an Eskimo (Inuit) kayak, moose and caribou heads, furs from the Hudson's Bay Company, and a fire engine faced with copper and painted over with scenes from the Montreal fire.

The India Gallery glittered with riches. The centrepiece was the huge elephant and howdah, but the most valuable exhibit in the entire collection was the Koh-I-Noor diamond, the 'Mountain of Light', valued at £2 million in 1851, and weighing 186 carats. A French visitor wrote: 'It is exposed in its great cage, ornamented by a policeman…The Koh-I-Noor is well secured; it is placed on a machine which causes it, at the slightest touch, to enter an iron box. It is thus put to bed every evening, and does not get up till towards noon.'

In 1851 Prince Albert suggested that the profits from the Great Exhibition should be used to build libraries, museums and colleges in the area to the west of Hyde Park. After Albert's death in 1861 a public fund was opened to finance a memorial to the Prince. The architect selected to design both the Albert Hall (*above*) and the Albert Memorial (*opposite, left*) was Sir Giles Gilbert Scott (*opposite, right*), though Scott's plans were subsequently altered by Captain Francis Fowke of the Royal Engineers. The Hall was opened by the Prince of Wales in 1871, Victoria being too overcome by emotion to do so.

The design of the Albert Memorial was entirely Scott's work, and in 1863 Parliament voted £50,000 for the cost of its erection. Gladstone delayed the project, for he believed it was too expensive. Victoria, deeply concerned, never forgave him. The Memorial was completed in 1876. The total cost was £126,000.

Victoria remained devoted to Albert all her life (*left*) After their first meeting she wrote in her diary: 'Albert is extremely good-looking…very amiable, very kind and good, and extremely merry.' Within a few days she had written a letter to her uncle, King Leopold, telling him that she accepted the husband he had chosen for her. Three and a half years passed before they were married on 10 February 1840. Victoria slept well on the night before the wedding. She was not nervous, though she did record that the only thing she dreaded about marriage was the possibility of having a large family…

…which they did (*above,* Albert and Victoria with their nine children). Albert's death on 14 December 1861 threw Victoria into an agony of mourning. 'I kissed his dear heavenly forehead and called out in a bitter and agonising cry "Oh! My dear darling!" and then dropped on my knees in mute, distracted despair, unable to utter a word or shed a tear!' Later Victoria found some consolation in her Scottish ghillie, John Brown (*right*).

Henry Temple Palmerston (*opposite, left*) was Prime Minister of Britain from 1855 to 1858 and from 1859 to 1865. His years in office were characterised by an aggressive foreign policy to support British interests throughout the world. (*Opposite, right*) A Chinese depiction of fire-eating Europeans. (*Below*) Chinese junks are destroyed in the First Opium War. (*Right*) British artillery at rest after capturing Pehtang Fort in the Second Opium War.

The Crimean War was the first to be covered by modern reportage. The public at home were intrigued by the photographs of Roger Fenton (*above*), but shocked and distressed by the descriptions of bungle and blunder despatched from the Crimea by William Howard Russell of *The Times* (*opposite, below*). Russell's reports revealed how poorly led, equipped and organised the British army was, and led to later reforms in training and structure.

(*Above*) Fenton's photograph of the Allied fleet in Balaclava harbour. Neither Fenton's pictures nor Russell's communications was censored. The nation was roused to anger by reports that British troops were ill-clothed, ill-housed, ill-fed and receiving scant medical attention. Russell's accounts of the conditions endured by the wounded at Scutari were especially distressing. There were no drugs for the 14,000 men in the hospitals, and the usual diet of boiled beef and potatoes was supplied. In one hospital half the patients died in a single month.

(*Left*) The Allied commanders in the Crimea gather round a table to discuss tactics – from the left, Lord Raglan, Omar Pasha and General Pelisier. Part of the problem in the Crimea was that Raglan kept referring to the Russian enemy as 'the French'. (*Below*) Sir George Brown, seated on chair, with his staff before the Battle of Sebastopol.

(*Right*) Members of the 8th Hussars prepare a meal in the field during the Crimean campaign. (*Below*) A picket of British troops poses for the camera – all pictures on these two pages are by Roger Fenton.

Few heroines of the 19th century have achieved such long-lasting fame and respect as Florence Nightingale (*right*). With the help of Sidney Herbert, Secretary at War (*above*), she obtained permission to take thirty-eight nurses to the Crimea to work at Scutari. Here she organised a barracks hospital (*opposite, top*) which put all existing army hospitals to shame. As the wounded were brought down from the battlefields of Inkerman and Sebastopol, more beds were needed, and the Lady with the Lamp opened another hospital at Therapia (*opposite, below*).

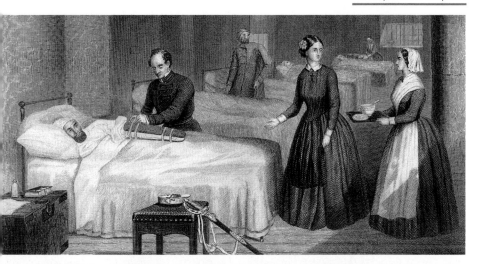

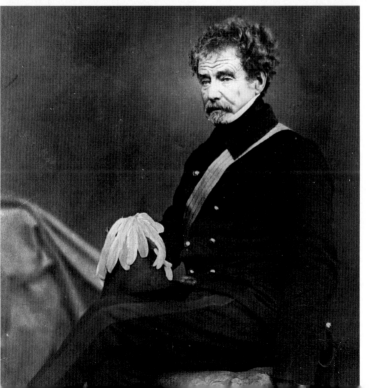

The Indian Mutiny began at Meerut on 10 May 1857, when Bengali troops marched to Delhi and proclaimed King Bahadur Shah emperor. They were incensed by attempts to reform their institutions, by the forcible introduction of Christianity, and by abuse of their religious laws. British troops and citizens were besieged in Cawnpore and Lucknow (*above, and opposite, above*). Sir Colin Campbell (*left*) was appointed to crush the Mutiny, and eventually succeeded in raising the siege of Lucknow, leading out a six-mile column of women and children, soldiers, bullock carts, elephants, horsemen, Sepoys and camp followers.

Though most of the Bengali regiments joined the Mutiny, the British could rely on the loyalty of most Sikh officers (*far right*), and some irregular forces. Hodson's Horse (*right*) was a mixed force of British and Indian troops, commanded by William Hodson, who galloped with fifty followers to Delhi and captured Bahadur Shah. He was later killed at the relief of Lucknow. (Photographs on this page by Felice Beato.)

Like George Stephenson, Brunel (*above*) was a brilliant, if eccentric, engineer. He once designed a makeshift hoist from which he could be suspended to dislodge a guinea piece that had stuck in his throat. Besides the Great Western Railway, Brunel designed many bridges, including the Royal Albert Bridge to carry the track over the River Tamar at Saltash (*right*). His greatest shipbuilding feat was the Great Eastern (*far right, below*). (*Far right, above*) From left – John Scott Russell, Henry Wakefield, Brunel and Lord Derby at the launching of the *Great Eastern*.

In 1862 Henry Cole repeated the success of the Great Exhibition of 1851. The International Exhibition was held in South Kensington and attracted even more visitors. The main building (*above*) was designed by Captain Fowke, later to work on the Albert Hall. Crowds flocked to the Main Hall (*opposite*) where the centrepiece was a majolica fountain surmounted by a statue of St George. Others were impressed by the brewery exhibits and the zinc baths (*right*).

Despite the widespread exploitation of labour by most factory and mine owners, there were some who wished to provide their workers with better housing, conditions and pay. One of the earliest of these was Robert Owen (*above*) whose New Lanark Mills were run on a largely cooperative basis. Sir Titus Salt (*right*) was a wool manufacturer whose main works were at Saltaire, near Bradford (*opposite, above*). Around the factory, Salt built a model village to house his workers. (*Opposite, below*) The Rochdale Pioneers, founders of the first retail cooperative movement.

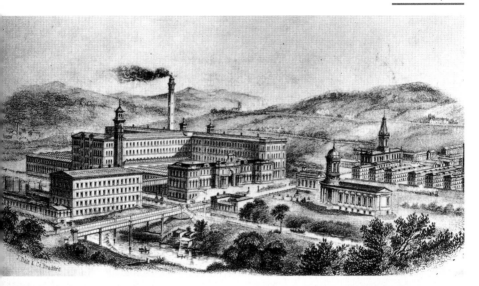

William Makepeace Thackeray (*left*) was born in 1811. He was a satirist and contributor to *Punch* magazine, who turned to novel writing in his mid-thirties. His first, and greatest, novel was *Vanity Fair*, published in 1848, the story of the amorous adventures of Becky Sharp. (*Opposite, clockwise from top left*) Four scenes from *Vanity Fair*: Sir Pitt Crawley goes on his knees to propose to Becky; Captain William Dobbin and Miss Amelia Sedley; Captain Rawden Crawley is taken in hand; and Jos Sedley, Amelia's brother, 'shaves off his moustachios'.

The great British sports were rough and ready pastimes in the mid-19th century. A game of football could mean anything from a wild scramble of dozens of combatants (*right, above*) to the more organised contest on Parker's Piece at Cambridge (*opposite, below*). It was the public schools and the universities that civilised football, and in 1846 the first serious attempt to codify the rules was made at Cambridge University. At Rugby School (*right, below*) the great game was rugger, probably invented by William Webb Ellis, who, one day in 1823, 'picked up the ball and ran with it' during a game of soccer.

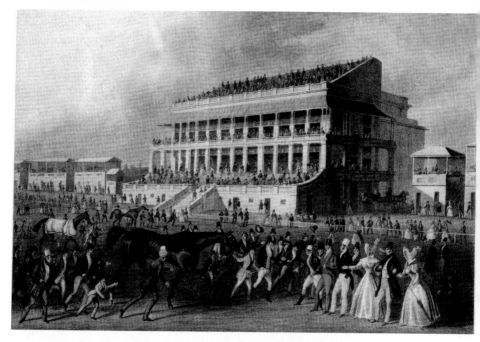

To be a sportsman (or woman) and to play 'fair' was the hallmark of the British character. Horse racing was increasingly popular, and Epsom Grandstand was crowded in June 1836 with people watching Lord Jersey's bay Middleton win the Derby (*above*). Others gathered for a more sedate afternoon of cricket, as Kent played Sussex at Brighton (*left*).

The steeplechase (*above*) promised excitement and the chance to see horse and rider 'come a cropper'. Alfred Mynn (*right*) was the Pride of Kent, a cricketing giant who weighed 20 stone and yet was said to be elegant in every movement. Lieutenant Colonel Henry Stracey (*far right*) of the Scots Guards was a champion fencer, 'an epigrammatic writer', 'a clever talker' and an all-round good chap.

Ballooning became all the rage in the mid-19th century. It began in France, but was quickly taken up in Britain. The principle London sites for ascents were Batty's Royal Hippodrome in Kensington (*left*), Spring Gardens in Vauxhall, and Cremorne Gardens, Chelsea (*below*) It was from here that Charles Green, 'the Intrepid Aeronaut', made one of his five hundred and twenty-seven flights, this one in a balloon accompanied by a lady and a leopard (*opposite, above*).

Vincent van Goof was an early glider pilot. After some success in France, he tried his luck in Britain. Sadly, he was killed on 9 July 1874 when his glider crashed to the ground in Chelsea Street after being released from a balloon (*right*). (*Far right*) Mr Godard takes off in his hot air balloon, *Montgolfier*, from Cremorne Gardens.

17
RELIEF AND REFORM
1850–1880

By the middle of the 19th century, the Thames had become a foul
and stinking sewer running through the heart of London. On hot
days, Members of the House of Commons had to leave their
offices, overcome by the smell. Something had to be done. The
man responsible for the great clean-up was Sir William Bazalgette,
who constructed a labyrinthine system of sewers beneath the city,
leading to a giant outfall on the Essex marshes (*right*). Thanks to
his engineering genius, the inhabitants slept sweetly and soundly
at night, and MPs could sleep soundly by day.

Introduction

The mid-Victorian years produced a hard core of men and women possessed of great reforming zeal. From the lower strata of society came the socialists and trade unionists – Keir Hardie (who founded the Scottish Labour Party), Alexander Macdonald (ex-Lanarkshire miner and Liberal MP), and Thomas Burt (ex-miner who sponsored the Employers' Liability Act of 1880). From the middle classes came the professional specialists: Florence Nightingale (who reformed the nursing service), Dr John Snow (who identified a deadly source of cholera in the heart of London), Dr Thomas Barnardo (who opened his first refuge for destitute children in Stepney in 1866), and William Booth (the fiery-eyed evangelist who founded the Salvation Army in 1878).

The aristocracy provided the most famous reformer of them all, Anthony Ashley Cooper, 7th Earl of Shaftesbury. He devoted his life to improving working conditions, in limiting the hours of toil, and in freeing children from near slavery. It was a long and hard battle. Employers were loathe to spend good money on safety, or to employ a man where a woman or a child could do the same work for less money. The workers themselves were not always eager for reform. Many families desperately needed the money that their children were able to earn as chimney boys, mineworkers and factory hands. Government inspectors were horrified by the prevalence and severity of the abuses that they discovered – but much had to be done between discovery and remedy.

Slowly and steadily the battle was won. In 1847 came the first Factory Act; others followed in 1850 and 1859. In 1842 Shaftesbury piloted the Mines Act through Parliament. A grateful nation later raised a monument to him – the fine statue of Eros in London's Piccadilly Circus.

The pace of change quickened. Life improved on many fronts. In 1876 Samuel Plimsoll persuaded Parliament to pass an act that has since carried his name and did much to prevent the dangerous overloading of merchant ships. Thomas Cook had introduced Britain to the excursion train in 1841, and now ran regular 'day trips'. George Peabody, an American philanthropist, established a trust that provided good, cheap housing for the poor. Joseph Lister pioneered the use of antiseptics in surgery in 1867. Sir Joseph Bazalgette engineered a system of sewers that made London a sweeter, safer place to live. And Thomas Crapper created the first flush lavatory, which made excellent use of Bazalgette's sewers, and proved a convenience for all.

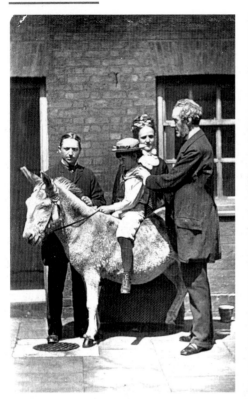

Anthony Ashley Cooper Shaftesbury (*above right, and left*, with his hand on the shoulder of a child at a donkey sanctuary) was a politician and philanthropist responsible for many of the reforms that radically improved the lives of working people. His Factory Acts limited the working day to ten hours. His Coal Mines Act of 1842 prohibited the underground employment of women and children under thirteen (*opposite, above*). Shaftesbury also worked to provide lodging houses for the poor, thousands of whom lived and even slept in the street (*opposite, below*).

Gustave Doré's engraving of the terraces meanly clustered around the arches of Waterloo (*above*) illustrates some of the appalling – but not the worst – conditions in which the poor lived in later Victorian times. It was usual for several families to share one small house, sleeping on bundles of rags, using an outside lavatory if they were lucky, and breathing the foetid air. Conditions in most work places were even worse (*left*). Hours were long, safety was ignored, and the noise was insufferable.

To escape the stench of the slum tenements, women and children, and the old, spent much of the day in the street (*right*). In the winter months, some heat was provided by coal or coke fires in the tiny grates, giving little warmth but making work for the sweep (*above*). Henry Mayhew observed: 'They are clever fellows...known in many instances to be shrewd, intelligent and active.'

Annie Besant (*above*) was an early socialist and member of the Fabian Society. In 1877 she was heavily fined and deprived of her children for publishing an American booklet on birth control. She led the Match Girls strike of 1888. The young women (*above, right*) were employed by Bryant and May, making and packing matches. Their conditions of work were appalling, their hours long, the work dangerous, and the pay minimal.

With reform went an increasing support for the ideas of socialism and trade unionism. More and more groups of workers banded together to demand better pay and conditions. Joseph Arch (*above*) was a preacher and reformer who founded the National Agricultural Labourers' Union in 1872. (*Right*) The ornate and beautiful membership card of the Amalgamated Society of Engineers, Machinists, Millwrights, Smiths and Pattern Makers.

BE UNITED AND INDUSTRIOUS

AMALGAMATED SOCIETY OF ENGINEERS, MACHINISTS, MILLWRIGHTS, SMITHS, AND PATTERN MAKERS.

This is to Certify that ___ was admitted a Member of the ___ Branch on the ___ day of ___ 18 . In witness whereof we have subscribed our names and affixed the Society's Seal.

PRESIDENT ___ SECRETARY

Most Victorian reformers were devout Christians. One who put his faith into practice was William Booth, founder of the Salvation Army in 1878. His eldest son was William Bramwell Booth (*left*), who became Chief of Staff of the 'Sally Army' in 1880 and later succeeded his father as General. (*Above*) William Bramwell Booth with his wife and three children, all of whom worked in the Army.

As late as 1869 George Cruikshank was still casting a cynical eye on British society, as in this cartoon, of the appalling treatment of street children (*right*). Their plight moved a young Irish medical student named Thomas Barnardo (*above, left*) to found the East End Mission at Stepney, the first of more than one hundred Dr Barnardo's Homes. William Stead (*above, right*) was a campaigning journalist who exposed the trade in children, by buying a child for £5, and then describing what he had done in an article.

The Metropolitan Board of Works received many ideas for disposing of London's sewage. One project suggested a system of sewers running like the spokes of a wheel from central London into the country, where the sewage could be sold in shops. Another advocated atmospheric tubes to suck the sewage from the rich parts of the city to the East End, where the poor lived. The problem was eventually solved by Sir Joseph William Bazalgette (*above, right*). (*Above, left*) Digging out the sewer in Fleet Street. (*Opposite, top*) Bazalgette, with hands on hips, surveys the Northern Outfall sewer at Abbey Mills, 1862. (*Opposite, bottom*) The sewer reaches the Essex marshes.

Benjamin Disraeli and William Ewart Gladstone were the leading statesmen of the middle years of Victoria's reign. The young Disraeli (*above, top left*) made an inauspicious maiden speech in the Commons, his words being drowned by jeers and laughter. 'Though I sit down now,' he concluded, 'the time will come when you will hear me.' The time came indeed. Disraeli was Prime Minister from 1867 to 1868 and from 1874 to 1878 (*above, bottom left*). Victoria adored him, not least for his insistence that she become Empress of India. (*Above, right*) Sir John Tenniel's drawing of Disraeli as Aladdin, offering new crowns for old.

The young Gladstone (*top right*) held many Government posts before becoming Prime Minister for the first time in 1868 (*bottom right*). He fought all his life for international understanding and Home Rule for Ireland. This *Punch* cartoon of 1879 (*above*) shows Gladstone as the new Colossus of Rhodes, straddling Peace and Retrenchment, grasping Finance and Foreign Policy, while the Ship of Reform sails between his legs.

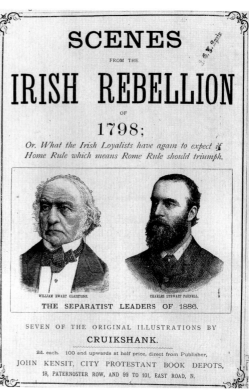

To Irish nationalists it made nonsense that they should be ruled from Westminster. Ireland was a conquered nation that had suffered poverty and neglect for hundreds of years. Charles Stewart Parnell (*above*) was a vociferous advocate of Irish Home Rule who campaigned in the United States on behalf of Ireland and brought back £70,000 for the cause. But there were others who regarded Home Rule as a nightmare. In 1856 John Kensit of the City Protestant Book Depot in London published *Scenes from the Irish Rebellion* which included Cruikshank's illustrations of Protestant massacres by Catholics back in 1798.

Parnell fought on. He found an ally in Gladstone, but in 1889 he was cited as correspondent in a divorce action brought by Captain William O'Shea against his wife Katherine. The scandal wrecked Parnell's political career, though he worked on, addressing many hostile crowds, as at this by-election meeting in Kilkenny in 1890. He died at Brighton in 1891, five months after his marriage to Katherine.

Perhaps the most famous greeting of all time has been that of Stanley to Livingstone in the village of Manyema: 'Dr Livingstone, I presume.' Henry Morton Stanley (*above, right*) led an adventurous life. He was, in turn, a cabin boy, a Confederate soldier and a US sailor before becoming a journalist for the *New York Herald*. In March 1871 he set off to track down the Scottish missionary David Livingstone (*above, left*), who had spent the last five years seeking the sources of the River Nile. Livingstone never found them, though he did discover Lake Ngami (*opposite, above*). It took Stanley eight months to reach Livingstone, but the two eventually came face to face on 10 November 1871 (*opposite, below*)

In 1841 Thomas Cook (*left*) organised the first of his 'excursions'. It was an outing from Leicester to Loughborough, some fifteen miles away, to enable teetotallers to attend a temperance meeting. It was a success and Cook's business quickly grew. By the 1870s Cook was offering package tours to Europe and the Near East costing as little as £10, chartering special boats and trains, and setting up hundreds of agents in cities abroad.

One popular port of call was Thomas Cook's Ticket Office in Jerusalem (*right*), which advertised '…the largest staff of dragomen and muleteers…the best landaus and carriages, camp equipment etc in Palestine and Syria'. The adventurous delighted in such bold journeys as being carried up Mount Vesuvius (*below, right*) for a picnic on the lava bed in 1880.

Wider yet and wider roamed the intrepid Victorians. Hardly had Egypt and the Sudan come under British control than tourists were swarming over the Pyramids (*opposite*). Athens (*right*) was an agreeable destination, and the top-hatted and full-skirted even made their perilous way over the Mer de Glace at Chamonix (*below*). Henry James disapproved: 'They are always and everywhere the same, carrying with them that indefinable expression of not considering anything out of England worth making a toilet for.'

The seaside holiday had become a joyful annual event for those who could afford it. Many had to be content with a day trip, sampling the delights of a stroll along the pier at Clacton-on-Sea (*opposite, above*), a gentle doze on the sands of Margate (*opposite, below*), a plunge in the sea from one of the remaining bathing machines at Swanage (*above*), or an afternoon's sail at Brighton (*right*).

The world's first underground railway (*left*) was opened in London in 1863. It ran for 6.5 kilometres, from Paddington to Farringdon Street in the City. It was built by the 'cut and cover' method (*below*) – digging a ditch, laying the track, and then covering the line.

The grand opening of the Metropolitan Line (as it became known) was held on 24 May.
Dignitaries were taken on a tour of inspection (*above*) in open trucks. Among them was
Gladstone, then Chancellor of the Exchequer – seen here in truck No. 23, in front of the man in
the light-coloured top hat. Passengers suffered from the effects of smoke, for the trains were
hauled through the tunnels by steam locomotives. Sir John Fowler developed a smokeless engine
powered by red-hot bricks under the boiler, but it made only one run.

The great Gothic buildings of Britain were monuments to Victorian prosperity and grandeur.
One of the finest was St Pancras Station (*opposite, below*). It was built between 1863 and 1867 by
W.H. Barlow and R. M. Ordish for the Midland Railway on the site of the old slums of Agars
Town. While the station was under construction the Company commissioned Sir George Gilbert
Scott to build the neighbouring Midland Grand Hotel (*above*). Scott later wrote of it: 'It is often
spoken of to me as the finest building in London; my own belief is that it is possibly too good for
its purpose…' (*Opposite, above*) John O'Connor's painting of *Pentonville Road*, with St Pancras in
the background.

George Edward Street (*opposite, below right*) was the architect of the new Royal Courts of Justice in London (*below and right*). Work began in 1871 and took over ten years to complete, at a cost of £826,000. Supervising the construction of the one-thousand room palace was too much for Street, and he died a year before the official opening by Queen Victoria. The style was Victorian High Gothic, with heavy emphasis on Portland stone and marble (*opposite, below left*).

9068. THE LAW COURTS.

Few children received more than a rudimentary education. The country relied on the zeal of such reformers as Thomas Guthrie (*left*, at blackboard) to provide schooling for the poor. His Ragged School was held in a church hall in Princes Street, Edinburgh. The Forster Act of 1870 brought education to the masses, though early provision fell well short of that at the best private establishments, such as Richmond School (*above*). Outshining all others were Eton and Harrow, Eton with its boating (and song to match) (*opposite, above*), Harrow with its soccer XI (*opposite, below*) (though Harrow may have cheated by fielding a team of twelve).

Charles Robert Darwin (*left*) was born in 1809, the grandson of Erasmus Darwin and Josiah Wedgwood. In 1831 he joined the company on board HMS *Beagle* for the voyage to South America, Australasia and the Galapagos Islands. His detailed studies of the flora and fauna discovered on the voyage led him to formulate his theory of evolution, though many years passed before he published his *The Origin of Species by Means of Natural Selection* in 1859.

The book rattled the complacency of Victorian society. *Punch* magazine published a satirical cartoon entitled *Man is But a Worm* (*right*), capturing the mixture of hilarity and outrage directed at Darwin. The idea that the human race could in any way be related to the orang utan, the chimpanzee and the gorilla was regarded as ludicrous. And, as for his theories of sexual selection… well, they were too dreadful to contemplate.

PUNCH'S ALMANACK FOR 1882. [December 6, 1881.

MAN·IS·BVT·A·WORM·

PUNCH'S VOICE OF THE STARS.
FOR AUGUST.

THIS is the month of Virgo. Pic-nics and river parties will be very popular. Most of the stars will now be in the provinces, consequently the London theatres will be under-let to speculators. Mars enters the scales on the 18th, and are found much heavier. This will be favourable to manufacturers of Anti-Fat, and other remedies for removing corpulency. The Crown Prince of GERMANY gains by the transit of Jupiter, which is now sent to him post paid direct from the head-office. The Emperor of AUSTRIA, if he has not bought a new hat since the commencement of the year, may now be expected to supply the omission in his outfit.

INFANTRY, BUT NOT FOOT.—Children in Arms.

PUNCH'S VOICE OF THE STARS.
FOR SEPTEMBER.

As Saturn halts in 26° 11′ of Taurus, *id est*, exactly on the place of the Solar Eclipse (8° 26′ 15′) of last May, several birds may be expected to be shot in England on the 1st. A per-centage of these birds will be called partridges. Persia will have a bad time of it. People living in Krim Tartary or Margate, should be careful to avoid catching cold on or about the 16th. BISMARCK will be seen smoking during this month. Should the Sun be in good aspect with the Moon on the 22nd, his highness will drink a glass of beer. Certain acquaintances of Mr. MARWOOD will find this month unfavourable to their health.

CON. FOR CASUISTS.—Can a man be said to indulge in the lie circumstantial when he lies at full length?

The literary genius of the age was George Eliot (*opposite, far right*). Her real name was Mary Ann Evans and she was born on a farm in Warwickshire in 1819. After her father's death she travelled in Europe before settling in North Bank, St John's Wood, London (*above*). Here she produced some of her finest work, including the novels *Middlemarch* and *Daniel Deronda*. She moved from North Bank when she married John Walter Cross in May 1880, but died the following December at the age of sixty-one.

Perhaps Eliot's best-loved work is *The Mill on the Floss*, the story of Maggie Tulliver and her conflict with society and her beloved brother Tom. The book ends with an account of the flood that seals their fate (*above*). '…A new danger was being carried towards them by the river. Some wooden machinery had just given way on one of the wharves, and huge fragments were being floated along… "It is coming, Maggie!" Tom said, in a deep hoarse voice, loosing the oars and clasping her.'

British art revived under the influence of John Ruskin (*left*), the art critic who resurrected Turner's reputation and championed the cause of the Pre-Raphaelites. William Holman Hunt (*above, right*) joined forces with Millais (*opposite, below*) and Dante Gabriel Rossetti to found the Pre-Raphaelite Brotherhood in 1848. They were joined by Edward Burne-Jones (*above left*, arms folded, with William Morris). The Rossettis were a talented family. (*Opposite, above*, from left) The Rossettis – Dante Gabriel (poet and painter); Christina (poet); Gabriele, their mother; and William Michael Rossetti (art critic).

With improvements in working conditions and public health came revolutionary changes in medical science. James Simpson (*opposite, above left*) was a gynaecologist who pioneered the use of chloroform as an anaesthetic. Sir William Bowman (*opposite, above right*) was an outstanding ophthalmic surgeon. Benjamin Brodie (*opposite, below left*) was an expert on diseases of the joints, whose work led to a dramatic reduction in the number of amputations. Dr William Budd (*opposite, below right*) published a classic work on typhoid in 1873. Joseph Lister (*right*) was the first surgeon to use antiseptics in the operating theatre.

Cycling was the rage. Undiscovered villages became the objective for outings by clubs and individuals. For many years the King of the Road was the Penny Farthing (*above and opposite, above*), a vehicle that was almost impossible to mount, difficult to balance, but delightful to propel. One revolution of the pedals produced enough power to cover several metres. Then came an even bigger revolution. In 1887 the Scottish inventor John Boyd Dunlop (*above, right*, with beard) fitted his child's tricycle with inflated rubber hoses instead of solid rubber tyres. Comfort and punctures were born.

A few years later, John Boyd Dunlop's son had grown and graduated to a two-wheeler, also with pneumatic tyres (*right*). The idea had already been patented by Robert William Thompson, but Dunlop founded a business, credited himself with the invention and went on to make a fortune.

18
IMPERIAL SPLENDOUR
1880–1910

The most dazzling moment in the history of the British Empire – Queen Victoria arrives at St Paul's Cathedral on 22 June 1897 for the thanksgiving service to mark her Diamond Jubilee. Never again would Britain be so powerful, so wealthy, so proud, so monstrous in its supremacy. The *Daily Mail* boasted that it was 'a pageant which for splendour of appearance has never been paralleled in the history of the world'. 'History may be searched in vain,' echoed *The Times*, 'to discover so wonderful an exhibition of allegiance and brotherhood...' All were agreed, this was 'the mightiest and most beneficial Empire ever known in the annals of mankind'.

Introduction

It was Benjamin Disraeli's idea that Queen Victoria should promote herself to Empress. The Queen was greatly amused and rewarded Disraeli by promoting him to Earl. On 1 January 1877 Victoria sat on the ivory throne presented to her by the Rajah of Travar, while, away in Delhi, her Viceroy Lord Lytton read the proclamation that formally gave her imperial power over the entire sub-continent. It was a production to rival those spectacles staged at the Theatre Royal, Drury Lane.

The event released a surge of patriotic – some would say, jingoistic – emotion in the British people. 'By being born British,' observed Lord Milner, 'one has won first prize in the lottery of life.' Who would argue? The riches of the world filled warehouses along the docksides of Britain – gold, ivory, diamonds, furs, copper, timber, rubber, fruit, cocoa, wine, spices, perfumes, tinned food, frozen meat, grain, and oil to power the new motor cars that hicoughed their way along hitherto quiet lanes.

Rudyard Kipling was the Empire's unofficial Poet Laureate. His jaunty verses caught the imagination of rich and poor alike, blending low-class heroism with high-flying aspirations:

Take up the White Man's burden –
Send forth the best ye breed –
Go, bind your sons to exile
To serve your captives need...

Wherever the armies of Victoria marched, Kipling's verses followed, capturing the drunken boredom of life in Aldershot barracks and the terrifying frenzy of action in Afghanistan. His thoughts and images became part of the everyday language of imperial Britain.

The anthems of the age were composed by Sir Edward Elgar, chief among them his *Pomp and Circumstance March No.1.* Elgar wrote this as an orchestral piece. Edward VII wanted words added. In 1902 A.C. Benson supplied them, and *Land of Hope and Glory* was born.

To those who loved the Empire, everything about it was glorious, even its faults, defeats and the deaths of its heroes. When news reached London that the tiny garrison at Mafeking in the Transvaal had been saved and the siege lifted, the entire city threw itself into an orgy of joy. Artists laboured long and lovingly to portray the drama of imperial life and death, though the camera was now bringing a harsher reality to the images of war. For the moment, however, only the minority could find fault with the Empire.

And there were precious few who foresaw that the triumphant progress was over, and the imperial trumpets would soon have to sound 'Retreat'.

'Sooner or later,' wrote Winston Churchill, 'in a righteous cause or a picked quarrel…for the sake of our Empire, for the sake of our honour, for the sake of the race, we must fight the Boers.' But it was the Boers who started the war when they crossed the frontiers of Natal and Cape province, and lay siege to Mafeking and Ladysmith. They were hopelessly outnumbered. The British army in South Africa numbered 85,000. At the most, the Boers could put 35,000 men in the field – though Mrs Otto Kranz (*left*) and other women were prepared to fight alongside their husbands. What they lacked in numbers the Boers made up in spirit. (*Above*) Boer reinforcements are addressed by Commandant Schutte before leaving Pretoria.

They were fighting for their independence and for the land that they believed they held by God-given right. They mustered in local mounted units called 'commandos', under democratically elected officers. They were crack shots and superb horsemen, though their discipline was irregular, and it was not uncommon for troops to disappear when they felt their farms needed them more than the war did. There were no age limits for recruits to the Boer cause. (*Above*) Three generations of Boer warriors – (from left) P.Lemmer (aged sixty-five), J.Botha (fifteen), G.Pretorius (forty-three).

The British army was shocked by the fighting skill and determination of the Boers. Defeat and disease resulted in an embarrassing need for reinforcements – (*left*) Canadian, Australian and New Zealand troops on the march. (*Below*) The Guards march on Brandfort. (*Opposite*) Soldiers of the Royal Canadian Regiment attack a *kopje* during the battle for Sunnyside Farm.

Three photographs by Reinhold Thiele of some of the personalities of the Boer War. (*Above*) General Cronje, the Boer commander, slumps in a chair with members of Lord Roberts' staff after surrendering at Paardeberg, February 1900. (*Left*) The British commander-in-chief, Lord Roberts, leans on a balustrade in Pretoria, October 1900. (*Opposite*) A group of war correspondents on Glovers Island. Rudyard Kipling is nearest Thiele's camera.

Her reign was the longest in British history. The devotion of her people was unquestioned and unquestioning. Most European rulers were relations in awe of her. Victoria (*opposite*) was the most famous person in the world. (*Above*) Victoria and members of the royal family at Osborne House. (Left to right) Prince Leopold of Battenberg, the Princess of Anhalt, Prince Edward of York, a nurse holding Princess Victoria of York, Princess Margaret of Connaught, Prince Alexander of Battenberg, the Duke of York and Prince Albert, Victoria, Prince Arthur of Connaught, the Duchess of Connaught, Princess Patricia of Connaught, Princess Henry and Princess Ena of Battenberg, Princess Victoria of Schleswig-Holstein, Prince Maurice of Battenberg.

No one has waited as long to ascend the British throne as Edward, Prince of Wales (*above, left*, with Scottish shooting trophy). He was twenty-one when he married the nineteen-year-old Alexandra, daughter of the King of Denmark (*above, right*, in one of the last photographs taken together), but he had to wait until he was sixty before he became King. In the meantime, he took care to enjoy himself in a variety of sporting ways. One of the more acceptable of these was dancing. (*Opposite, above*) Edward, third from left, at a house party at Mar Lodge, Scotland. And even when he was King, Edward still found time to go to the races. (*Opposite, below*) Edward visits Epsom racecourse for the 1909 Derby.

The early career of Winston Spencer Churchill (*left*) set the pattern for much of what was to follow – a mixture of the brilliant and the boastful, the audacious and the outrageous. In 1910 Churchill, as President of the Board of Trade, was largely instrumental in introducing Labour Exchanges, to make it easier for ordinary people to find work (*below*).

In the early years of the 20th century, Churchill (*right*, third from left) worked closely with David Lloyd George (second from left), the Liberal Chancellor of the Exchequer, introducing National Insurance and reforming the tax system. In 1910 Churchill became Home Secretary and was present at the siege of Sidney Street, London (*below*), when police and soldiers fought an armed battle against a group of anarchists.

Churchill addresses a crowd from the top of a car in Manchester, April 1908. Churchill was often at his best in such a situation. He excelled as an orator, and, in the days before radio and television, crowds had to be held by the force of the speaker's personality. Churchill's almost unique combination of wit and vision invariably compelled his audience to listen, even though they may not have agreed with what he said, and even though he was capable of upsetting the whole gamut of society, from the very rich (who disapproved of the introduction of death duties), to the coal miners, who felt cheated by him.

There were those who thought the Liberals were pushing reform too far, and there were those who thought the Liberals were not going far enough. Among the latter were the founders of the Labour Party. John Burns (*above, left*) was a trade unionist who was elected as MP for Battersea in 1892, the same year that James Keir Hardie (*above, right*) entered Parliament as MP for West Ham South. A year later the Independent Labour Party was formed. Socialism was a vigorous creed, as evidenced by these ILP members on a cycling trip in 1910 (*opposite, above*). Supporters were in many ways ahead of their time. This rally against racism took place in 1910 (*opposite, below*). The placard reads 'WHITE, BROWN AND BLACK UNITE AND CONQUER.'

(*Above*) William Arrol, who began his working life as a thread boy in a cotton mill at the age of ten, and thirty-four years later built the Forth Bridge.

Arrol studied mechanics at night classes and began his own engineering business in 1868. Work began on the Forth Bridge in 1883. It was an immense achievement. The bridge was designed by John Fowler and Benjamin Baker. It was over a mile long, and its steel cantilever construction (*opposite, below and right*) enabled it to carry a double track railway and a road across the Firth of Forth. When it was completed in 1890 (*above*) it was the longest bridge of its kind in the world.

William Arrol was also responsible for the construction of Tower Bridge in the 1890s (*opposite*). The bridge was built in response to a great many petitions from Londoners for a river crossing below London Bridge. Earlier designs (among them one by Sir Joseph Bazalgette) were rejected in favour of the bascule bridge of Sir Henry Jones. The grand opening was held on 30 June 1894. (*Above*) Crowds cheered and bands played. The bridge was described as 'a colossal symbol of the British genius'. But there were those who disliked it intensely. H.G. Wells likened it to 'a stock-broker in armour'.

In the last days before the cinema pushed all opposition aside, the music halls were the venues for mass entertainment. They offered a mixed programme – dancers, singers, jugglers, acrobats, comics and comediennes. The best acts were outstanding: the worst were atrocious. Top of the bill were Lotte Collins (*left*) and Marie Lloyd (*below*). Collins's most famous song was *Ta-Ra-Ra-Boom-De-Ay*, a song and dance routine that brought the house down. She was paid $1,000 a week to take the song to America. Lloyd had many hits, including *Oh, Mr Porter!*, *My Old Man Said Follow the Van*, and *I'm One of the Ruins that Cromwell Knocked Abaht [About] a Bit*.

Harry Lauder (*top left*) was a Scots comedian and singer, best known for such sentimental numbers as *Roamin' in the Gloamin'* and *I Love a Lassie*. George Robey (*top right*) was nicknamed 'The Prime Minister of Mirth'. He was a great Dame in pantomime, and, like Collins, was popular in the United States. Dan Leno (*bottom left*) was one of the best loved stars of the Music Hall. Sadly he broke down from overwork and became insane. Many of the stars performed in four or five different theatres a night. Vesta Tilley (*bottom right*) was a male impersonator and originator of the song *Burlington Bertie*.

The epitome of modern luxury in Edwardian days was the Rolls-Royce limousine. It was the creation of two remarkable engineers. Sir Frederick Henry Royce (*above, left*) was apprenticed to the Great Northern Railway, but became more interested in the motor car. He made his first car in 1904, the year he met Rolls, and their company began production two years later. Charles S. Rolls was an aviator as well as a maker of motor cars. He made the first double crossing of the Channel in 1910. The picture of him (*opposite*) was taken at an aviation meet in Bournemouth on 27 July 1910, shortly before he crashed and was killed. To many the most beautiful car of all time was the Rolls-Royce Silver Ghost. (*Above, right*) J. Doran and partner pose in their Silver Ghost in the warm up to the Leicester Automobile Club's Kettleby Hill Climb, 16 July 1910.

The genius of Oscar Wilde (*opposite, top left*) was never disputed. He had a wit that could be charming or withering, as occasion demanded. His plays were enormously successful, and audiences packed London theatres to see *A Woman of No Importance*, *Lady Windermere's Fan* and *The Importance of Being Earnest* (*opposite, below*). Professionally, he was the darling of London society. The problem was his private life, and especially his friendship with Lord Alfred Douglas (*left*).

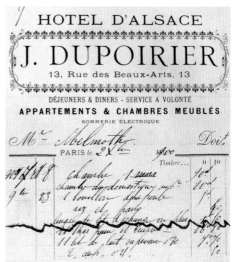

Douglas was the son of the 8th Marquis of Queensbury (*opposite, top right*). The Marquis strongly objected to their relationship, and insulted Wilde publicly. Wilde made the mistake of suing the Marquis for slander. His case was thrown out, and Wilde himself was then prosecuted and imprisoned for homosexuality. On his release, Wilde left England, never to return. (*Top right*) A hotel bill made out to 'Melmoth' (one of Wilde's pseudonyms) just before he died in 1900.

Universal education and cheap newspapers led to a reading public that was hungry for literature, and in Edwardian Britain there was an abundance of good writers. One of the most popular was Herbert George Wells (*top left*), better known as 'H.G.', author of *The Invisible Man*, *The War of the Worlds* and *The History of Mr Polly*. The works of Thomas Hardy (*top right*) were deeper and sadder – *Jude the Obscure*, *Tess of the d'Urbevilles* and *The Mayor of Casterbridge* offered little in the way of make-believe. That was provided by J.M. Barrie (*left*), the Scottish playwright and creator of *Peter Pan* .

Oscar Wilde's only rival in the theatre was George Bernard Shaw (*top left*), another Irish playwright who made his name and his fortune in England. Unlike Wilde, Shaw formally expounded his political beliefs and his 'kindly dislike' of capitalism. The poet of the age was Rudyard Kipling (*top right*). Although often criticised as the creator of jingoistic verse, much of Kipling's best known work was more a comment on the life of the British soldier than the glories of the Empire. Perhaps the most lasting literary creation was that of Sir Arthur Conan Doyle *(right)*. Sherlock Holmes entered the 20th century in *The Hound of the Baskervilles* and has been solving mysteries ever since.

In the late 19th century, British music was revived by a handful of composers and two brilliant entrepreneurs. Head and shoulders above all other British composers was Edward Elgar (*above, right*), a violinist and amateur conductor whose symphonies, oratorios and concertos achieved immediate popularity at home and abroad. The entrepreneurs were the conductor Sir Henry Wood (*below, left*), who initiated the Promenade Concerts and did much to improve British orchestral playing, and Richard D'Oyly Carte (*above, left*), who shouldered the almost impossible task of keeping the peace between Gilbert and Sullivan.

The partnership of Sir William Schwenk Gilbert (*above, left*) and Sir Arthur Seymour Sullivan (*above, right*) was often acrimonious – they once worked together for a year without exchanging a single word. But the string of light operas that they produced together were unsurpassed for melody, inventiveness and the fun that they provided. Like Gilbert and Sullivan, Frederick Delius (*below, right*) had a champion, though decades had to pass before Sir Thomas Beecham had finally convinced audiences of the haunting beauty of much of Delius's work.

The *crème de la crème* of society gathered at Cowes each summer for a week of sailing or, more often, watching the ships slip by. Edward, both as Prince of Wales and as King, was an enthusiastic sailor and it was deemed a high honour to be one of the King's party. The place to be seen was at the Royal Yacht Club, though the nearest many visitors got to actually being afloat in 1909 was the end of the Club pier (*right*).

For the rich, the summer was a time of well-regulated enjoyment. Dukes and earls, viscounts and baronets converged on their London houses for the 'Season'. This was a round of balls and dances, cricket matches and regattas, promenades and parades. One of the high points of the season was a visit to Ascot Races, held annually at the beginning of June. This was a day at the races *par excellence* (*above*).

Among those seen in 1908 were Constance Edwina, Duchess of Westminster, and Anthony Ashley Cooper, 8th Earl of Shaftesbury (*opposite, below*), son of the reforming Earl, strolling from the grandstand to the paddock. For eligible young ladies, visits to Cowes, Henley, Lord's and Ascot offered a chance to meet eligible young men. The only trouble was, once the cry, 'They're off!', went up and the race began, most men directed their concentration on the wrong sort of filly (*right*).

Tennis was played at all levels. (*Opposite, above left*) Spencer Gore, winner of the first Men's Singles Championship at Wimbledon in 1877. (*Opposite, above right*) Arthur Gore at Wimbledon 1905. (*Opposite, below*) A more relaxed game on the court at home, 1888. (*Right*) Dora Boothby serving in a Ladies' Singles at Wimbledon in 1910. (*Far right*) Mrs Albu at Knebworth House. (*Below*) The Eastbourne Tournament, September 1889.

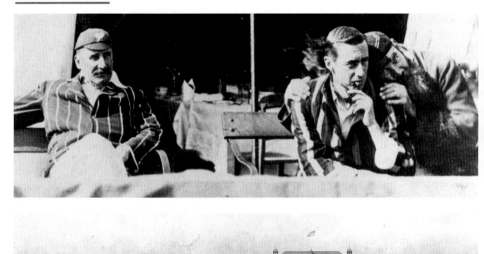

Apart from the Queen, the most instantly recognisable Victorian was W.G. Grace (*right, and opposite, top*, resting his head on a colleague's shoulder), the greatest English cricketer of all time. Crowds swarmed to see him wherever he played – at the Oval (*opposite, centre*) or Lord's (*opposite, below*). (*Far right and below*) The luncheon interval, Oxford v Cambridge, Lord's.

The White City Stadium, London, was selected as the venue for the 1908 Olympics. (*Opposite, above*) The City Toast-master uses a giant megaphone to announce the next event. In track and field, the Americans carried all before them. Edward Cooke (*left*) won the gold medal for the pole vault with an Olympic record of 3.71 metres. First to finish the Marathon was Dorando Pietri of Italy (*opposite, below*). He was on the point of collapse when he entered the stadium for the last lap. Just metres from the tape, he staggered and was helped across the line. He was subsequently disqualified.

19
KING AND COUNTRY
1910–1920

A 200bhp Blitzen Benz makes an attempt to break the world's land speed record on the banked track at Brooklands, Surrey, 16 May 1914. Brooklands, near Weybridge in Surrey, was the first purpose-built motor racing circuit in the world, completed in 1907. Amateurs as well as professionals flocked there to try their driving skills (and their luck) on the steep banking. What they were often unprepared for were the stiff breezes that blew across the track. The circuit remained in use until the Second World War.

Introduction

In the second decade of the 20th century, two polar explorers set out on Antarctic expeditions. The first was that of Robert Falcon Scott from 1910 to 1912, the second that of Ernest Shackleton from 1914 to 1916. The first was a tragic success – Scott reached the South Pole but perished with his comrades on the awful return journey. The second was a triumphant failure – Shackleton failed to make the first ever crossing of the Antarctic, but every member of his expedition survived, even the perilous crossing of eight hundred miles of the wildest and coldest seas in the world in an open boat.

Such contrasts characterise British fortunes during the decade. Glory and tragedy were inextricably mixed. The suffragettes were imprisoned and tortured before they won a limited right for women to vote. In 1912 the SS *Titanic* was launched, emblem of the unsinkable pride of a seafaring nation. A few months later 1,513 passengers and crew were drowned when the ship struck an iceberg on her maiden voyage to New York.

British troops fought long and hard to thwart the ambitions of the Kaiser and German militarists. Their efforts were crowned with victory in the autumn of 1918, but over a million lives were lost in the mud and filth of Flanders, the heat of Gallipoli and the dark waters off Jutland. The hell of war was recorded in some of the finest poetry ever written in the English language.

In 1919, piloted by Alcock and Brown, the Vickers Vimy, developed as a bomber in the First World War, became the first aircraft to fly across the Atlantic. It was a golden age for the English theatre – pantomimes and musicals at Drury Lane were the most lavish ever seen, the London Palladium first opened its doors on 26 December 1910, and Sir Herbert Beerbohm Tree created the role of Professor Higgins in George Bernard Shaw's *Pygmalion* in 1914.

It was also a time of magic and mystery. J.M. Barrie's *Peter Pan* captured the hearts of the simple and the sophisticated in equal numbers. And, in 1919, two Yorkshire schoolgirls convinced scientists, journalists and a large slice of the British public that they had seen, and photographed, fairies at the bottom of their garden.

After the horrors of the First World War such concepts came as welcome balm for the shattered minds of those who had lost their loved ones.

Shackleton (*above*) was one of Scott's party who had almost reached the Pole in 1902 and had survived (*opposite, below* – Shackleton is the second from the left). In 1908 Shackleton returned to the Antarctic in *Nimrod* (*opposite, above*), and again in 1914 in *Endeavour*. When this ship was crushed by the pack ice (*right*), Shackleton and his men had to cross eight hundred miles of sea in an open boat. It was Shackleton's proud boast that in all his expeditions he never lost a man.

Captain Robert Falcon Scott (*opposite, top left and right*) led two expeditions to the Antarctic. In 1902 members of his *Discovery* expedition struggled to within one hundred and fifty miles of the South Pole – at that time a record. It was an ill-prepared attempt, however, and the much-vaunted balloon proved useless (*above*). Scott returned in a new ship, the *Terra Nova* (*left*) in 1910, with a better equipped expedition.

Scott knew that Roald Amundsen was also heading for the Pole. Five members of the British team made the last run but were too late – Amundsen arrived at the South Pole one month ahead of Scott in December 1911. Scott and his companions all perished on the way back. (*Above*) Scott's last entry in his journal: 'For God's sake look after our people.'

In 1899 the Marchese Guglielmo Marconi formed the Marconi Telegraph Company in London. By 1910, there was a steady output of radios from the Marconi Works in Essex (*opposite, above*). Company headquarters were at Marconi House, where operators received their training (*above*). The development of radio was swift. Portable equipment was in the field long before this picture was taken in 1919 (*opposite, below*). And it was not long before radio was seen as a medium for mass entertainment: (*right*) a young Hughie Greene at the microphone.

Theatres were crowded. It was the era of the actor-manager, of Sir Herbert Beerbohm Tree, whose repertoire ranged from the dramatic Lord Illingworth in *A Woman of No Importance* (*below, right*) to Professor Higgins in *Pygmalion* (*below*).

On the lighter side, Fred Emney, Harry Fragson, Harry Randall and Walter Passmore delighted audiences in the pantomime Sinbad (*above, left*), Dorothy Ward (*above, right*) brought glamour to variety and panto, and George Robey (*below, left*) was billed as the 'Prime Minister of Mirth'.

(*Right*) Vera Hamilton's poster for Henry Irving's production of Dr Jekyll and Mr Hyde at the Queen's Theatre, London, 1910.

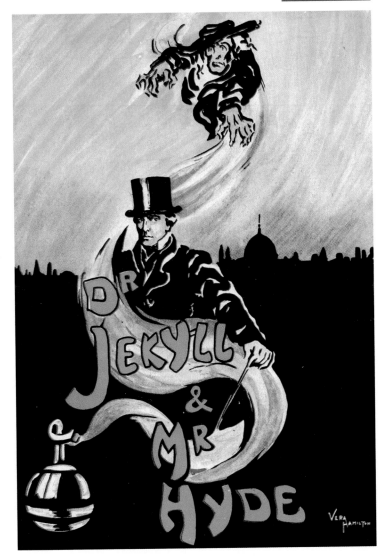

In 1910 Dr Hawley Harvey Crippen (*opposite, left*) murdered his second wife, Cora Turner (*opposite, below right*), a music hall artiste whose stage name was Belle Ellmore. Crippen fled with his lover, Ethel Le Neve (*opposite, above right*). The pair took ship for the United States, with Le Neve disguised as a young boy. They were spotted by a passenger on board and the captain contacted Scotland Yard by radio-telegraphy – the first use of the radio for police purposes. Crippen and Le Neve were arrested and returned to England on the SS *Megantic.* Crowds waited at the Liverpool dockside for a glimpse of them (*above*). Both were tried at the Old Bailey (*right*). Crippen was executed at Pentonville.

The White Star liner SS *Titanic* was built at the Harland and Wolff shipyard, Belfast, between 1910 and 1912 (*left*). The liner was the pride of the merchant marine – grand, graceful and, it was claimed, unsinkable. Sea trials were completed in March 1912 (*below*), and the ship set out on her maiden voyage the following month.

There were 2,224 people on board, but sufficient lifeboats (*below*) for only a third of that number. When the *Titanic* hit an iceberg on 12 April, more than 1,500 of the passengers and crew were drowned. (*Right*) Ned Parfitt sells copies of the newspaper with details of the disaster. He was killed in the last days of the First World War.

One of the greatest spectacles of the age was the Delhi Durbar of December 1911, celebrating the accession of George V as King and Emperor (*opposite*). Attended by young Indian princes, King George and Queen Mary viewed the procession from the Red Fort (*top*). Other celebrations included a tiger shoot, which was followed by a picnic in the field (*bottom*) – George V is on the left, nearest the camera. In 1922 it was the turn of George's son Edward, Prince of Wales, to visit the Jewel in the British Crown (*centre*). He is here accompanied by the Dowager Begum of Bhopal, titular Ruler of India.

In the early 19th century the suffragettes were at their most active. (*Opposite, above*) The death of Emily Davison, Epsom, 1913. (*Opposite, below left*) Lady Emmeline Pethick-Lawrence celebrates her release from prison, 1909. (*Opposite, below right*) Sylvia Pankhurst, Bow Road, 1912. Emmeline Pankhurst (*right*) and other suffragettes (*below*) are arrested, May 1914.

The Royal Air Force became an independent branch of Britain's armed forces in 1917. It grew rapidly in the closing stages of the First World War, and in the years immediately following. Queues formed at recruiting offices (*left*) for a service that promised 'Good Pay and Good Prospects'. The RAF equivalent of the army's Sandhurst and the navy's Dartmouth was Cranwell, where officer cadets learned carpentry (*left, below*), an essential skill in the days when aircraft frames were made of wood.

The young RAF developed an optimistic *esprit de corps*, as seen in this picture of an RAF sports meeting at Hastings, Sussex, on 5 August 1918 (*right*). There was no record of past defeat, no top-heavy chain of command, no straitjacket of tradition. (*Below, right*) RAF No. 1 Squadron pose for the camera in Claremarais, France. The squadron was older than the service, for it was originally formed in 1878 as No. 1 Balloon Company, and had been in continuous operation since 1912.

The most successful British campaigns in the First World War were those fought against the Turks in Mesopotamia. The regular troops were led by Edmund Allenby (*opposite*), who captured Jerusalem in 1917, entering the city on foot, like a pilgrim. More flamboyant operations were conducted by T.E. Lawrence (*right*), more famously known as Lawrence of Arabia. After the war Allenby became High Commissioner in Egypt, and Lawrence flirted with obscurity.

"WHAT IS THE WORTHIEST THING TO DO?
BEST FOR THE COUNTRY-A CREDIT TO YOU;
WHAT WORTHIER DEED COULD EVER BE DONE,
THAN SETTING TO WORK WITH A WILL & A GUN."

A.ADLINGTON. COPYRIGHT.1914.

The horrors of the First World War produced some of the most moving poetry in the English language. Rupert Brooke (*opposite, above right*), Wilfred Owen (*opposite, below right*) and Edward Thomas died in the War. Siegfried Sassoon (*opposite, left*) and Robert Graves survived. But there were other poets at work, composing song lyrics and poetic propaganda. This postcard (*left*) was used for recruiting purposes. Its blunt call to arms reads:

'*What is the worthiest thing to do?*
Best for the country – a credit to you;
What worthier deed could ever be done,
Than setting to work with a will & a gun.'

(*Above*) The start of a relay race on the Brooklands circuit, 31 July 1909. Brooklands was regarded with affection by many racing drivers, but they were conscious of the many dangers that the track posed for the lightweight racing cars of the early days. There was the unbanked blind curve made to negotiate the Vickers aircraft factory, the Big Bump on the viaduct over the River Wey, and, in some competitions, New Hill (*left*), constructed in 1909. The enthusiasts who went to Brooklands (*opposite, below*) had a mixed fare. As well as lap and relay races, there were also competitions to see how far a car could go in a given time. (*Opposite, above*) L.G. Hornsted (at the wheel) and S. A. Gibbons before their attempt to break the One-Hour Record, 16 May 1914.

From the time that J.M. Barrie (*opposite, bottom left*) created Peter Pan in 1904, the 'boy who never grew up' remained a favourite with British theatre audiences. On stage, the part was always played by a woman. Among notable Peter Pans were Stephanie Stevens in 1906 (*left*); Gladys Cooper (*opposite, top left* – perhaps a little old at thirty-five); Betty Bronson (*opposite, top right*), the silent film star; and Jean Forbes-Robertson, who played the part in London's West End for eight consecutive years (*opposite, bottom right*).

On 14 June 1919, a Vickers Vimy biplane took off from St John's, Newfoundland (*above, left*). Its destination was Ireland, for the flight was an attempt at the first non-stop crossing of the Atlantic. Sixteen hours and twenty-eight minutes later, the plane nose-dived into a bog at Clifden, County Galway. Four days later the pilot, John Alcock (on left with macintosh), and navigator, Arthur Whitten Brown, arrived at Windsor Station (*below, left*) on their way to receive knighthoods. In November, Vickers entered another Vimy (*opposite, below*) in the £10,000 competition for the first plane to fly to Australia. The winners were Ross and Smith (*opposite, above*) who completed the 11,294 mile flight in twenty-eight days.

20
DEPRESSION AND APPEASEMENT
1920–1939

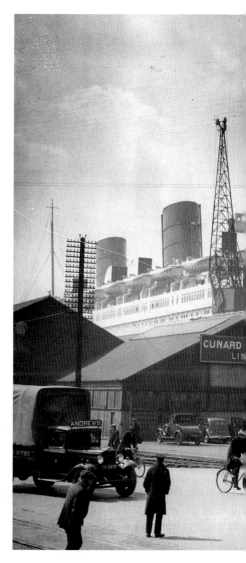

It was the heyday of ocean liners. French, German, Italian and British liners competed for the Blue Riband awarded to the ship that made the fastest crossing of the Atlantic. These floating palaces offered a degree of luxury and style that it would have been hard to rival on dry land. One of the largest was the Cunard Line's *Queen Mary*, seen here at her home port of Southampton on 22 April 1936. The *Queen Mary* was built at Brown's on Clydeside in 1934 and was the largest liner afloat until the building of her sister ship, *Queen Elizabeth*, in 1938.

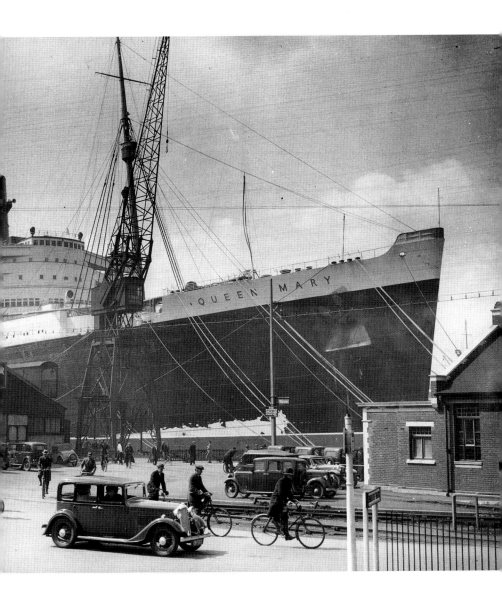

Introduction

Old ways of life had one last fling in the twenty years that separated the two World Wars. Though complaining bitterly about death duties and income tax, the rich preserved their ancient grandeur. There were balls and presentations at Court, regattas, days at the races, nights at the opera, and everyday splendour in stately homes.

The masses had to be content with the new wonders of radio, gramophone and cinema. Millions tuned in to the broadcasts of the best of British dance bands (Jack Payne, Henry Hall, Harry Roy and Ambrose), transmitted from the hotels and night clubs of London's West End, or from the granite magnificence of the London Midland and Scottish Railway's Gleneagles Hotel. The poor had to be content with love on the dole, the Means Test and the lock-out.

Streamlined trains left London for most

points of the compass – the *Flying Scotsman*, the *Coronation Scot* for Edinburgh and Glasgow; the *Cornish Riviera* for Penzance; the *Golden Arrow* for Folkestone and then Paris. At sea, the SS *Queen Mary* and the SS *Queen Elizabeth* joined the ever-expanding fleet of transatlantic liners. Imperial Airways travelled even further, linking the far flung outposts of the Empire.

Alfred Hitchcock directed his first films, bridging the change from silent films to talkies with ease and assurance. Noël Coward wrote his finest plays and songs that were witty and wistful by turn. Ivor Novello captured the hearts of theatregoers, and George Formby tickled the ribs of variety audiences.

The Prince of Wales dictated taste in men's fashions, but failed to rule his country, precipitating the monarchy into an unexpected crisis when he gave up the throne to marry the woman he loved. When he departed for France, he left behind the Windsor knot, Oxford bags and plus fours. Other innovations included safety glass, Billy Butlin's first holiday camp, the Lambeth Walk, *Picture Post* and bodyline bowling.

Britain flirted with Fascism. Sir Oswald Mosley strutted and boasted, but his Blackshirts failed to appeal and occasionally needed considerable and unwarranted police support to survive. Ramsay MacDonald became Prime Minister when the Labour Party came to power for the first time in 1924. Both leader and party surrendered their principles and their policies within a shamefully short time. For the Tories, Stanley Baldwin smoked his pipe and appeared reassuringly unflappable. Flappers, on the other hand, danced the night away as the country staggered through strikes and depressions, appeasement and re-armament.

The General Strike began on 3 May 1926. Although armoured cars patrolled Oxford Street (*left*) and troops guarded convoys of food and distribution centres, the Strike was a very British attempt at revolution. Those not directly involved saw it as a nuisance, which necessitated cycling to work (*below, left*), or pinning one's faith in volunteer drivers of buses and trains (*opposite, top right*). Football matches were arranged between strikers and police. Strikers marched to church services at St Andrew's Church, Plymouth (*opposite, below*), and elsewhere, seeking God's blessing on their industrial action. The Government took matters more seriously, publishing its own newspaper, which even the strikers read (*opposite, top left*).

In the post-war optimism of the 1920s, one of the loudest cries was the call for better housing. In most major cities there were still appalling slums, as in Great Peter Street, London (*above, left*). A massive building programme was launched, and hundreds of thousands of new houses were built (*above, right*), like these in Warrington, Cheshire (*left*).

By the 1930s the standard design of the lower middle-class home was the three-bedroom, semi-detached house, as modelled at the North London Exhibition at Alexandra Palace in 1932 (*above, right*). For the working class in the inner cities, large blocks of flats were built. One of the largest developments was at Quarry Hill in Leeds, West Yorkshire (*below, right*).

Imperial Airways had its headquarters at Croydon Airport (*below*). It was primarily a passenger airline with routes connecting the British Empire, though it was also used to carry important freight. (*Left*) A cargo of gold from the Lena mines in the USSR arrives at Croydon, 17 August 1926.

Most of Imperial's fleet consisted of twin- or four-engined biplanes, with exotic names such as *Hanno, Hengist* and *Scylla* (*right*, being serviced in 1935). Some of the destinations were less exotic – a group of race-goers board for a flight to Liverpool's Grand National, 25 March 1930 (*below*).

Trains had never been so fast, so beautiful or so comfortable. The *Cheltenham Flyer*, the *Royal Scot*, the *Cornish Riviera* and, above all, the *Flying Scotsman* (*left*) ushered in a new age of travel. The first-class saloon on the LNER's *Flying Scotsman* (*below*) and the first-class lounge on top LMSR trains (*opposite, above*) offered service to rival that of the best hotels. By the late 1930s, many of the most powerful locomotives had been streamlined, some of the most beautiful being those of the 'Coronation' class on the London, Midland and Scottish Railway (*opposite, below*).

The London Underground network was enlarged in the 1920s and 1930s with the building of the Piccadilly Line (*left*) and extensions to many of the other routes, pushing outwards from the centre of London as suburbia invaded the countryside. New stations were opened, with gleaming escalators (*below*), smart staff (*opposite, above left*), and automatic ticket machines (*opposite, below*). The new trains were lighter and more comfortable (*opposite, above right*).

If there was one single 'darling' of the 1930s, it was Amy Johnson...in the words of the song 'Amy, beautiful Amy...'. She was born in 1903, the daughter of a fish merchant in Hull. At the age of twenty-six she became the first woman to gain certificates as both ground engineer and pilot. Within a year she had become the first woman to fly solo from London to Australia. She took off on 5 May 1930 in her single-engine Gypsy Moth *Jason* (*opposite, above*), arriving in Australia nineteen days later. On her return to England, crowds went wild. (*Above*) Amy waves from a car as she is driven in triumph past the Dorchester Hotel, 6 August 1930.

In 1932 Amy married Captain Jim Mollison (*opposite, below*), a Scottish aviator who had already made a record solo flight from Australia to England in just under nine days. The following year he made the first east-west crossing of the Atlantic, and the year after that the first solo flight from England to South America. It was not a happy marriage, however. Amy had better luck in the air. In 1936 she made a new record flight from Capetown, South Africa, to London, to be greeted by wildly cheering crowds (*below, right*). Amy's luck ran out in 1941 when she was forced to bale out of an Air Transport Auxiliary plane and was never seen again.

Malcolm Campbell and John Cobb both held the world land speed record in the 1930s. (*Opposite, above*) Campbell streaks across the Pendine Sands, January 1927. (*Opposite, below left*) Campbell with his twelve-year-old son Donald at the wheel of *Bluebird*, 1933. (*Opposite, below right*) Campbell prepares to take part in a Belfast road race. He is driving a Bugatti. (*Above*) Cobb and T.E. Rose-Richards at Brooklands, 1935. (*Right*) Cobb roars round Brooklands, March 1937.

Women's clothes in the 1920s ranged from the outstanding to the outlandish. White crèpe and crystal beads were all the rage at this garden party in 1925 (*left*). For a day at the races you couldn't beat a tunic coat with fur stole and a cloche hat (*opposite, above left*). Negligees were silky if not subtle (*opposite, above right*). Jessie Matthews knew what to wear on a chaise longue (*opposite, below left*). Flappers knew what to wear anywhere (*opposite, below right*).

'Cocktails and laughter,'
wrote Noël Coward in the
lyric to his song *Poor
Little Rich Girl*, 'but what
comes after?' Probably
more cocktails and
laughter. It was the age
of the Gimlet, the
Screwdriver, the
Snowball, the Gin and It,
the Gin and Orange, the
Gin and Lime, the gin
and anything.

All you needed was a bar and a barman (*opposite, above left, and below right*), and a glamorous evening dress (*opposite, above right*), and, if you really wanted to make a night of it, a floor show (*opposite, below*). There would always be some (certainly) handsome and (possibly) intelligent young men to enliven the party, and a hot band to set the toes tapping. For those of a more sober demeanour, there was a living to be made as professional drinkers (*right*).

C.B. Cochran specialised in producing revues – shows made up of songs, dances and sketches. *Wake Up and Dream* at the London Pavilion in 1929 (*right, below*) was a typical example. Almost every revue featured a troupe of 'Cockie's' Young Ladies (*opposite, above right*). In the *Streamline Revue* of 1934, these included Nijinsky's daughter Kyra (*opposite, above left*), Bubbly Rogers, Helena Taylor and Sylvia Pearman (*right*). Among the stars of his *Midnight Matinee* in 1930 (*opposite, below*) was Barbara Cartland (far left), who also designed the costumes.

Noël Coward (*opposite, above left*) and Ivor Novello (*opposite, above right*) were the darlings of the English stage in the 1930s. Both were composers, actors and playwrights, though Coward's rapier-like wit gave his work a wider audience and a longer shelf life than that of Novello. Coward owed much to the English theatrical impressario Charles B. Cochran (*opposite, below*, fourth from left, returning with Coward from New York on board the SS *Berengaria*). The most famous scene in all Coward's plays is the Balcony Scene in *Private Lives* in which he and Gertrude Lawrence starred at the Phoenix Theatre, London in 1930 (*right*).

By the time he got married on 16 December 1926 (*above*), Alfred Hitchcock had already worked for seven years in the film industry. The first film he directed was *The Pleasure Garden* in 1925. This was followed by *The Lodger* in 1926, and his first sound film, *Blackmail*, in 1929. By then Hitchcock had established some of his early trademarks as a director. Bold cutting, almost melodramatic close-ups, and, in the case of *Blackmail*, highly innovative use of sound, were all means by which Hitchcock could startle his audiences.

His greatest early success was his screen adaptation of John Buchan's *The Thirty-Nine Steps*. Robert Donat (*above*, leaning anxiously forward in his seat) played the role of Richard Hannay, wrongly suspected of murder, who flees from London on the *Flying Scotsman*. The film was made in 1935 and was described by critics as 'a miracle of speed and light...a humorous, exciting, dramatic, entertaining, pictorial, vivid tale told with a keen grasp of the cinematic idea'. Five years later, Hitchcock went on to Hollywood, and to greater fame and fortune.

There was a thriving British film industry in the 1930s. Among the female film stars were Vivien
Leigh (*above, left*, photographed by Sasha), Madeleine Carroll, Wendy Hiller, Cicely Courtneidge,
Ida Lupino (*above, right*), Elsa Lanchester (*opposite, above*), Olivia de Havilland, Valerie Hobson,
Anna Neagle, Merle Oberon and Gracie Fields (*opposite*). Vivien Leigh made her professional
debut in a film called *Things Are Looking Up* in 1934. Ida Lupino's first film was a year earlier –
Her First Affair. Elsa Lanchester appeared in a series of comedy two-reel silent films of H.G.
Wells' short stories.

'Our Gracie' was born over a fish and chip shop in Rochdale in 1898. Like Leigh, Lupino and Lanchester, she tried her luck in the United States, but she was not a success there and returned to Britain in 1931 to make her first film, *Sally in Our Alley*. Lanchester went to Hollywood with her husband, Charles Laughton. Vivien Leigh went with Laurence Olivier, and there found fame and fortune when she was cast as Scarlett O'Hara in *Gone With the Wind*. Ida Lupino fought hard for her career and eventually succeeded in Hollywood, both as actor and director.

Evelyn Waugh (*opposite, above left*) was the bright young thing among English novelists. W.H. Auden and Christopher Isherwood (*opposite, above right*) shocked and delighted in equal measure. Aldous Huxley (*opposite, below left*) produced a chilling view of the future with his *Brave New World*. Daphne du Maurier (*opposite, below right*) was perhaps the most financially successful writer. T.S. Eliot (*above, left*) was respected for his poetry, Somerset Maugham (*above, right*) for his novels and plays. Two of the most interesting writers were Virginia Woolf (*below, left*) and Marguerite Radclyffe Hall (*below, right*). Both struggled emotionally through the 1920s and 1930s.

In the 1920s and 1930s the Tennis Championships at Wimbledon, run by the All England Lawn Tennis and Croquet Club, were a strictly amateur affair; no professional players were allowed to enter. The Club had moved from Worple Road to its grand new premises in 1922, and the new Centre Court became the magnet to draw tennis fans from all over the world (*opposite*). Almost the last British tennis hero (as opposed to heroine) was Fred Perry (*above*) who won the Men's Singles title three years running, from 1934 to 1936. Here he is fighting his way through the 1936 semi-final match against Don Budge of the United States.

Perry was originally the world's table tennis champion, and only took up lawn tennis in 1928 at the age of nineteen. As well as his Wimbledon titles, he was US champion three times, and winner of the Australian and French championships. He also helped England win the Davis Cup four times in the 1930s. For all that, Perry had a love-hate relationship with the All England club. He was the son of a Labour MP, and lacked the breeding and background that the Club officials preferred. Even while champion he had to use a side entrance into the clubhouse. The Spirit of Bolshevism made little headway in Wimbledon.

In 1936 the Prime Minister, Stanley Baldwin, demanded that Edward VIII end his love affair with the twice divorced Mrs Simpson (*left*). The alternative was abdication. Edward, who had already made radio broadcasts to the nation (*below*), asked for a chance to put his case. Baldwin refused. On 11 December 1936, Edward abdicated. When the news broke, the press made much of it (*opposite*).

21
ONE NATION
1939–1951

The Dome of Discovery, on London's South Bank, site of the
Festival of Britain, 1951. The Festival was in part a celebration
of the one hundredth anniversary of the 1851 Great Exhibition,
but more an attempt by the Labour Government to persuade a
nation, bruised by six years of war and another five years of
austerity rationing, that a bright new dawn was breaking. The
Dome housed all that was best in British science, engineering
and technology. Little remains now but some fond memories
and the Royal Festival Hall.

Introduction

There'll be bluebirds over
The White Cliffs of Dover
Tomorrow, just you wait and see...
(Popular song of the Second World War)

Britain went to war in 1939 with mild-mannered and ill-prepared courage. Having capitulated to all Hitler's requests until that year, Prime Minister Neville Chamberlain surprised himself by declaring war on Germany. For the first two years, Britain grimly hung on, rescuing its pride and its army from Dunkirk, enduring the Blitz and winning the crucial Battle of Britain. Winston Churchill took over from Chamberlain, rallied the country with a series of masterly speeches, and identified the battle of El Alamein as the end of the beginning of the war. Ahead, however, lay another three years of bombing, rationing, and surviving – with a separate war to be fought against Japan in the Pacific.

Great minds went to work, inventing everything from ASDIC to the Anderson Shelter. Even greater minds spent the duration of the war in Bletchley Park, cracking Germany's Enigma Code. Women were conscripted into the forces for the first time, providing a welcome new way of life for many. Children were evacuated from the major cities, providing working-class boys and girls with a taste of the joys and horrors of middle-class life.

When the radioactive dust finally settled on Hiroshima and Nagasaki, Britain was all but bankrupt. Attlee's Labour Government flexed its political muscles, nationalised the mines, railways, gas and electricity industries and the Bank of England, and created the National Health Service. Industry switched back to peacetime production as quickly as it could, but hundreds of factories had been destroyed and many of the tools and machines that survived were outmoded.

The winter of 1946–7 was one of the worst on record. British Railways did its frozen best to keep trains running, and those motorists who managed to eke out their petrol ration dug their way out of snow drifts and slithered over icy roads. Coal was rationed, and its comically named substitute – nutty slack – gave off a warmth that bordered on the dismal. Meat was rationed, and its comically named substitute – snoek – turned out to be the off-cuts of whale. A housing crisis was thwarted by the production of tens of thousands of prefabs. British sport produced several heroes (Denis Compton, Stanley Matthews, Gordon Richards) but few victories.

After six years of austerity, the Government encouraged the country to celebrate a hoped-for new dawn with the Festival of Britain in 1951. But the voters had lost patience with Labour, and Churchill returned to power. He was seventy-seven years old. Youth was not at the prow.

Another Government aim was to ensure that, wherever possible, life continued as normal, though sometimes this needed extra effort and ingenuity. (*Opposite*) A couple emerge from the sandbagged Islington Registry Office after their wedding in 1939. (*Above, right*) A telephone callbox still in use after an air raid in 1941. (*Above, left, and right*) Gas masks worn on point duty, and at the ready while their owners go for a swim in Hyde Park.

Sir John Anderson (*above*) introduced the prefabricated air raid shelter that bore his name at the beginning of the war. It consisted of sections of corrugated iron, which were bolted together and then covered with earth (*left*).

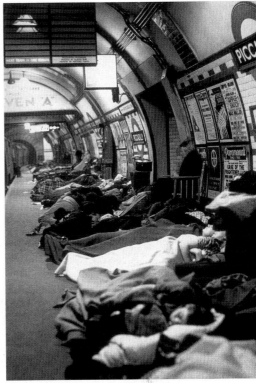

For those who lived or worked in London, the Underground system provided regular shelter from the Blitz. At first, the authorities tried to prevent people taking cover in the Tube, but people forced their way in. Once in the stations, the public sought to make a home from home, taking with them bedding (*above, right*), changes of clothes, and even alarm clocks to make sure they woke in time for work the next morning. (*Above, left*) A woman applies make-up while waiting in a shelter during a bombing raid.

Old and young were evacuated from areas likely to bear the brunt of enemy air raids (*opposite, bottom left and right*). In 1940 the decision was taken to send 120,000 children from London (*opposite, top left*) to the country (*opposite, top right*). The Government insisted that city children were taking happily to country life (*above and right*). Only after the war did stories emerge of unhappiness.

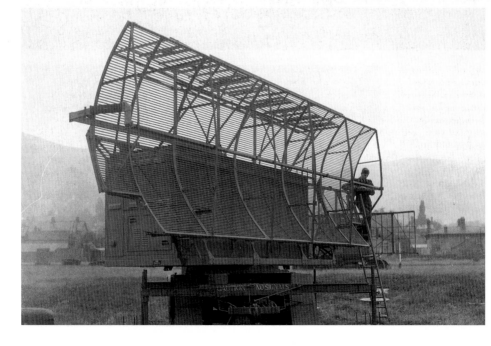

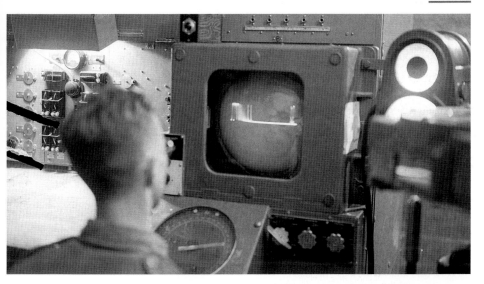

Sir Robert Watson-Watt was the pioneer of radar, the use of radio signals to detect the position of planes and ships. Its existence was kept secret for most of the war, and all these photographs date from the immediate post-war period. (*Opposite, above left*) The nose of a Halifax bomber fitted with night fighting radar equipment. (*Opposite, above right*) A map and a plain screen in an RAF radar centre. (*Above*) A coastal artillery operator scans a battery fire direction set, used in the war to detect approaching enemy ships. (*Opposite, below*) A radar aerial used by the RAF to detect the height of enemy aircraft during and after the Battle of Britain. (*Right*) Preparing a wide-angle radar lens for installation.

One of the most successful Home Front campaigns of the war was 'Dig for Victory'. Every available scrap of land was used to grow food, from farms (*above, left*) to allotments, sports grounds, school fields and suburban gardens (*opposite, above left*). Everyone was urged to take part. (*Above, right*) Two evacuee children carry a 44 lb (20 kilo) cabbage, grown by J.W. Buckland of Oxford, 22 October 1940. (*Opposite, above right*) A young sailor from Chatham Barracks helps to bring in the potato harvest on a farm at Codling, near Rochester, 22 June 1945. (*Opposite, below*) Two members of the Women's Auxiliary Air Force arrive at the RAF Fruit and Vegetables Show, Royal Horticultural Society Hall, London, 25 September 1945.

The governments of all combatants in the Second World War were much occupied with the problem of keeping up morale. In Britain, the BBC had a key role, especially in the field of light entertainment. The most popular radio programme of its kind was *ITMA* (*It's That Man Again*), which was fronted by the fast-talking Liverpool comedian Tommy Handley (*above left, and right*). The show was a mixture of satire, parody and slapstick, larded with catch phrases ('Can I do you now, sir…', 'Don't forget the diver…', 'It's being so cheerful as keeps me going…').

'The Forces' Sweetheart' was the young singer Vera Lynn (*above*), here presenting a canteen to the YMCA on behalf of the Variety Artistes Ladies' Guild in 1942. Her voice rang with sincerity, and was often likened to that of the 'girl next door', albeit a very talented 'girl next door'. Her songs emphasised this 'homely' quality. Among her biggest hits were *The White Cliffs of Dover* and *We'll Meet Again*. Vera Lynn's career continued long after the war ended, in both Britain and the United States. (*Right*) 'The Forces' Sweetheart' boards the *Queen Mary* en route to America, 30 December 1951.

In 1944 'Rab' Butler, President of the Board of Education (*opposite*), presented his report on education in England and Wales. It recommended that all children should receive an education that matched their 'age, aptitude and ability' and promised free secondary education for all. From the age of eleven, children were to be divided into three groups. Those who had passed the Eleven Plus examination would be offered places at grammar schools, the others would go to modern or technical schools. (*Left*) Pupils at the Beckenham and Penge Grammar School, January 1950.

The report was implemented by the Education Act of 1944, popularly known as the Butler Act. It also created a whole series of special schools, for pupils with physical, emotional or learning problems. Much of the report was far-sighted, for Butler was a thoughtful and progressive man. He was not easy to deal with, however, and was described as 'both irreproachable and unapproachable'.

Clement Attlee (*above*) became Labour Prime Minister following the election of 1945. His government embarked on a programme of radical reform, nationalising the railways, mines, Bank of England, steel industry and docks. It was a staggering achievement, but, despite a vigorous campaign (*opposite, top*), the Labour Party only just scraped home in the election of 1950, and another election was held in 1951. The *Daily Mirror* used its front page to back Labour, asking 'whose finger on the trigger?', and presenting Churchill as a warmonger. The message backfired, and Labour lost power.

(*Right*) Attlee in happier times, on the platform of the first Labour Party Conference following the great victory of 1945.

In December 1942 William Beveridge recommended the creation of a National Health Service, providing free treatment and medicines to everyone. As the war neared its end, the public were canvassed for their views on such a scheme (*above, left*). The landslide success of the Labour Party in the 1945 General Election gave Aneurin Bevan, Minister of Health (*opposite, top, and below left*), the chance to make his dream come true, and the NHS came into being in 1948.

Despite the post-war weakness of the British economy, much was done to provide the country with health care. (*Opposite, below*) Princess Elizabeth visits the Princess Elizabeth Hospital in Guernsey, 24 June 1949. (*Below, right*) Mother and child visit one of the new Child Clinics, 1950.

'...all the world is coming to London in 1951...all the world is coming to London to see what we have done...' (popular song at the time of the Festival of Britain – emblem *below*).

(*Above*) The Dome of Discovery, packed with exhibits great and small (*opposite, above left*). A great many people did come – Betty Barks and John Brown (*opposite, above right*) were the millionth visitors to pass through the turnstiles. (*Below, right*) A special train brings the employees of the Van Houten cocoa factory to London from Taunton. (*Opposite, below left*) Special glasses were needed for the screening of the three-dimensional films.

The 1948 Olympic Games were held in London, with Wembley Stadium as the main arena. The torch to light the flame at the Games was carried by a relay of runners from Athens across the ruins of Europe. (*Above, left*) The flame reaches Redhill on the final section of its journey from Dover to London. (*Below, left*) The first cars approach Wembley Stadium along the newly built Wembley Way.

(*Above*) The opening ceremony of the 1948 Olympics, 29 July 1948. (*Right*) The finish of the mens' 100 metres final. The winner is Harrison Dillard of the United States (nearest the camera), followed in order by Norwood 'Barney' Ewell, Lloyd Labeach, Alistair McCorquodale, Melvin Patton and E. Macdonald Bailey.

(*Left*) Gordon Richards, champion jockey. (*Below left*) Stanley Matthews, in white shorts, in a 1948 FA Cup semi-final. (*Below right*) Len Hutton batting for England v South Africa. (*Opposite, above*) Denis Compton, the most glamorous of England's cricketers. (*Opposite, below*) World champion cyclist Reg Harris, 1950.

On 27 July 1949 the De Haviland *Comet* (*above*) made its maiden flight. It was the first jet airliner, sleek, beautiful and powerful. It was designed by H.E. Bishop (*left*) and gave Britain a lead in aviation. Unhappily, a series of crashes in the early 1950s led to the *Comet* being withdrawn from service. It returned a few years later in an improved and strengthened form, though by then the Boeing 707 ruled the skies.

The man responsible for the jet engine was Frank Whittle (*above*, signing autographs at the Schoolboys' Own Exhibition, 1954). Whittle was an aeronautical engineer and inventor who began work on the project in the late 1920s. Despite official opposition, his jet engine (*right*) made its first flight in 1941, powering a Gloster aircraft.

Sir Alexander Fleming (*left*) received the Nobel Prize for Physiology or Medicine in 1945. It was in recognition of the work he had done in the discovery and development of penicillin, the first antibiotic. Fleming had been a student at St Mary's Hospital, Paddington, where he had his laboratory (*opposite*) and where he spent his entire professional life. It was thanks to his skill as a marksman in the St Mary's rifle team that he came to the attention of Sir Almoth Wright, who employed Fleming as a researcher in bacteriology.

The British film industry thrived both during and after the war. (*Left, clockwise from top left*) John Mills in *In Which We Serve*; James Mason and Margaret Lockwood in *The Wicked Lady*; Alec Guinness in *The Man in the White Suit*; and Laurence Olivier and Joan Fontaine in *Rebecca*. (*Opposite, clockwise from top left*) Alastair Sim as Scrooge in *A Christmas Carol*; Richard Attenborough in *Brighton Rock*; Roger Livesey as *Colonel Blimp*; and David Niven.

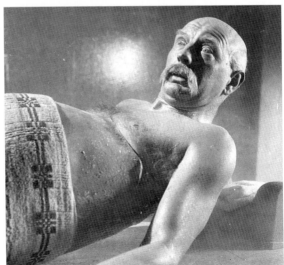

(*Opposite, above left*) Hollywood comes to Britain – Gregory Peck and Ann Todd in Hitchcock's *The Paradine Affair.* (*Opposite, below left*) Britain goes to Hollywood – Montgomery Clift and Elizabeth Taylor in *A Duel in the Sun.* (*Opposite, above right*) Joan Greenwood (*opposite, below right*) Flora Robson. (*Right, clockwise from top left*) Peggy Ashcroft; Trevor Howard and Celia Johnson in *Brief Encounter*; Jean Simmons; and Deborah Kerr.

22
RECOVERY AND RENAISSANCE
1951–1970

The greatest moment in the history of English football. (*Right*)
Bobby Moore holds the Jules Rimet trophy aloft after England's
victory over West Germany in the World Cup Final, Wembley
Stadium, London, 30 July 1966. In the closing seconds of extra
time, as Geoff Hurst dribbled the ball towards the German goal,
the crowd spilled on to the pitch in the belief that the referee had
blown the final whistle. 'They think it's all over...' said the BBC
television commentator Kenneth Wolstenholme. Hurst drove the
ball into the net. '...it is now,' added Wolstenholme, in what was
to become the most famous sporting soundbite of the century.

Introduction

The Coronation of Queen Elizabeth II in June 1953 was hailed as a bright new dawn for Britain. There were those who promised a second Elizabethan Age, and pointed to the conquest of Everest by Hillary and Tenzing as early evidence of glories to come. Four years later, Harold Macmillan, the Conservative Prime Minister, proudly said: 'Let's be frank about it, most of our people have never had it so good.' But Britain's fortunes were mixed for most of this period.

On the credit side were a host of airborne inventions. The de Haviland *Comet* became the world's first jet passenger airliner in 1951. The Flying Bedstead first appeared in 1954, and a more practical successor, the Hovercraft, in 1958. The Anglo-French Concorde made its maiden flight in 1969. A further wonder, the Bristol *Brabazon*, made a brief appearance before being wrapped in mighty mothballs. The largest radio telescope in the world came into commission at Jodrell Bank in 1957, the *QE2* was launched ten years later. Sir Francis Chichester sailed alone round the world in *Gipsy Moth IV*. Cars from the last great age of the British motor industry sped along the first motorways. The Clean Air Act of 1955 brought an end to smog.

Britain's first nuclear power station opened at Windscale, but a little later 200 square miles of surrounding countryside were contaminated by radioactive iodine after a fire at the plant. Also on the debit side were the Aberfan disaster, the Suez debacle, insurrections in Kenya and Cyprus, and the proliferation of atomic weapons. Ardent believers in peace formed CND and marched in protest.

Much of what had been promised ten years earlier came to pass in the Swinging Sixties. For a few years, a brightly coloured Britain became the focus of world attention. The Beatles and the Rolling Stones carried all before them in pop music. England won football's World Cup in 1966. The designs of Mary Quant, the hairstyles of Vidal Sassoon, and the glossy pictures of Twiggy and Jean Shrimpton shaped the look of much of the world. The King's Road in Chelsea was the place to buy your clothes. Benny Hill brought simple-minded television comedy to a new high or low, depending on how you viewed him. London Bridge was sold to an American oil tycoon for £1 million.

But the decade ended with rioting on the streets of Derry and Belfast in Northern Ireland. British troops were hastily posted there to keep order.

A day to remember, weather to forget. (*Above, left*) Crowds line the South Carriage Drive, Hyde Park, as the Royal Navy contingent of the Coronation procession march past, 2 June 1953. (*Below, left*) Drenched crowds in Trafalgar Square.

(*Right*) One of the thousands of street parties that took place on Coronation Day. This one is in Morpeth Street in London's East End.

(*Below, right*) Rockets and flares light up the fleet, part of the Coronation Naval Review to celebrate the Coronation.

The dawn of a bright new age – the Coronation of Elizabeth II in Westminster Abbey, 2 June 1953. George VI had been a popular King, but it was believed that the young Queen would preside over a spiritual, cultural and economic renaissance for Britain. (*Left*) Elizabeth and her Maids of Honour arrive at the Abbey for the long ordeal of the Coronation service. (*Above*) Following the crowning moment of the celebration, the Duke of Edinburgh pays homage to his wife and Queen.

There was still much to be done after the Queen returned to Buckingham Palace. (*Above*) The royal family, complete with Prince Charles and Princess Anne, appears on the balcony. (*Right*) The Queen and her Maids of Honour in the Throne Room of Buckingham Palace.

News broke in London early on the morning of Coronation Day that members of a British expedition had succeeded in being the first known to reach the summit of Mount Everest (*left*), the highest mountain in the world. One month later, the team arrived at London Airport (*below, left*).

The expedition was led by an ex-army officer named John Hunt (*above, right*), a man nobody had heard of until this time. The two climbers who had reached the peak were Sherpa Tenzing Norgay (*above*) and Edmund Hillary (*right*). Tenzing was a professional Everest guide. Hillary was a New Zealand bee-keeper. The two never revealed which of them was first to the top. They left the Union Jack, the Nepalese flag, and the flag of the United Nations on the summit.

On 6 May 1954, a small crowd gathered at the Iffley Road athletics track, Oxford. It was widely rumoured that a twenty-five-year-old student named Roger Bannister, from St Mary's Hospital, Paddington, was to attempt a Four-Minute Mile. No one had succeeded before. Two athletes taking part had no interest in winning. They were Chris Brasher (*above, left*, in glasses) and Christopher Chataway, who acted as Bannister's pacemakers. Bannister broke the tape (*opposite*) in 3 minutes 59.4 seconds, and the small crowd went mad. (*Above, right*) Churchill congratulates Brasher, Chataway and Bannister, Downing Street, June 1954.

The new phenomenon in Soho and in towns throughout Britain was the coffee bar, with its gleaming coffee machine, its glass cups and saucers, and its live music. King of the Coffee Bars was Tommy Steele (*above*, with guitar), here 'sending' one and all at the Bread Basket, London, 25 February 1957.

Steele became Britain's first rock 'n' roll star, leaving his coffee bar roots far behind. Within a couple of years he was a sensation, and crowds (*above*) wrestled with police in their frantic desire just to catch a glimpse of their idol. The alternative to rock 'n' roll was skiffle, acoustic music played on guitar, bass, and washboard, and the King of Skiffle was Lonnie Donegan. There were thousands of youngsters who emulated Steele and Donegan in bedsits and garages all over Britain. (*Opposite, below*) Bert Hardy's picture of Lonnie Donegan on the *Six Five Special* TV show.

Soho (all pictures) was a lively place in the 1950s. (*Opposite, above right*) Ronnie Scott's Jazz Club. (*Opposite, bottom right*) Andria Loran, the elected Queen of Soho. (*Above, left*) Dancers at the Gargoyle Club. (*Above, right*) Hanging out on the streets. (*Below, right*) The Kittens 'hand jive'.

In 1950 Randolph Turpin (*opposite*) became British Middleweight Boxing champion. The following year he won the European title, and then went on to the greatest moment in his career. On 10 July 1951 Turpin met the American champion Sugar Ray Robinson in a fifteen-round fight for the World Middleweight title at Earl's Court, London. Robinson was the favourite to win, but Turpin was faster and more pugnacious. (*Above*) Robinson swings and misses with his left. After the final bell, Turpin was declared the winner on points.

Sir Alec Issigonis (*left*), the Turkish-born designer of the Mini, on his way to receive a knighthood at Buckingham Palace, 22 July 1969. The Mini became the darling of the roads – small and cute, cheap to run and fun to drive. There were contests to see how many people could fit into a Mini, how far a Mini would go on a gallon of petrol, in how small a space the car could be parked.

Minis became popular rally cars (*above*), and the Mini-Cooper was much in demand as a sporting version. Everyone loved the Mini, including Christine Keeler (*right*), though the passing vicar may have wondered why she was getting in the back of the car.

A new breed of Grand Prix cars and a new breed of drivers hit the circuits in the 1950s. Britain's top driver was Stirling Moss (*left*), who had the misfortune to follow Juan Manuel Fangio round many European tracks. (*Below*) Moss in a Maserati at Monza, 1 June 1954.

Safety was a side issue in the 1950s, with only a few bales of straw separating spectators from Moss on a rain-soaked track (*above*). (*Right*) A mechanic cleans the bottom of Moss's boots.

The Campaign for Nuclear Disarmament was formed in the 1950s to rid the world of nuclear weapons. Each year its supporters held an Easter march from the Atomic Weapons establishment at Aldermaston, in Hampshire, to London's Trafalgar Square. (*Above, left*) Marchers gather in the Square, 30 March 1959. (*Below, left*) CND protesters stage a symbolic 'slaughter' on the steps of Westminster Pier, June 1962.

One of the founding figures of CND was Canon John Collins (*above*). (*Above, right*) Rain-soaked CND marchers carry their banners through the streets of Aldermaston, 17 April 1958. (*Below, right*) Bertrand Russell and Edith Finch, his wife, on the platform at a CND rally, Trafalgar Square, 1961. It was the year both were imprisoned for taking part in a protest in Whitehall.

Throughout the late 1960s protests against the Vietnam War increased in size and determination. As on 18 March 1968 (*below, left*), the target for most of these demonstrations was the American Embassy in Grosvenor Square. (*Above, left*) Vanessa and Corin Redgrave join the protest. They are wearing paper headbands, the traditional Vietnamese sign of mourning.

Many of the protests were peaceful enough. On 19 February 1968, more than four hundred women marched in silence from Grosvenor Square to Downing Street (*below, right*). The most violent of the protests took place on the night of 27 October 1968 (*right*), when police and protesters fought for control of the Square. Next day, supporters of the war were outraged by the treatment of the police horses at the demonstration.

The rise was meteoric. The Beatles signed their first record contract in 1962. By February 1964 it was reckoned that their recordings accounted for 60 per cent of all records sold in North America. By 1965 they were an unprecedented showbiz phenomenon. (*Above*) The Beatles warm up in the recording studio – (left to right) Ringo Starr, George Harrison, Paul McCartney and John Lennon. (*Left*) Paul and John on stage at the Hammersmith Odeon, London, 17 December 1965.

Onwards and upwards, the Beatles rose. By 1965, when this picture (*above*) was taken, they were making films as well as albums. Later that year their concert at Shea Stadium in New York was filmed for American TV. In 1968 (*right*) they were working together on *Yellow Submarine*, having received a Grammy Award for *Sergeant Pepper*, but the writing was on the wall.

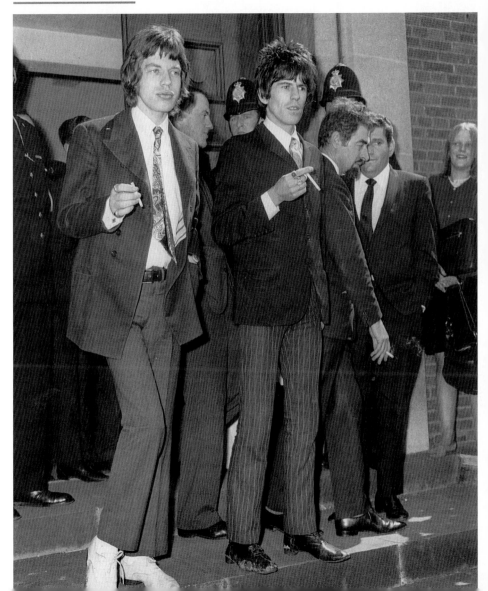

The Rolling Stones (*right*) were the tougher alternative to the Beatles. Mick Jagger and Keith Richards (*opposite*) were hard enough to be called before the Chichester Magistrates Court in May 1967, for offences under the (not very) Dangerous Drugs Act. (*Above*) The Stones at the Richmond Jazz Festival, 1964.

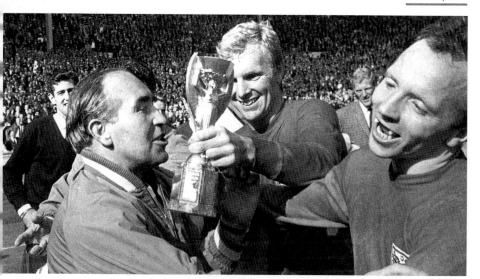

(*Opposite*) Geoff Hurst (left) and Ray Wilson carry the World Cup and their captain, Bobby Moore, on their shoulders as the England team revel in their lap of honour. (*Above*) The England manager, Alf Ramsey, prepares to kiss the cup rather than Nobby Stiles (right). (*Below, right*) Bobby Moore collects the Jules Rimet trophy from Queen Elizabeth II. Behind Moore is Hurst, who scored a hat trick.

British fashion had never been so popular. British designers had never been so sharp. There was the mini-dress (*top left*), and the maxi coat (*top right*). There was Sandie Shaw in her glamorous boutique *(bottom left)*, barefoot as always. There were the boutiques in Chelsea's King's Road (*bottom right*).

Designs were bold and colourful, like this batique printed mini-dress (*top left*). (*Top right*) Models display Mary Quant footwear at the Quant's Afoot fashion show. (*Centre left*) Vidal Sassoon cuts Quant's hair. (*Centre right*) Dedicated followers of fashion hang out in Swinging London. (*Bottom right*) Watching the girls go by in Carnaby Street, 1965.

At a time when clothes and style played such an unusually large part in British life, models became celebrities. Two of the most famous, on or off the catwalk, were Jean Shrimpton (*left*) and Twiggy (*opposite*). Shrimpton was better known by her nickname – 'The Shrimp'. Twiggy was only known by her nickname. Few ever knew her as Lesley Hornby. Both flirted with the pop scene and the film world, but they needed little more than a stunning little dress to stay in the limelight.

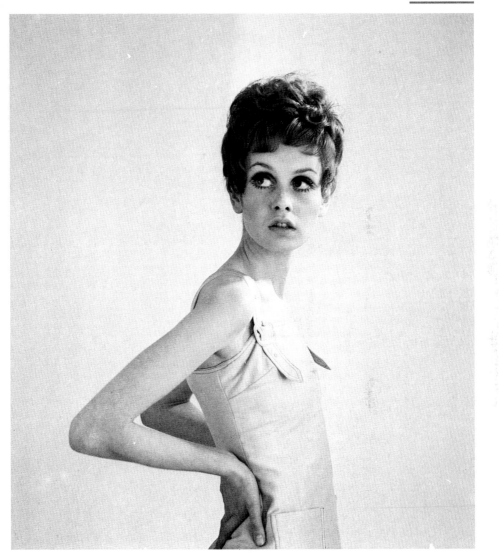

Ian Fleming (*opposite*) created James Bond in 1953. Sean Connery (*above, left*) first played Bond in 1962. From then on, it was success all the way, for books as well as for films: (*above, right*) *You Only Live Twice*, 1966, (*below, right*) *Goldfinger*, 1964.

In 1961 the young cellist Jacqueline du Pré made her concert debut at the Wigmore Hall in London. She was immediately hailed as a major musical talent and was booked for a series of international tours. She began a musical partnership with the French pianist and conductor, Daniel Barenboim, and the two married in 1967. For a brief while she was the most renowned British concert artist, but in 1972 she developed multiple sclerosis and her performing career came to an end. (*Left*) Erich Auerbach's portrait of du Pré and Barenboim at the Queen Elizabeth Hall, London in 1967.

Not all British aviation innovations made the grade. The Bristol *Brabazon* airliner (*above, left*) was the world's largest land plane. It made a two-day visit to Heathrow in July 1951, but never came into service. The Flying Bedstead (*below, left*) was the forerunner of most vertical take-off machines.

More successful were Christopher Cockerell's Hovercraft (*right*), here arriving at Ramsgate on 25 July 1959, and the Concorde (*below*), which made its maiden flight in April 1969.

In 1966 the yachtsman Francis Chichester completed plans for a solo circumnavigation of the world. The boat in which he pinned his faith was *Gipsy Moth IV* (*left*), here undergoing sea trials. Chichester set out from Plymouth on 27 August 1966. His plan was to sail westwards to Sydney, Australia, and then back to Plymouth by way of Cape Horn.

By May the following year, Chichester had all but completed the voyage. In late May he was waving from *Gipsy Moth* as he approached Plymouth (*right*), and a few days later he was greeted by cheering crowds outside Astor House (*above*).

23
MARKET FORCES
1970–1990

The best is yet to come. (*Right*) Margaret Thatcher basks in glory after the Conservative General Election victory, 11 June 1987. It was the beginning of her third term in office as Prime Minister. Ahead lay the challenge of continuing high unemployment, the Poll Tax and the stirrings of discontent among her followers. But these were also the golden years of Thatcherism, when her strength of personality overran friend and foe alike. Cabinet, Opposition, the British press, and much of Europe had little to stand in the way of Thatcher's immense energy and determination.

Introduction

In the 1970s Britain experienced sporting success such as had not been known since the beginning of the 20th century. Mary Peters and Daley Thompson won Olympic gold. Lester Piggott was a famous jockey on the racecourses of Europe and America. Red Rum was the most famous horse and most loved steeplechaser of all time. Eddie 'the Eagle' Edwards happily revealed the limitations of British ski-jumping. Chay Blyth followed in the wake of Sir Francis Chichester and sailed single-handed round the world. Virginia Wade became Women's Singles Champion at Wimbledon in 1977, Silver Jubilee year. Sebastian Coe broke a succession of world athletic records. Jane Torvil and Christopher Dean spun and sped their way to ice-skating glory.

British popular music increased its sales with *con brio* offerings from Andrew Lloyd Webber as composer, Elton John, David Bowie, Tom Jones, Lulu, Cilla Black, and the Sex Pistols. Bob Geldof was a determined promoter of Live Aid. It was carnival time in Notting Hill, and white-knuckle thrills abounded in newly established theme parks.

But the most influential event of the period was the election of a Conservative Government in 1979. Margaret Thatcher became Britain's first woman Prime Minister, and introduced a staggering succession of changes to the political, economic and social life of the country. For those that had, it was a time of unbelievable sweetness. Property dealers gorged themselves on the tasty pickings of a rapidly rising market. Employers rubbed their hands as trade unions were battered and broken by irresistible waves of legislation. Consultants, lobbyists and financiers delighted at the speed with which their coffers swelled. Entrepreneurs, great and small, relished the privatisation of vast industries.

For the have-nots, life was less sweet, but Thatcherism – as it came to be known – was temptingly packaged. In their millions, those who could scarce afford to, bought. They bought shares. They took out mortgages on their council houses and flats. They used their newly acquired pieces of plastic to buy cars and consumer goods. They bought holidays on credit – tan now, pay later.

The writing was on the wall. On Monday 19 October 1987, the London Stock Exchange fell by two hundred and fifty points, threatening the latest privatisation deal and hinting that there might one day be an end to the bonanza. A new phrase – 'negative equity' – was creeping into the property market. And the Prime Minister herself had made some powerful enemies, several of them from within her own Cabinet. A little queue was forming with scores to settle.

Edward Heath (*left*, addressing Conservatives in 1971) spent much of his political life seeking Britain's entry into the EEC. Finally, he was successful. On 1 January 1973, newspaper headlines (*below*) greeted 'A Day in History' and 'Happy New Europe!'.

It was not an easy marriage. (*Right*) Margaret Thatcher and Francois Mitterand meet to discuss EEC sanctions against Argentina, 1982. (*Below*) Vicky Crankshaw compares shopping baskets inside and outside the EEC, and recommends that Britain should stay in Europe, 1975.

Margaret Thatcher (with Denis) waves to crowds after winning the 1979 election (*above, left*). Eight years later the crowds wave back after the 1987 victory (*below, left*). Cautious optimism (*opposite, above*) – Margaret Thatcher (with Alan Clark in background) meets Mikhail Gorbachev at RAF Brize Norton, 7 December 1988. Effusive joy (*opposite, below*) Thatcher and Ronald Reagan at Downing Street, 5 June 1984.

The first British motorways led into and out of London. Eventually there was the likelihood that some of them would meet somewhere.

That 'somewhere' was Birmingham, in the heart of the Midlands. On 24 May 1972, the Gravelly Hill Interchange, popularly known as Spaghetti Junction, opened (*left*). It had cost £30 million to build, and was the largest multi-level motorway interchange in Europe. No one ever claimed it would be pretty, but from the air it has a certain crazy charm.

In the 1970s British Petroleum and other companies opened up the vast North Sea oil fields, a fuel and power bonanza that went a long way towards solving Britain's balance of payments problems. The oil lay deep underwater in the roughest of Britain's territorial waters, but its extraction meant jobs for thousands of people, and brought hitherto unexpected prosperity to the north of Scotland. (*Right*) The *Beryl A* oil rig in October 1980.

(*Above, right*) Oil rig workers position a new length of pipe on the North Sea drilling rig, *Transworld 61*, exploring the Beryl Field for the Mobil oil company. (*Below, right*) A BP worker perched high above the deck of the oil rig, *Sea Quest*, 30 November 1973. The harvesting of oil from the North Sea was one of the major engineering successes of the 1970s and 1980s.

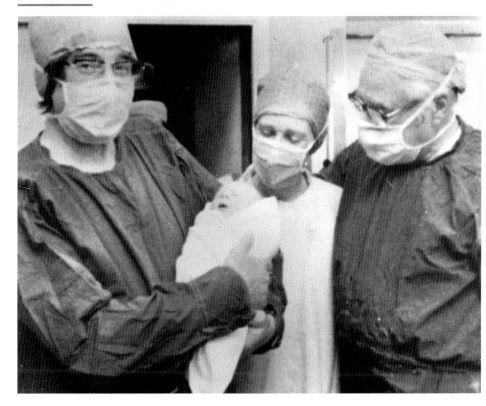

The Pill had liberated many families in the 1960s by allowing women a safe and reliable means of contraception. Couples could now decide when they wished to have children. Not until the 1970s was comparable attention paid to families who were unable to have children. What had previously seemed an unavoidable tragedy now became a problem for science to solve. The solution was provided by two doctors at the Oldham General Hospital, Lancashire – (*above*) Dr Robert Edwards (left) and Dr Patrick Steptoe (right). The work had taken them ten years.

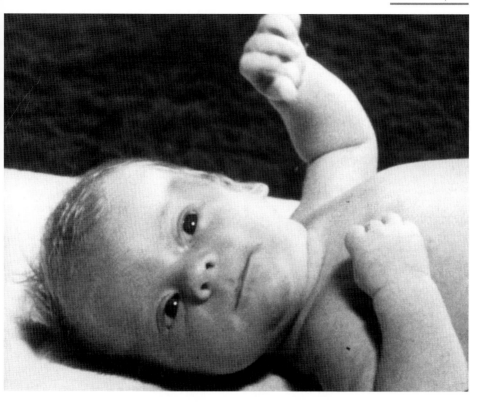

The fruit of their labour, and of the test tube, was Louise Joy Brown (*above*), born on 25 July 1978. Louise was conceived by *in vitro* fertilisation and then implanted in her mother's uterus. There were those who had doubts about the ethics of all this. The doctors were accused of playing God. Some people worried about the possible trauma to which Louise might have been subjected even before her birth. But others hailed the work as a wonderful breakthrough.

(*Left, clockwise from top left*) BBC Radio 1 disc jockey John Peel at the Reading Pop Festival, 1975; Elvis Costello, Stockholm, 1977; Ziggy Stardust, aka David Bowie, Hammersmith, 1973; Mickey Finn and Marc Bolan of T Rex, 1972. (*Opposite, clockwise from top left*) Freddie Mercury; the Bay City Rollers with Princess Anne and Eric Morley, 1975; Rod Stewart and Mia, 1973; and the Sex Pistols (from left, Steve Jones, Glen Matlock, Johnny Rotten and Paul Cook).

It was the time of Telethons and sponsored swims, of mass rallies and monster fund-raising events. Charity often began at home, with the money collected going to schools, hospitals and children's homes. But the world was shrinking. Television had brought the horrors of drought and famine-stricken Africa into the sitting rooms of the nation. Live Aid was Bob Geldof's inspiration, all-day concerts in Philadelphia and London to be broadcast simultaneously to one hundred and fifty-two satellite-linked countries. (*Left*) Part of the huge crowd at Wembley Stadium on 13 July 1985 for the Live Aid concert. Switchboards were jammed with calls pledging money.

Stars of the Eighties –
(*opposite, clockwise from
top left*) Bucks Fizz,
winners of the Eurovision
Song Contest in 1981
with *Making
Your Mind Up*; Andrew
Ridgeley and George
Michael of Wham! at the
film premiere of *Dune*,
1984; Boy George at the
Sony Radio Awards,
1984; and Toyah Wilcox,
1980. (*Right*) Elton John
in ebullient mood and
dazzling costume at the
Hammersmith Odeon,
London, 16 December
1982.

(*Clockwise, across spread from top left*) Michael Caine; Glenda Jackson as Hedda Gabler, 1975; Oliver Reed in customary pose; Donald Pleasance; Judi Dench in *Waste*, 1985, Sir John Gielgud; Vanessa Redgrave; and Jane Seymour and Roger Moore in the 1973 Bond movie *Live and Let Die*.

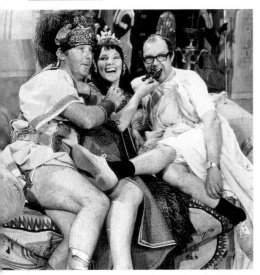

And perhaps the cream of British television was comedy. (*Opposite, clockwise from top left*) Ernie Wise (left), Glenda Jackson and Eric Morecambe, 1971; Benny Hill, who even managed to make playing the guitar look suggestive, 1970; Richard Beckinsale and Ronnie Barker in *Porridge*, 1979; Dudley Moore and Peter Cook, 1973. (*Above, clockwise from top left*) The cast of *Dad's Army*, 1974; Harry H. Corbett and Wilfrid Brambell, better known as *Steptoe and Son,* 1971; Griff Rhys-Jones (left) and Mel Smith, 1987; and five versions of Alan Whicker from the *Monty Python* cast, 1971.

It was firmly believed, at least by the British, that Britain produced the best television programmes in the 1970s and 1980s. (*Above, clockwise from top left*) Tom Baker (*Doctor Who*) with a Cyberman, 1974; John Thaw (left) and Dennis Waterman in *The Sweeney*, 1974; Martin Shaw (left), Gordon Jackson and Lewis Collins in *The Professionals*, 1978; and Joanna Lumley, Gareth Hunt and Patrick MacNee in *The New Avengers*, 1976. (*Opposite, top*) Some of the cast of the long-running TV soap opera *Coronation Street* in the bar of the Rover's Return, 1978. (*Opposite, bottom right*) Jeremy Irons and Diana Quick in Granada Television's adaptation of Evelyn Waugh's *Brideshead Revisited*. (*Opposite, bottom left*) Leonard Rossiter signing copies of the book of his TV series *Reginald Perrin*.

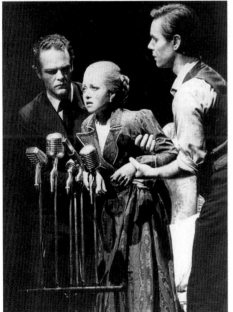

The composer/lyricist team of Andrew Lloyd Webber and Tim Rice (*opposite, top left*) had their first West End success when *Jesus Christ Superstar* opened at the Palace Theatre in 1972, with Paul Nicholas and Dana Gillespie (*opposite, top right*). Then came Elaine Page in *Evita* in 1978 (*opposite, bottom left*), and Michael Crawford and Sarah Brightman in *The Phantom of the Opera* in 1986 (*opposite, bottom right*). (*Above, right*) Christopher Gable and Twiggy (Lesley Hornby) in Ken Russell's film version of *The Boy Friend*, 1971. (*Above, left*) Ken Russell holds his BAFTA trophy from the same year. (*Right*) Roger Daltrey of the Who, as Liszt in Russell's film *Lisztomania*, 1975.

After the doldrums of the late 1940s and 1950s, British theatre was rescued by a bevy of great writers. (*Opposite clockwise from top left*) Tom Stoppard, 1978; Samuel Beckett, 1980; Steven Berkoff, Limehouse, 1980; and Alan Bennett, 1980. (*Right, clockwise from top left*) Alan Ayckbourn, 1975; Dennis Potter, who revolutionised TV drama, 1978; Harold Pinter, 1979; and John Osborne, whose *Look Back in Anger* began the new wave.

Sporting heroes of the 1970s. (*Opposite, clockwise from top left*) Mary Peters, winner of the pentathlon gold at the Munich Olympics, 1972; James Hunt, Formula 1 champion; Red Rum, opening a betting shop in Kilburn, 1979; and Virginia Wade, Women's Singles Champion at Wimbledon, 1977. Sporting heroes of the 1980s. (*Right, clockwise from top left*) Daley Thompson wins decathlon gold at the Moscow Olympics, 1980; Sebastian Coe wins the 1500 metres gold; world ice-skating champions Torvill and Dean; and champion jockey Lester Piggott.

Once upon a time there was a prince named Charles who was heir to the British throne. His advisers told him he should marry a beautiful young girl, and promised that they would help him find one. The beautiful young girl was Lady Diana Spencer.

On 29 June 1981 Charles and Diana were married in St Paul's Cathedral. After the ceremony, the couple were driven to Buckingham Palace where they appeared on the balcony (*above*). The public kiss was unprecedented in the annals of royal weddings. The honeymoon was spent in Balmoral Castle, where the couple were photographed on the banks of the River Dee (*opposite*), and Princess Diana began her round of royal duties. From then on, it was all downhill. The Prince and Princess did not live happily ever after, and one could be forgiven for reading too much into this picture of Diana, sheltering under an umbrella on 1 February 1981 (*right*).

24
AIMING FOR GLORY
1990–2000

Following the sudden death of John Smith, Tony Blair (*right*) became the youngest ever leader of the Labour Party. After years in the political wilderness, Labour was slowly struggling back into favour, helped enormously by Tory sleaze and incompetence. The crunch time came with the election of May 1997. Most people expected Labour to win, but then, most people had expected Labour to win in 1992. The result was a landslide victory. Labour had their biggest ever majority in the Commons, and Blair became Britain's youngest Prime Minister for a hundred and fifty years.

Introduction

At the end of the First Millennium, Britain did not exist. The disparate regions of England had recently united under one king, but Scotland, Wales and Ireland were independent nations. The Anglo-Saxon word for a Briton had come to be used as a common noun meaning 'slave'. The people who inhabited the British Isles viewed each other with suspicion, and only the brave, the greedy and the desperate were prepared to cross the Channel to see what life was like on the other side.

Over the next 1,000 years, England conquered Wales, merged with Scotland and plundered Ireland. Britain was created and British influence grew. In ever-increasing numbers, the British took sail across the oceans of the world until they were to be found everywhere – as rulers, administrators, advisers, engineers, explorers, missionaries and soldiers. Wherever they went, they had later to retreat, leaving behind their language and bits of their culture. Most international sport, from ping-pong to rugby football, is British in origin.

But, as the Second Millennium neared its end, Britain – or more particularly England – faced a crisis of confidence. The Welsh and the Scots have always known who they are. They have kept their own language and culture – the Scots have even exported much of theirs. The English have never had the certainty of knowing who they are, only of remembering what they have done. When they have been successful, this was enough.

But the 1990s were unsettling and unsteady times. Old themes – devolution and independence for Wales and Scotland – were revived. Old complaints were aired – that England was a land of two nations: north and south, rich and poor, industrious and dilettante, those who created wealth and those who pocketed it. Old spectres were dusted off – there was even talk of Britain becoming a republic.

With the departure of Margaret Thatcher in 1990, a vision faded. Her successor, John Major, surprised many by managing to win the 1992 General Election, but he was not the man for the moment. Britain withdrew from the ERM, suffered an epidemic of sleaze, lost her People's Princess, lost patience with the rest of the royal family (and then forgave them), and witnessed the destruction of Barings Bank by a single rogue trader.

A landslide victory in the General Election of 1997 brought New Labour to power and old Tory policies into play. Hopes ran high for a short while. Better, it seemed, that Scotland and Wales should legally separate from England than that they should have to tear themselves painfully away – as Ireland had done and was still doing. But, just a month or two into the Third Millennium, there were worrying signs that the Greenwich Dome – over-priced and under-attended – was all too fitting a symbol for Britain.

London's Docklands were a creation of the 1980s – a brand new financial hothouse on what had become the industrial wasteland of the Isle of Dogs. The centrepiece of the development was Canada Tower on Canary Wharf (*left*) At 250 metres high Canada Tower is the tallest building in London and the tallest office building in Europe. It was designed by Cesar Pelli and opened in 1991.

It was said to be a product of Thatcherism, but shows every sign of being able to outlast any transient political creed. Work began on the Docklands development in the late 1980s (*above, right*). Canary Wharf (*below, right*) was the first section to be completed, but Docklands was still pushing up and out well into the 21st century.

The idea was mooted in Napoleon's day – a tunnel under the Channel, linking France and England. A Bill for such a tunnel was presented to Parliament in 1907. An Anglo-French agreement was reached to build a tunnel in 1964, and, in the wake of the British entry into the EEC, work started at the Shakespeare Cliff near Folkestone early in 1973 (*above*). The Tunnel was driven several miles out under the sea (*opposite, right*). Costs began to soar way above expectation, however, and the project was abandoned in 1975.

In the late 1980s work started again. This time there was more determination and more money, improved equipment, and a greater financial incentive to speed road traffic between the European mainland and Britain. After seven years of digging, and at a cost of over £8 billion, the Channel Tunnel was inaugurated on 6 May 1994, and Britain was no longer an island. (*Above, left*) The Channel Tunnel lorry terminal at Folkestone.

John Smith (*opposite, below left*) was elected Labour leader in 1992, but died of a heart attack two years later. He was succeeded by Tony Blair (*opposite, below right*). Blair's leading lieutenants were Gordon Brown (*opposite, above*, on the left) and John Prescott (*right*). (*Above*) The launch of the Labour Manifesto, 4 July 1996.

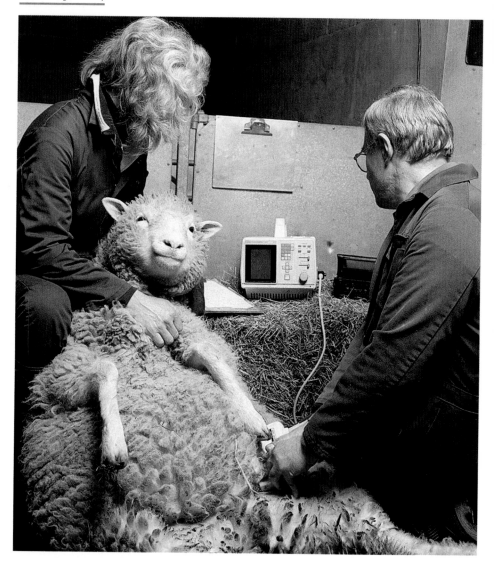

On 24 February 1997, Dolly was introduced to the public by scientists at the Roslin Institute in Edinburgh. She had been cloned from a single cell of her mother. A year later Dolly hit the headlines again, with the news that she was pregnant by a Welsh Mountain ram. (*Opposite*) Dolly undergoes an ultrasound scan at the Roslin Institute. (*Right*) Ten-day-old Bonnie, the lamb born to Dolly, makes her first public appearance, 23 April 1998.

Like an unwanted child, there were those who hated the Millennium Dome from the moment of its conception. It was said to be too expensive, in the wrong place, poorly planned, ugly. Slowly the poor child rose from the wastes of North Greenwich (*left*). When it seemed that it might open on time, there was a scramble to find ideas of what to put in it, and to find sponsors willing to pay. When it was empty it was beautiful. When paying customers came there weren't enough of them. Before it was two months old there were worries about what to do with it after the year 2000, when it would be up for adoption.

(*Left*) A Virgin airship pokes fun at the British Airways London Eye, after engineers failed to raise the giant wheel, 28 September 1999. (*Opposite, above*) Seven weeks later all was well, and the wheel and its gondolas ('pods') were in position on London's South Bank. (*Opposite, below*) Poppy Holden (*left*) and Rosie Sewell were among the first members of the public to see the sights of London from the top of the wheel, 1 February 2000.

The soccer team of the millennium was Manchester United, whose English League, FA Cup and UEFA Champions' League treble in 1999 was the stuff of which football legends are rapidly made. It was a team of stars, whose individual brilliance knitted together to produce some of the most exciting games ever seen. (*Left*) Ryan Giggs in action at Wembley Stadium as Manchester United beat Newcastle United 4-0 in the FA Charity Shield, 11 August 1996.

Oo, ah! Cantona! (*Right*) Jason McAteer of Liverpool is brought down by Eric Cantona, Old Trafford, 12 October 1996. United went on to win 1-0. (*Below*) David Beckham strides past Gary Speed of Newcastle United in the 1999 FA Cup Final at Wembley Stadium. Their 2-0 win gave United the Double of League and Cup for the third time in six years.

It had been a long time since Britain held the World Heavyweight Boxing title. Bob Fitzsimmons was the only British-born champion, back in 1897. Then, on 13 November 1999, Lennox Lewis (*opposite, below right*) stepped into the ring at the Thomas and Mack Center in Las Vegas to fight Evander Holyfield (*opposite, above and below left*). Lewis won on points (*left*).

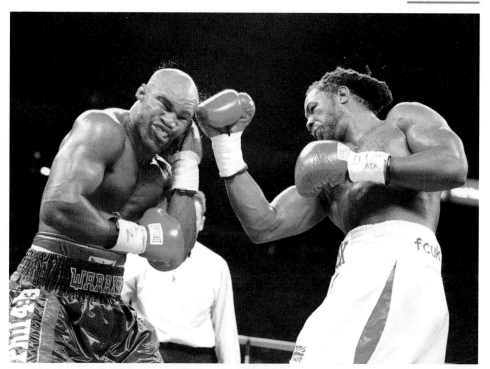

The Formula 1 World Championship was a year or two in coming. (*Opposite, below right*) Damon Hill in pensive mood after winning the Italian Grand Prix, Monza, 12 September 1993. (*Right*) Jubilation when Hill (flanked by Michael Schumacher and Jean Alesi) wins the British Grand Prix, 10 July 1994. (*Opposite, above*) Hill back at Monza, 8 September 1996. (*Opposite, below left*) Hill at Suzuka, Japan, needing just one point from the final Grand Prix for the Championship, 12 October 1996. He got it.

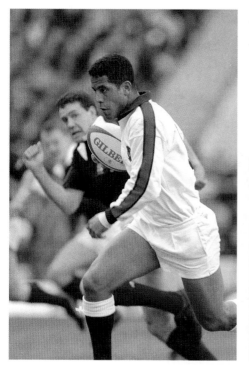

The years of Five Nations glory – (*opposite, above*) Rob Andrew kicks a penalty in England's 18-14 victory over France at the Parc des Princes, 5 March 1994. (*Opposite, below left*) Martin Johnson and Graham Rowntree of England struggle with the Scottish defence at Murrayfield, 4 March 1996. England won 18-9. (*Opposite, below right*) Rory Underwood sidesteps Simon Geoghegan's tackle at Twickenham, 16 March 1996. England beat Ireland 28-15. (*Above, left*) Jeremy Guscott beats the Scots to the line, Twickenham, 18 March 1995. England won 24-12. (*Above, right*) The England captain Will Carling runs from the field after the victory.

Linford Christie (*left*) was Britain's fastest sprinter of all time. In 1988 he took the silver medal at the Seoul Olympics, after Ben Johnson had been disqualified. He then undertook a training regime that was said to be tougher than any other sprinter's. It paid off. Four years later, he was the clear winner in the final of the men's 100 metres final at the Barcelona Olympics (*opposite*) in July 1992.

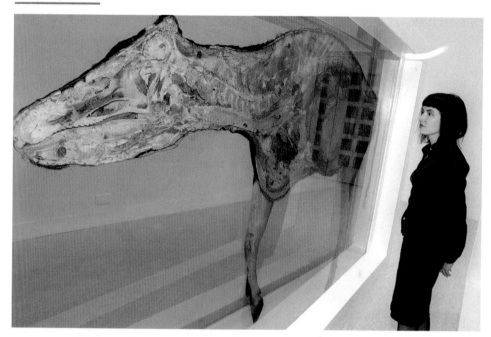

Concept Art received enormous publicity, some acclaim and much hostility when Damien Hirst's *Mother and Child Divided* went on display at the Tate Gallery, London, in November 1995 (*above*). The exhibit – a pregnant cow sawn in half and pickled in a glass container – managed to shock, disgust, amuse, thrill and bore people, and gained further notoriety for the Turner Prize. Later exhibitions of Hirst's work, in New York, ran into trouble with hygiene inspectors, who viewed carcasses, even when soaked in formaldehyde, as more suitable for the abattoir than the gallery.

Hirst (*right*) studied art at the Goldsmiths College of Art in south London. In the early 1990s he was the *enfant terrible* of British art, making his mark with *The Physical Impossibility of Death in the Mind of Someone Living* – a dead tiger shark floating in preservative. Unsurprisingly, some critics remarked on his apparent obsessive fascination with death.

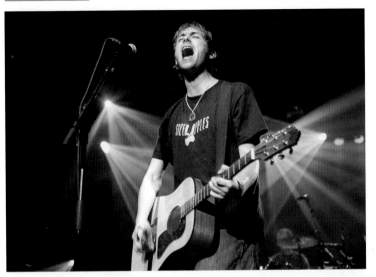

(*Left*) Damon Albarn, lead singer with Blur, at full throttle during the band's Mutualité concert in Paris, 16 September 1999. (*Below left*) Liam and Noël Gallagher in quieter mode, 25 August 1999. They were attending a press conference to announce that bass player Paul 'Guigsy' McGuigan had quit Oasis, just two weeks after Paul 'Bonehead' Arthurs left.

(*Above*) The Spice Girls in their heyday, at the Brit Awards, London, 24 February 1997 – (from left) Mel C (Sporty), Emma Bunton (Baby), Mel B (Scary), Geri Halliwell (Ginger) and Victoria Adams (Posh). (*Right*) A year later, and Robbie Williams (left) has some new tricks for an old dog, Tom Jones (right), at the London Docklands Arena, 9 February 1998.

Index

About the pictures in this book

This book was created by The Hulton Getty Picture Collection which comprises over 300 separate collections and 18 million images. It is a part of Getty Images, Inc. with over 70 million images and 30,000 hours of film. Picture sources for this book include:

Hulton Getty, Archive Photos and **FPG** (archival photographs and film)
Allsport (sports photography)
Liaison Agency (news and reportage)
Online USA (celebrity photography)

All are part of Getty's press and editorial sales channel, **www.gettysource.com**
In addition to gettysource suppliers, images were supplied by Stone, The Image Bank and Telegraph Colour Library, who are all part of Getty's online solution for creative access, gettyone, **www.gettyone.com**

How to buy or license a picture from this book

All non-Hulton images are credited individually below.

Picture licensing information
For information about licensing any image in this book, please phone **+ 44 (0)20 7579 5731**, fax: **44 (0)20 7266 3154** or e-mail **chris.barwick@getty-images.com**

Online access
For information about Getty Images and for access to individual collections go to **www.hultongetty.com.**
Go to **www.gettyone.com** for creative and conceptually oriented imagery and (in third quarter 2000) **www.gettysource.com** for editorial images.

Buying a print
For details on how to purchase exhibition quality prints call The Hulton Getty Picture Gallery, phone **+ 44 (0)20 7276 4525** or e-mail **hulton.gallery@getty-images.com**

Acknowledgements

p. 54 © Klaus Frahm; p. 75 © Klaus Frahm; pp. 73 (*left and right*), 130, 185 © Könemann Verlagsgesellschaft mbH/Photo: Achim Bednorz.

PA Photos: pp. 968-9 Roslin Institute/PA Photos; p. 972 Tom Hevezi/PA Photos; p. 973 (*above*) Michael Walter/PA Photos, (*below*) Toby Melville/PA Photos; pp. 984, 986 (*below*), 987 Fiona Hanson/PA Photos; p. 985 Tony Harris/PA Photos; p. 986 (*above*) Kipa Press/PA Photos.

Allsport: p. 974 Gary Prior; p. 975 (*above*) Clive Brunskill, (*below*) Stu Forster; p. 976 John Gichigi; p. 977 Al Bello; p. 978 (*above*) Mike Cooper; pp 978 (*below, left* and *right*), 979 Pascal Rondeau; p. 980 (*above* and *below, left*); pp 980 (*below, right*), 981 (*left*) David Rogers; p. 981 (*right*) David Cannon; p. 982 Mike Hewitt; p. 983 Tony Duffy.

Maps, pp. viii-xvi © Studio für Landkartentechnik, Norderstedt